W9-DFC-112

Architecture in France 1800–1900

Editor, English-language edition: Elisa Urbanelli
Designer, English-language edition: Robert McKee

Library of Congress Cataloging-in-Publication Data
Lemoine, Bertrand.
[France du XIXe siècle. English]
Architecture in France 1800–1900 / Bertrand Lemoine ;
translated from the French by Alexandra Bonfante-Warren.
p. cm.
Includes bibliographical references and index.
ISBN 0–8109–4090–6 (clothbound)
1. Architecture—France. 2. Architecture, Modern—19th century—France. 3. Architecture and society—France—History—19th century.
I. Title.
NA1047.L4713 1998
720'.944'09034—dc21 97–45861

Published in 1998 by Harry N. Abrams, Incorporated, New York

Printed and bound in Spain

Harry N. Abrams, Inc.
100 Fifth Avenue
New York, N.Y. 10011
www.abramsbooks.com

Bertrand Lemoine

Architecture in France 1800–1900

Translated from the French by

Alexandra Bonfante-Warren

Harry N. Abrams, Inc., Publishers

Contents

INTRODUCTION

A period known for its opulence, eclecticism, and innovation, the nineteenth century left an extraordinary architectural legacy in France. The Industrial Revolution, political change, economic expansion, and the power of the emerging middle class were all catalysts for prolific architectural development. France underwent a profound transformation, as towns appeared where none had been before and existing cities grew at an unprecedented rate.

This urban development was facilitated by designs for numerous types of buildings that addressed the needs of a newly industrialized society. Some, such as courthouses, were traditional buildings adapted from ancient models, while others, such as train stations, were entirely unprecedented. Influenced by the ideals of the esteemed École des Beaux-Arts, which championed a universal aesthetic based on the classical tradition, as well as by the tenets of Rationalism promoted by certain architects and theorists, French architects both mined the past and looked to the future for inspiration in meeting the architectural challenges of the era.

Architecture in the nineteenth century was invested with representative value because it translated into practical built form the aspirations and needs of the culture. It came to play a major part in the forging of a social unity that was essential to progress in French society. History served a creative role by opening up architecture's referential repertoire. Architectural types never became wholly standardized, however, even when they were followed for identical programs, as there were always stylistic interpretations and considerations of site and context. The freedom of choice available to the architect was more than a question of personal taste. It corresponded to the democratic condition to which the society as a whole aspired.

Eclecticism, which was manifested in specific reference to periods or styles, was in large measure a function of a building's particular program. Churches were Neo-Romanesque or Neo-Gothic, town halls Neo-Renaissance, courthouses Neoclassical, theaters Neo-Baroque. These revivals were not only driven by aesthetic considerations, but also inspired by the resonance of a particular historical period whose characteristics were intended to reinforce the building's meaning. The integration of different styles within a single building or interior reveals the design approach that typified the nineteenth century: borrowing freely from the catalogue of the past, including the recent past, in order to produce an entirely new architecture appropriate to the era. What today may seem like mere quotation, which some consider to be creative regression, was a means to design for the age, as eclecticism was one of its key defining attributes.

Technological innovation also had a profound impact on the development of the architecture of the period. The introduction of iron and steel, by radically revising the methods of construction and opening up new aesthetic possibilities, revitalized design and provoked passionate debate and discussion among architects seeking a new language to express the century's social and cultural ambitions. Architects looked to engineers, who were largely responsible for the new building technology, for creative stimulation.

Thus, overlaying a respect for the history of built form based upon scholarly knowledge was an extraordinary desire to invent something new by exploiting the material and technical possibilities of the era. The nineteenth century is marked by a fascination with novelty and progress, an optimistic belief in the future—whether that future was to arise from the ceaselessly accruing production of wealth or from the social revolution prophesied by some. It is this modern attitude that makes the period so intriguing, and so close to our own.

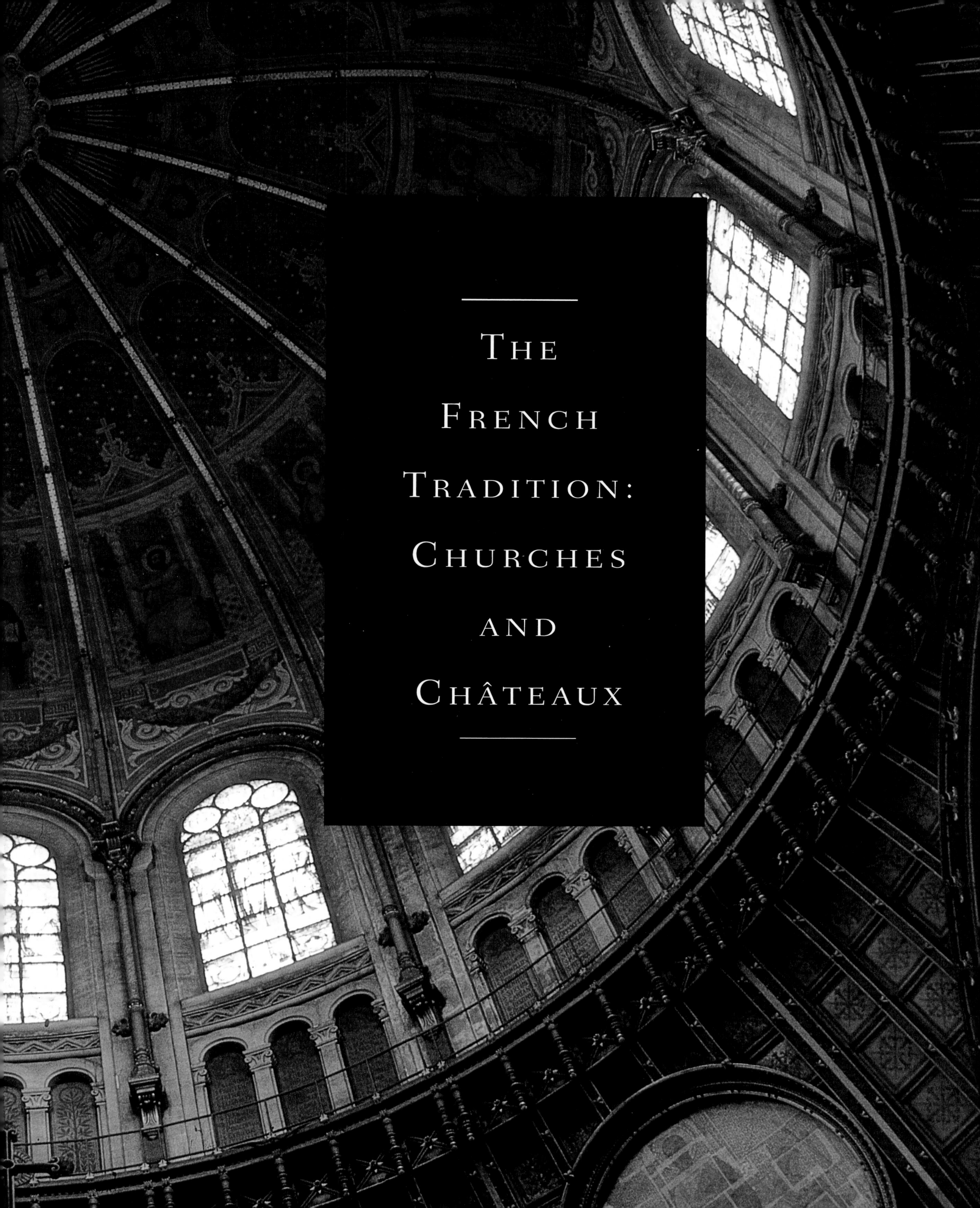

The French Tradition: Churches and Châteaux

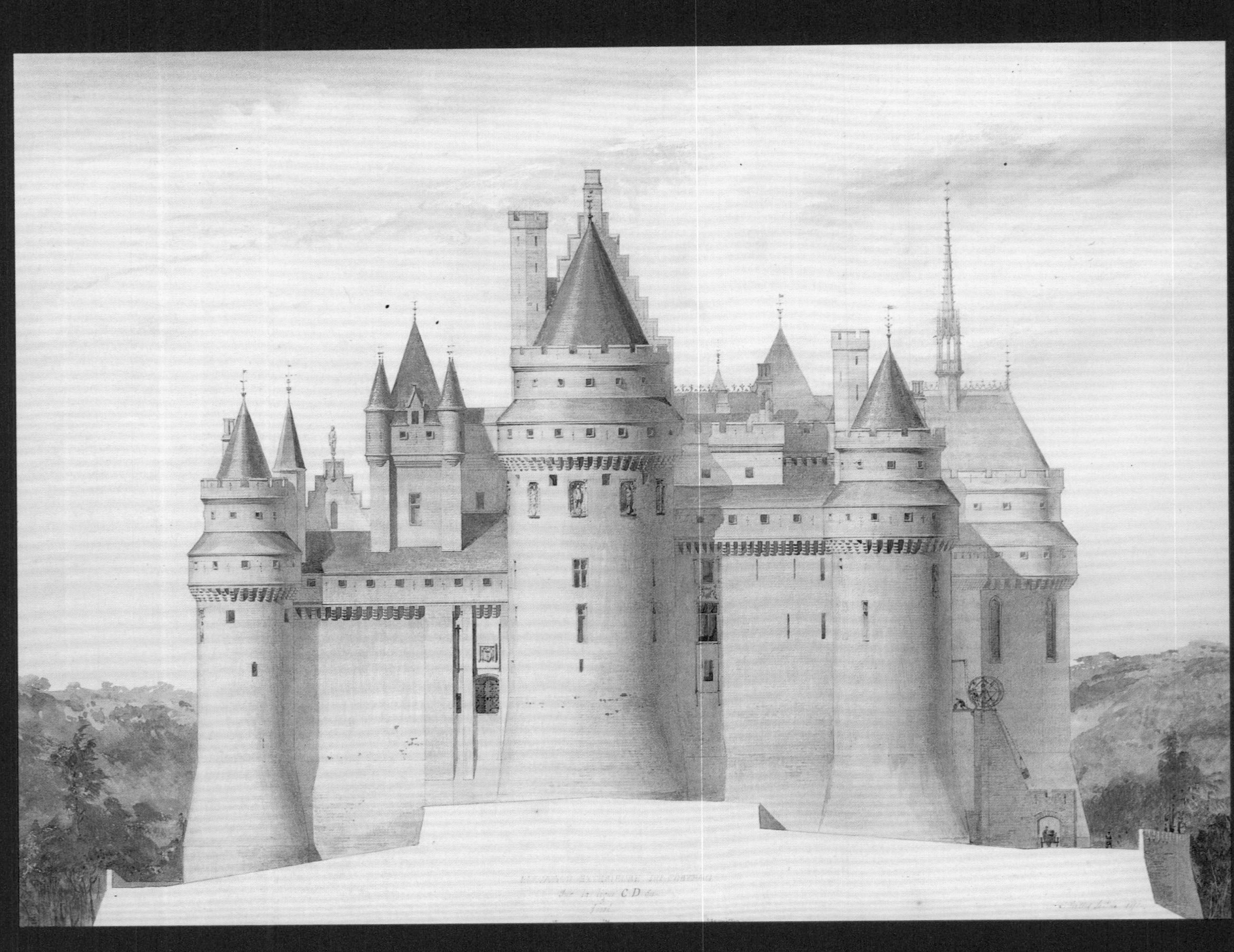

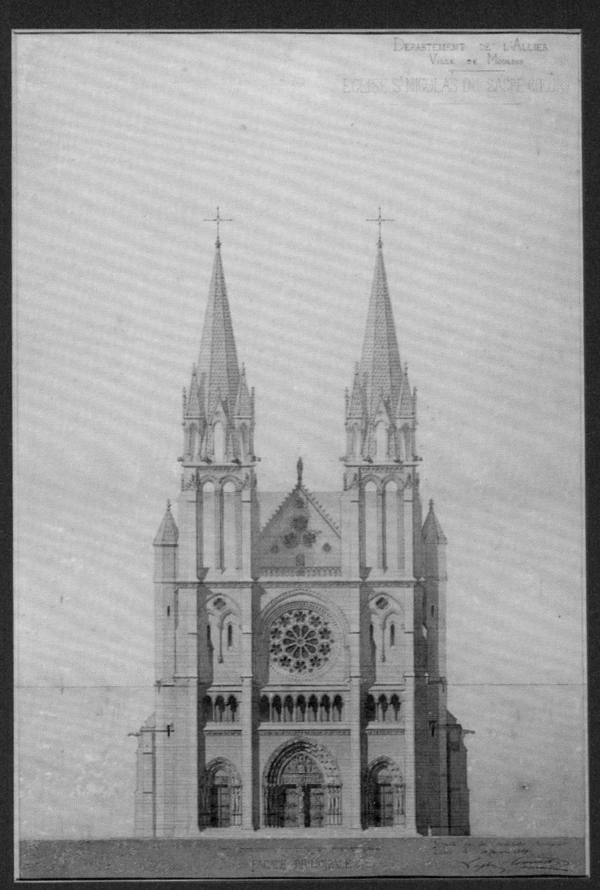
Departement de l'Allier

In the nineteenth century, churches and châteaux were the buildings that most embodied France's traditional values. As expressions of the two dominant classes of the ancien régime—the clergy and the aristocracy—they represented the continuity of old power structure in the face of the revolutionary upheavals that marked the century. Although churches and châteaux could be said to epitomize the reactionary impulse, they were not necessarily conservative in design: they were also sites of architectural experimentation.

The early years of the century still belonged to the Enlightenment. The rhetoric of the period's architecture was in the Neoclassical mold, and the monuments of antiquity were the architects' stock in trade. There was little distinction between history and creativity: reference to tradition was the basis of all architectural design in the Napoleonic era. Charles Percier and Pierre-François-Léonard Fontaine—Napoleon I's favorite architects—championed an elegant and delicate reinterpretation of classical antiquity, solemn on the exterior but rich with the colors of Pompeii on the interior. An outstanding example of the work of Percier and Fontaine is the renovation of the Château de Malmaison, executed with great refinement in 1799, which anticipates the features of the Empire style.

At times, the more important the architectural project, the more excessive the reinterpretation of classical antiquity became. Pierre Vignon's competition-winning design for the church of La Madeleine, conceived as a "Temple to Glory," was begun in 1807 on Pierre Contant d'Ivry's foundations. Isolated on its podium, with a row of Corinthian columns supporting a pediment, the church is practically a replica of a Roman peripteral temple. The exterior is a somewhat chilly pastiche, but the interior, completed in 1828 by Vignon's successor, Jean-Jacques Huvé, is almost baroque. La Madeleine was not finished until 1845, and clearly reveals the transition from an austere Neoclassicism to a richer, more ornate style.

The Roman tendency is even more obvious in the church of Notre-Dame-de-Lorette in Paris, built to designs by Hippolyte Lebas in 1823–36, which was directly inspired by the Early Christian basilica of Santa Maria Maggiore in Rome. Lebas's church was very much acclaimed in its day, despite the contrast between its severe facade and its heavily gilded interior with an ornate coffered ceiling. Similarly, the church of Saint-Vincent-de-Paul, built in 1830–46 from plans drawn in 1824 by Jean-Baptiste Lepère and Jacques-Ignace Hittorff, echoes the architectural style of Rome's Trinità dei Monti, with a pediment flanked by square towers. The interior also recalls the Early Christian basilica, a comparison that extends to the polychromy and frescoes lavished on every flat surface.

PICTURESQUE NEO-GOTHIC

During the Restoration period (1814–30), French architecture remained within the narrow confines of the Neoclassical canon, but in the 1830s architects began to abandon seventeenth- and eighteenth-century models, turning instead to the Gothic style of the Middle Ages. Gothic architecture became a veritable craze, amplified by a sense of historical legitimacy on the part of the nobility, who were then returning to live on ancestral land and who hoped to regain the peasantry to their cause. The passage in 1825 of a law that restored the estates of a certain number of émigré families had already resulted in a movement back to the countryside, which intensified under the July Monarchy of Louis Philippe beginning in 1830. A desire to revive the feudal tradition by re-creating its most tangible expression inspired a great many Neo-Gothic and Neo-Renaissance châteaux, built into the early twentieth century. Likewise, church architecture became liberated from the prevailing Neoclassical style, returning instead to the Gothic roots of French Christianity. The Church was influenced by writers such as René Vicomte de Châteaubriand, who, in his *Génie du christianisme*, published in 1801, argued for a return to the Gothic, the "national architecture," which he considered both Sublime and Picturesque, qualities indivisible from religious sentiment:

> *Those ceilings sculpted into foliage of different kinds, those buttresses which prop the walls and terminate abruptly like the broken trunks of trees, the coolness of the vaults, the darkness of the sanctuary, the dim twilight of*

Chapter opening spread: The dome of the church of Saint-Augustin in Paris, with its exposed metal skeleton, adapted modern technology to a design that reinterpreted the Byzantine style.

Preceding spread, left to right: The Château de Pierrefonds, an archaeologically correct, yet richly imaginative reconstruction by Viollet-le-Duc from a medieval ruin, 1858; the eclectic facade of the church of Saint-Augustin, by Victor Baltard, 1868; the church of Saint-Nicolas du Sacré-Coeur in Moulins, by Jean-Baptiste Lassus, faithfully in the Gothic style, 1850.

The church of La Madeleine, completed in 1845 from a design of 1806, is a paragon of Neoclassicism.

> *the aisles, . . . in a word, every thing in a Gothic church reminds you of the labyrinths of a wood; every thing excites a feeling of religious awe, of mystery, and of the Divinity.*
>
> *The two lofty towers erected at the entrance of the edifice overtop the elms and yew-trees of the churchyard, and produce the most picturesque effect on the azure of heaven.*

Other writers, such as Jules Michelet and Victor Hugo, took up the cause; in Hugo's *Notre-Dame de Paris,* published in 1831, the author's evocative force infused the great cathedral with new life. The Neo-Gothic arose simultaneously with the fledgling concept of the historical monument, which was embodied in 1837 in the establishment of the Commission des Monuments Historiques, at the urging of Ludovic Vitet and Prosper Mérimée. In the first ranks of a generation of architects enthusiastically rediscovering this national patrimony was Eugène-Emmanuel Viollet-le-Duc. A self-taught architect, he had refused to attend the École des Beaux-Arts, preferring to practice his talents for observation and drawing on his own, in the study of French and Italian medieval monuments. This legacy was becoming better known, thanks in large part to Baron Isidore-Justin-Séverin Taylor and Charles Nodier, who, beginning in 1820, published the twenty-one beautiful volumes of *Voyages pittoresques et romantiques dans l'ancienne France,* to which a number of artists contributed, including Viollet-le-Duc. This utterly charming survey brought Gothic churches and ruins to the fore by emphasizing their poetic atmosphere and their dilapidated state, in effect, their Picturesque qualities.

This literary and cultural movement was inseparable from the rage for Neo-Gothic architecture—long a popular style for landscape follies and garden pavilions, but limited to less important buildings. Architects sought to re-create the sensibility and atmosphere of the period's novels in fanciful buildings unencumbered by archaeological accuracy. A typical example of the passage from Neoclassicism to Picturesque Neo-Gothic is the royal chapel erected at Dreux as the Orléans family mausoleum. Using Flamboyant Gothic motifs, Pierre Bernard Lefranc completely redesigned the Neoclassical rotunda that an architect named Cramail had built in 1816–22 after a Doric temple.

In the realm of châteaux, the works of the architect René Hodé in Anjou are particularly good examples of Picturesque Neo-Gothic in the French manner, also represented by the Château de Challain-la-Potherie, in Maine-et-Loire, built in 1846–54 for Comte Albert de La Rochefoucauld-Bayers. One of the earliest and most spectacular Neo-Gothic structures, which unfortunately was demolished in 1962, was the Château de Comacre, erected in 1845–48 by Sylvain-Philippe Chateigner, the Touraine native master of the genre. The château's combination of French Flamboyant details and English motifs, such as bow windows, revealed the influence of architects from across the English Channel, who demonstrated a particularly strong predilection for the Picturesque. The many books on Elizabethan architecture published between 1830 and 1840 contributed widely to the proliferation of Neo-Gothic models in England. The Neo-Renaissance château built near Marly by J.-N.-L. Durand for Alexandre Dumas and known as the castle of Monte Cristo was another extravagance, drawn directly from the writer's wishes. Dumas wanted statuary "by Jean Goujon, as well as by Germain Pilon," and so casts were made from the sculptural motifs at the Château d'Anet and from the salamanders—emblems of Francis I—at Villers-Cotterêts. Dumas also commissioned a tiny Gothic castle in which to work, called by André Maurois "a miniature keep, a doll's fortress."

THE ARCHAEOLOGISTS

The Neo-Gothic fashion of the years 1830–45 left much to the imaginative fancy of architects, who were inspired more by a Romantic approach than by a concern for faithfulness to historic sources. Beginning in the mid-nineteenth century, however, the work of a new generation of architects profoundly transformed how the architecture of the Middle Ages was viewed. Although in both cases there was a return to tradition, the earlier Picturesque Neo-Gothic deliberately sought to emphasize the picturesque quality that characterizes the Flamboyant style, and to play with its exuberance in order to shape an architectural mode that would evoke the medieval tradition in a pleasing way. The subsequent period saw the rise of a more academic strain of Neo-Gothic architecture, as archaeological societies were established to study medieval monuments. At the forefront was the archaeological society of Normandy, founded in 1823, whose guiding light, Arcisse de Caumont, produced a primer on medieval architecture, first publishing a *Cours d'antiquités monumentales*, beginning in 1830, then in 1851 an *Abécédaire*. Architects began to build and restore chapels, churches, and cathedrals following the trend toward a more accurate, scholarly, and archaeological interpretation of the Gothic style that was far removed from the excesses of the Romantic approach. After 1850, the loosely interpreted, whimsical style was no longer in favor. The so-called diocesan architects—those charged with maintaining the churches—almost unanimously followed the doctrine of the "archaeologizing" Gothic style. Under their influence, churches and châteaux designed according to the canons of the Gothic style had to remain rigorously and rationally true to the models inherited from history, although there remained significant room for variation in the arrangement of the parts and the treatment of detail.

The church of Saint-Nicolas-de-Nantes is one of the best examples of this puritanism. In 1823, Jean-Baptiste Ogée had proposed a renovation project based on the Neoclassical model of Saint-Philippe-du-Roule, but another architect, Louis-Alexandre Piel, was commissioned in 1837 by the new young parish priest, Félix Fournier, who intended to remain faithful to the "true Christian style," that is, the Gothic style: "This style of architecture is more in harmony with Christian ideas, more appropriate to the needs of a cult, and [has] a greater religious effect upon the people," he wrote. Piel proposed looking to the churches of the thirteenth century, in particular, Notre-Dame de Paris, rather than to the Gothic style of the fourteenth century, which was "more deeply carved, more flowery, more pompous, thus more expensive." The final project was ultimately designed by Jean-Baptiste Lassus, who

Classical versus Gothic: Hippolyte Lebas's Notre-Dame-de-Lorette in Paris (left), built in 1823–36, and Saint-Nicolas in Nantes (right), built in 1837–76 to designs by Louis-Alexandre Piel and Jean-Baptiste Lassus.

broke ground in 1844. The church would not be completed until 1876.

Lassus's archaeologically faithful, but somewhat dry, reinterpretation of the Gothic was followed at Sainte-Clothilde in Paris, built in 1846–57 to plans by Franz-Christian Gau and Théodore Ballu. The commission came after a lively discussion between partisans of classicism and supporters of the Gothic style at the Conseil des Bâtiments Civils, the office charged with oversight of public works. In 1846, the Académie des Beaux-Arts, the bastion of classicism, publicly asked the question: "Is it fitting, in our time, to build a church in the so-called Gothic style?" and replied plainly:

> *Is it possible to go backward more than four hundred years and to offer as monumental expression to a society that has its own needs, customs, and habits, an architecture born of the needs, customs, and habits of thirteenth-century society? In short, we must determine if, at the heart of a nation such as ours, in the presence of a civilization that no longer has anything in common with the Middle Ages, it is fitting, I might even say possible, to build churches that would be oddities, anachronisms, and eccentricities, that would look like accidents amid the overall system of a new society.*

This defiance of destiny carried over into the government itself. On July 26, 1847, Comte Charles-Forbes-René de Montalembert, one of the militant supporters of the Gothic Revival, gave a "speech on vandalism in public works," in which he deplored France's backwardness in the area of religious architecture: "Must we, in this, as in the railroads, lag behind all our neighbors?"

THE GOTHIC STYLE OF VIOLLET-LE-DUC

The architect Eugène-Emmanuel Viollet-le-Duc continued to promote the Gothic vein, confirming his intellectual authority through many restoration projects and the publication, between 1854 and 1868, of a prodigious survey, the *Dictionnaire raisonné de l'architecture française*. Not only did he have a profound archaeological grasp of Gothic architecture, acquired on the job, but he turned it into a compositional method by transposing the rationalism of its construction, evident in its vaulting system, into contemporary architectural theory. Like their adversaries in the Académie, the archaeologists wished to avoid pastiches, and they sought in history's example an architectural language suitable to their time.

Viollet-le-Duc was trying to circumvent the Beaux-Arts tradition, which championed a universal

aesthetic based on classical ideas, and on which the architectural consensus of his time was based. Instead he favored an inventiveness made possible by the independence of reason, an innate quality, he argued, that alone can guarantee a genuinely creative approach. Thus, he situated architecture's rational foundations in "the clean expression of use, needs, and means of execution." "Let us be well persuaded, once again," he wrote around 1870 in his *Entretiens sur l'architecture*, "that architecture can take on new forms only if it seeks them by means of a rigorous application of a new structure." Paradoxically, Viollet-le-Duc relied upon a very literal reinterpretation of medieval architecture to put into practice a doctrine of modernist inspiration.

The example of the Château de Pierrefonds is particularly striking. Beginning with the ruined walls of a late-fourteenth-century château, Viollet-le-Duc re-created an entire medieval environment, down to the furniture. The exterior is quite faithful archaeologically, while the interior displays the decorative fancy of the Second Empire manner. His 1853–79 restoration of the old city of Carcassonne takes fewer liberties with history. The half-dozen private châteaux he built were experimental sites for developing his doctrine, yet the architect never allowed himself to be overly seduced by his own program. "A country that has suppressed the aristocracy and everything that it entails in terms of privileges," he wrote in his *Dictionnaire*, "cannot seriously build châteaux. For when there is division of property, what is a château but the whim of a day, an expensive home that dies with its owner, leaving no memory." Likewise, this restorer and builder of churches had a secular soul, yet that did not prevent him from endowing the cathedral of Clermont-Ferrand with two incredibly lofty spires. It was a step toward the ideal cathedral that he dreamed of building.

Viollet-le-Duc's students, especially Edmond Duthoit, continued to espouse his theories on medieval architecture. As with the Château de La

One of the most beautiful Neo-Renaissance creations in the Loire Valley, the Château de Challain-la-Potherie, built in 1854.

Far left: The facade of the Clermont-Ferrand cathedral, endowed with spires added by Viollet-le-Duc, embodies the architect's notion of the ideal cathedral.

Left: A mantel in the Château de Roquetaillade, near Langon, evokes the Middle Ages.

Flachère, built in 1863–67 in the Isère region from plans by Viollet-le-Duc, Duthoit built the château near Hendaye for the explorer and astronomer Antoine d'Abbadie from his teacher's sketches, but took their decorative exuberance much further. "My Gothic has Arab and Byzantine aftertastes," he acknowledged. While the exterior is a Picturesque Neo-Gothic creation, the interior is an extravagant, color-saturated design, its rich ornamentation evoking the owner's personal history of military campaigns, particularly in Ethiopia. The château that Duthoit built in 1864–68 in Roquetaillade, near Langon, from the remains of an ancient castle is in the same vein. The Château de Kériolet, near Concarneau, exhibits a Neo-Gothic interpretation that is both regional and political. Joseph Bigot, the architect for the department of Brittany, built it in 1862 for Charles de Chauveau, a department official, as an evocation of the Breton patrimony; its design refers to the style of the reign of Louis XII, who was responsible for integrating Brittany into France.

THE ECLECTICISM OF CHÂTEAUX

Curiously, châteaux were not built in Viollet-le-Duc's Rationalist Neo-Gothic style, considered too severe—in fact, too earnest—in the eyes of a clientele that preferred the more cheerful surroundings of Neo-Renaissance architecture. However, château architecture would be characterized by faithfulness to an identifiable style until the end of the century, thereby confirming the emblematic value of châteaux as signs of timeless social legitimacy.

The tradition of the aristocratic dwelling remained especially strong along the Loire Valley, and in Paris and its surrounding area, for obvious historical reasons. To a clientele made up of the newly rich, many of them recently ennobled during the Second Empire, ownership of a château was a requirement of rank. This tradition continued into the 1920s along the Loire, but primarily in Sologne, an area reclaimed in the mid-nineteenth century, when it was reforested and some of its marshes drained to make a vast hunting park. Most of these châteaux were designed in the tried-and-true styles of the past, pastiches in some cases; others dis-

The Picturesque reconstruction of the Château d'Abbadia, near Hendaye, by Edmond Duthoit, a student of Viollet-le-Duc.

played a creative freedom verging on eclecticism, although faithfulness to a specific period was the general rule.

Certain architects specialized in château design, such as Clément and Louis Parent, Paul-Ernest Sanson, and Joseph-Antoine Froelicher. The latter had connections among one of the great French families that had gone as refugees to Switzerland, and this gained him the wealthy clients of the Faubourg Saint-Germain, as well as a number of other projects that earned him the sobriquet "the château architect." The Château de Bonhôtel in the Loiret region, built in 1875–82 by Clément Parent, its gigantic hall derived from the Anglo-Saxon hall, fits perfectly into the tradition of the Loire's Renaissance châteaux. Sanson designed a number of châteaux, as well as *hôtels particuliers,* or grand town houses, in the Étoile section of Paris. For Menetou-Salon, in the Cher region, he looked to Bourges's Hôtel Jacques-Coeur. Of course, the Loire Valley is not the only place where these wealthy homes flourished. One could cite the Château de Saint-Roch, near the commune of Le Pin, in Tarn-et-Garonne. Georges de Montbrison, an art lover and man of letters, commissioned the Montauban architect Théodore Ollivier to design, in 1860, a remarkable Neo-Gothic cathedral on the banks of the Garonne; equally remarkable was the interior decoration, painted by Edmond Lechevallier-Chevignard in 1864–69.

In the area around Paris, an architect named Lesoufacher built the Château de Sceaux, a fairly successful pastiche in the Louis XIII style, for the duke of Treviso in 1858–62. Baron James de Rothschild's Château de Ferrières, built in 1860 by Joseph Paxton, the architect of the Crystal Palace for London's Great Exhibition of 1851, is interesting principally by virtue of its great glass-roofed central ballroom.

The fashion for classical models returned after mid-century. One of the great monuments of the Second Empire, Hector Lefuel's new wing for the Louvre, added in 1852–57, demonstrated that an eclectic integration of tectonic and decorative elements could produce a true nineteenth-century style. Lefuel reprised the dynamic lines of Louis XIV architecture and integrated a profusion of independently treated decorative and sculptural motifs, thereby giving the palace an eclectic appearance that is both weighty and magnificent. Similarly,

Henri Daumet's 1875 restoration of the Château de Chantilly referred literally to the Château de Fontainebleau, as well as incorporated freely motifs from Écouen, Anet, and the Tuileries. As César Daly, the editor in chief of *Revue générale de l'architecture et des travaux publics*, noted: "The eclectic school treats the entire past as a kind of store-room, taking out anything that looks useful or pleasing, as their needs or whims dictate. For the eclectics, the past is a portfolio of motifs."

More modest projects exhibit the same liberties that were taken in the construction of the great châteaux. Reference to the architecture of the Renaissance or of the preceding century seemed more suitable to bourgeois taste and desire for respectability than did the Neo-Gothic, which had become too specifically connotative. No longer the principal residence of a lord in his fiefdom, a château was now the summer home of a middle-class businessman anxious to be recognized. A series of handsome châteaux in the Loire Valley are examples of this trend: Arthur Froelicher's 1868–70 Château de la Rougellerie in the Louis XIII style; the important 1885–89 Château de Vaux in Eure-et-Loire, with elements of the Louis XIV and Louis XVI styles, and outbuildings in the Napoleon III style; the eclectic Château de La Frogerie in the Loiret region and Château des Ruets in the Loir-et-Cher; the Château de Charbonnière, of 1895–1900, in the Loiret region; and the 1902 Château de Rivaulde, whose design is eighteenth century in inspiration. Other châteaux of the early twentieth century are, in the Cher region, the Château de la Triboulette at Vouzeron and Château de Saint-Hubert, in the Louis XIII–Louis XIV style; and the Château du Puy-d'Artigny in the Indre-et-Loire, built in 1912–30 for the perfumer François Coty, in a manner that recalls the work of Jules Hardouin-Mansart.

THE RATIONALISM OF GOTHIC CHURCHES

Churches underwent a development parallel to that of châteaux. As of 1852, more than two hundred Gothic-inspired churches were under construction in France. These sacred monuments, which appeared in the Gothic mode as early as the 1830s, offered a few daring architects the opportunity for limited but spectacular experimentation, although the more innovative solutions never entered the architectural canon. Tradition weighed heavily in the design of churches, and for almost thirty years the archaeological school of thought imposed the Gothic standard as the only possible direction for church architecture. Jean-Baptiste-Antoine Lassus, an important figure in this movement, championed an academic but severe Neo-Gothic style, taken directly from thirteenth-century French cathedrals; examples are the church of the Sacré-Coeur in Moulins, built in 1850–69, and the church of Saint-Pierre in Dijon, of 1855–58.

The Rationalist rigor of the archaeology-minded architects was also manifested in technical experimentation, especially in the structural use of metal. The last Neoclassical churches, such as La Madeleine, already had iron roofs; when fire destroyed a number of preexisting roof frames, these were rebuilt in metal. The roofs of the chapel of the Palais Royal were replaced this way, by Pierre Fontaine and an ironsmith named Mignon, in 1828. The roof framing of Chartres Cathedral, composed of ten thousand pieces of wood, went up in flames in 1836, and was rebuilt in cast iron by Émile Martin and Mignon, after the examples of London's Southwark Cathedral of 1822 and Mainz Cathedral of 1827. Certain variants proposed by other ironsmiths display Neo-Gothic details, even though the roof frames were not designed to be seen. By contrast, the architect François Debret rebuilt the roof framing of the basilica of Saint-Denis in metal in 1842–45, using a fairly classical structure.

Cast iron was put to spectacular use in the reconstruction of the spire of Rouen Cathedral, according to plans by Jean-Antoine Alavoine. Begun in 1827, the project was not completed until 1884. Composed of metal pieces bolted together to form a filigree, this airy structure was an innovative demonstration of the possibilities of the new material. Yet, the method of construction created some problems, if we are to believe Viollet-le-Duc: "When the temperature changes suddenly, it hails bolt-heads around this scrap iron; when it rains, a torrent of iron oxide, despite the paint." The spire was restored in 1975. Among its descendants, which are more numerous than one might think, is

Top: Inspired by the Château de Fontainebleau, Henri Daumet renovated the Château de Chantilly in 1875.

Bottom: The north wing of the Cour Napoléon at the Louvre, in which Hector Lefuel achieved a perfect synthesis: the Second Empire style.

Auguste Magne's 1857 cast-iron spire on the church of Saint-Bernard in the eighteenth arrondissement in Paris.

From 1850, metal roofing became the rule in church architecture. Rolled iron usually replaced cast iron, as in Théodore Ballu's 1861–67 Neo-Renaissance church of La Trinité in Paris, which also has metal transverse ribs masked by plastered hollow-brick roughwork. Churches such as Saint-François-Xavier and Notre-Dame-des-Champs used similar systems. Most nineteenth-century Neo-Gothic churches are faced in stone, considered a noble material and better suited to express the sacred nature of the architecture; however, metal was most often used when there were time, cost, or space constraints.

The church of Saint-Eugène, on Rue Sainte-Cécile in Paris, was the first French church built with a metal skeletal frame. In response to the need to construct a series of six churches inexpensively and in less than a year for the new neighborhoods being developed under the city's urban plan, architect Adrien Lusson proposed a church with a metal structure that would nonetheless respect the style appropriate to the building's purpose. "In order to harmonize the decoration of the small [cast-iron] pillars, I thought it fitting to use Gothic architecture, whose elegance works quite well . . . and whose style generally suits religious monuments." Lusson was supported by the bishop, who considered the future church "a real jewel," but he resigned following an argument with the priest assigned to the future parish, who was in charge of supervising the construction. Lusson was replaced by Louis-Auguste Boileau, a former cabinetmaker who had specialized in church furniture. Though Boileau took credit for the building, he shared Lusson's point of view.

As an imitation of Gothic architecture was then desired for religious buildings, the prin-

> *cipal conditions of the program were as follows: 1) To make the most of the advantages of iron construction in order to use an expensive, limited plot of land to provide the faithful with as much room as possible, and furthermore to respect the financial limitations of a founder who has only private resources available; 2) To design the iron structure in such as way as to reproduce, especially inside, the decorative forms of the Gothic style.*

As a result, the metal ribs of the church's vaults are sheathed with Gothic moldings, supported by slender cast-iron columns.

> *For the isolated columns, an exceptional type, a tour de force in stone by medieval builders, provided a model that was perfectly applicable to cast iron. Thanks to their metallic appearance, the single-shafted stone columns in the former refectory of Saint-Martin-des-Champs [today the library of the École des Arts et Métiers] looked so suitable to the scale of a wrought-iron skeleton, were they to be reproduced in cast iron, that they were allowed for Saint-Eugène.*

The use of iron rendered unnecessary the flying buttresses that would have been required by a vault with stone ribs, and made it possible for the walls to be reduced functionally to partitions. The interior of Saint-Eugène is interesting, if somewhat dark because of its polychromatic decoration, but the exterior is rather ordinary. Boileau, who had been working on metal architecture for some time, and had just published a work titled *Nouvelle Forme architecturale*, presented himself as a theorist on architecture that made wide use of metal.

The church of Saint-Eugène was the subject of a paradigmatic debate between Boileau and Viollet-le-Duc, in which the latter emphatically criticized Boileau's translation of Gothic arches into iron, specifically "because one should not make cast iron look like stone; when one changes materials, one must change the forms." Boileau, with his fervent proselytizing for metal architecture, did not share this moral position: "The moderns can pass where the Gothics had to stop; they reconnect with the tradition that was interrupted in the fifteenth century." Boileau put his principles to work in several churches, among them, Notre-Dame-de-France in London, of 1868; the chapels of the Clermont (Oise) poorhouse and the Ajaccio seminary; the church in Juilly (Seine-et-Marne), of 1867; the church of Saint-Paul in Montluçon, of 1863–67; and Sainte-Marguerite in Le Vésinet, built in 1862–65 for the new garden city planned under the aegis of Alphonse Pallu. The exterior walls of the latter church are made of reinforced concrete, one of the earliest applications of this new material.

The vault of the church of Saint-Eugène in Paris. The secret of this colorful 1850s re-creation of the thirteenth century was the use of metal framing and supports, such as slender cast-iron columns in the style of those of the abbey refectory of Saint-Martin-des-Champs.

Above and following pages: The church of Sainte-Marie-Majeure in Marseilles, designed in 1845. The architect was inspired by Romanesque-Byzantine sources, evident in details such as the tympanum of the main portal.

Later, Boileau would try in vain to promote an even more ambitious project, for a "synthetic cathedral."

Other contemporary churches also employed metal structural framing, without any special impact on the exterior. For example, the church in Masny, in northern France, built in 1864, has visible cast-iron columns; and Notre-Dame-de-la-Croix in Ménilmontant, built to plans by J.-A. Héret in 1863–80, exhibits pierced cast-iron ribs supported by stone columns. Victor Baltard's 1868 church of Saint-Augustin features a wide nave and a dome, both with metal ribs that spring from conspicuous cast-iron columns. The plan allowed a very small triangular site to be used fully, while at the same time permitting a monumental, albeit rather heavy, Neo-Romanesque design, deemed suitable to the beginning of the recently opened Boulevard Malesherbes. Less well known, but worthy of note for its gallery supported by cast-iron columns, is the synagogue on Rue des Tournelles in Paris, designed by Marcellin Varcollier and erected in 1867 by Gustave Eiffel. There, too, the challenge was to make the most of a relatively small plot of land. The facade is in a Neo-Romanesque style, its gable adorned with a distinctive rose window, evidence of contemporary typological studies of synagogues. In that period, the symbolic expression of Judaism oscillated between the revival of Romanesque and Byzantine models, on the one hand, and a Moorish vein, paradoxically, on the other.

AN EXPLOSION OF STYLES

After 1860, the Neo-Gothic lost its stranglehold on church architecture, which nevertheless remained narrowly limited in its historical references. The stylistic repertory gradually broadened to include the Neo-Romanesque; the church of Saint-Paul in Nîmes, built in 1835–50 by Charles-Auguste Questel—an architect known chiefly for that city's classical courthouse—was one of the first churches to be designed in this mode. The other acceptable styles were Neo-Byzantine, Neo-Renaissance, and their regional variations. Faithful copies and literal translations of historic precedents gave way to freer interpretations and bold compositional inventions. A system of conventions evolved: small country churches tended to be in the Neo-Romanesque style, while the great urban basilicas were cast in the Neo-Byzantine mold.

One of the most successful examples of the latter style is Auguste Vaudremer's Saint-Pierre-de-Montrouge in Paris, of 1864–70, its vertical clock tower foreshadowing those of the churches that would be built between 1880 and 1900, such as Notre-Dame in Auteuil. Sainte-Marie-Majeure Cathedral in Marseilles, built to plans by Léon Vaudoyer, was originally designed in 1845; the polychrome bands that characterize the building

appeared in 1852. The church displays a variety of influences, anticipating the eclectic designs of twenty years later. The plan is Gothic in inspiration, the shapes Romanesque, and the dome is taken directly from that of the Baptistery in Florence. The highly colored interior, which was not completed until 1893, expresses fin-de-siècle exuberance. Constructed in 1853–64 by Jacques Espérandieu, a student and assistant of Vaudoyer, the church of Notre-Dame-de-la-Garde, overlooking the city of Marseilles, was inspired by this model, but lacks its vitality. Lyons's Fourvière basilica, built in 1872–96 by P. Bossan, is a strange assemblage of Gothic, Romanesque, and Byzantine elements, which the writer Joris-Karl Huysmans nicknamed "the upside-down elephant." Its interest lies principally in its location overlooking the city. The rich interior decoration emphasizes the simplicity of the basilican plan. Another example of a Romanesque-Byzantine amalgam is the basilica of Saint-Martin in Tours, built by Victor Laloux in 1886–1902 on the site of Saint Martin's tomb.

The influence of Byzantine polychromy is equally evident in the churches of Émile Boeswillwald, such as the one in Masny, near Douai, in northern France, and the curious chapel built of multicolored bricks in Biarritz, built in 1864–65 for the empress Eugénie. Boeswillwald studied with Pierre-François-Henri Labrouste, was a close friend of Viollet-le-Duc, and succeeded Mérimée as inspector of historical monuments. Wishing to please the empress, who had been born in Granada, Spain, Boeswillwald incorporated into the chapel's very ornate interior decoration Hispano-Moresque elements, such as the painted ceiling coffers and capitals chiseled with the initials *N* and *E*, inspired by those of Granada's Court of the Lions in the Alhambra.

The basilica of the Sacré-Coeur in Paris is perhaps the most characteristic example of the tension between the impulse to express with pomp and grandeur the institution of Christianity, on the one hand, and, on the other, the desire to renew the formal language of its architecture, to be of one's time. Designed in 1874 by Paul Abadie—who had won a competition among a field of seventy-eight architects—the basilica was not completed until 1919. Abadie, who had restored the cathedral of Saint-

Front in Périgueux, fully exploited the possibilities of the Neo-Byzantine and Neo-Romanesque vocabularies in composing the extravagant play of brilliant white stone domes that have become an unmistakable element of the Paris cityscape. The basilica should be viewed as an ambitious attempt, however clumsy in its details, that goes deliberately beyond the mere quotation of earlier styles to define an architectural style of its time.

The church of Notre-Dame-du-Travail on Rue Vercingétorix also attempts to portray a style appropriate to its time, but in an entirely different and highly original way. Built in 1892–1902 to designs by Alexandre Astruc, its interest lies entirely in its interior. The frankly utilitarian quality of the church, whose rolled-steel structure is wholly exposed, is very likely a product of both the severe economic constraints imposed upon the architect (whose initial design called for stone and iron) and the urban context of the industrial, working-class Plaisance neighborhood. Whatever the reasons, this church remains surprising evidence of a turn-of-the-century religious structure that tended toward a rigorous aesthetic, which, however free it was from the limitations of the archaeological Gothic models, still favored masonry as its material of choice.

By contrast, Montmartre's church of Saint-Jean, completed in 1904 and built entirely of reinforced concrete, signals a break with the traditional image of a church. For most of his career, the architect, Anatole de Baudot, had restored churches; influenced by his mentor, Viollet-le-Duc, de Baudot was committed to the archaeological Neo-Gothic style, notably in the church of Saint-Lubin in Rambouillet, of 1866. Late in life, de Baudot abandoned the aesthetic of his earlier career, adapting the principles implicit in Viollet-le-Duc's work to an entirely new formal and technical repertoire. De Baudot thus continued the technical experimentation of the mid-century Rationalists, while logically extending this approach toward a material that was still experimental, and unknown to his predecessors. Concrete does not lend itself as well as metal to a direct translation of Gothic forms, and so it required a new aesthetic. Beginning with a project apparently dating to 1894, de Baudot undertook a bold system "of buttress-spines," invented by an engineer named Cottancin. The choice of reinforced concrete for the ribs determined the structure of the church's piers and its vaults, even as it allowed an entirely new interpretation of this system. On the exterior, the concrete vaults form a covering, while on the interior, the complex overlapping of the slender ribs breaks with traditional medieval solutions. On the facade, the glazed sandstone trim highlights the curves of the concrete structure and contrasts with the the flat hues of the red brick infill. The austere and massive forms of Saint-Jean in Montmartre herald the modernism of the twentieth century.

Below left: The basilica of Notre-Dame de Fourvière in Lyons, an eclectic manifesto that made the most of its prominent site.

Opposite: Notre-Dame du Travail was built in a working-class neighborhood of Paris in 1902. The metal structure is stated with unusual frankness, which was justified by economic considerations.

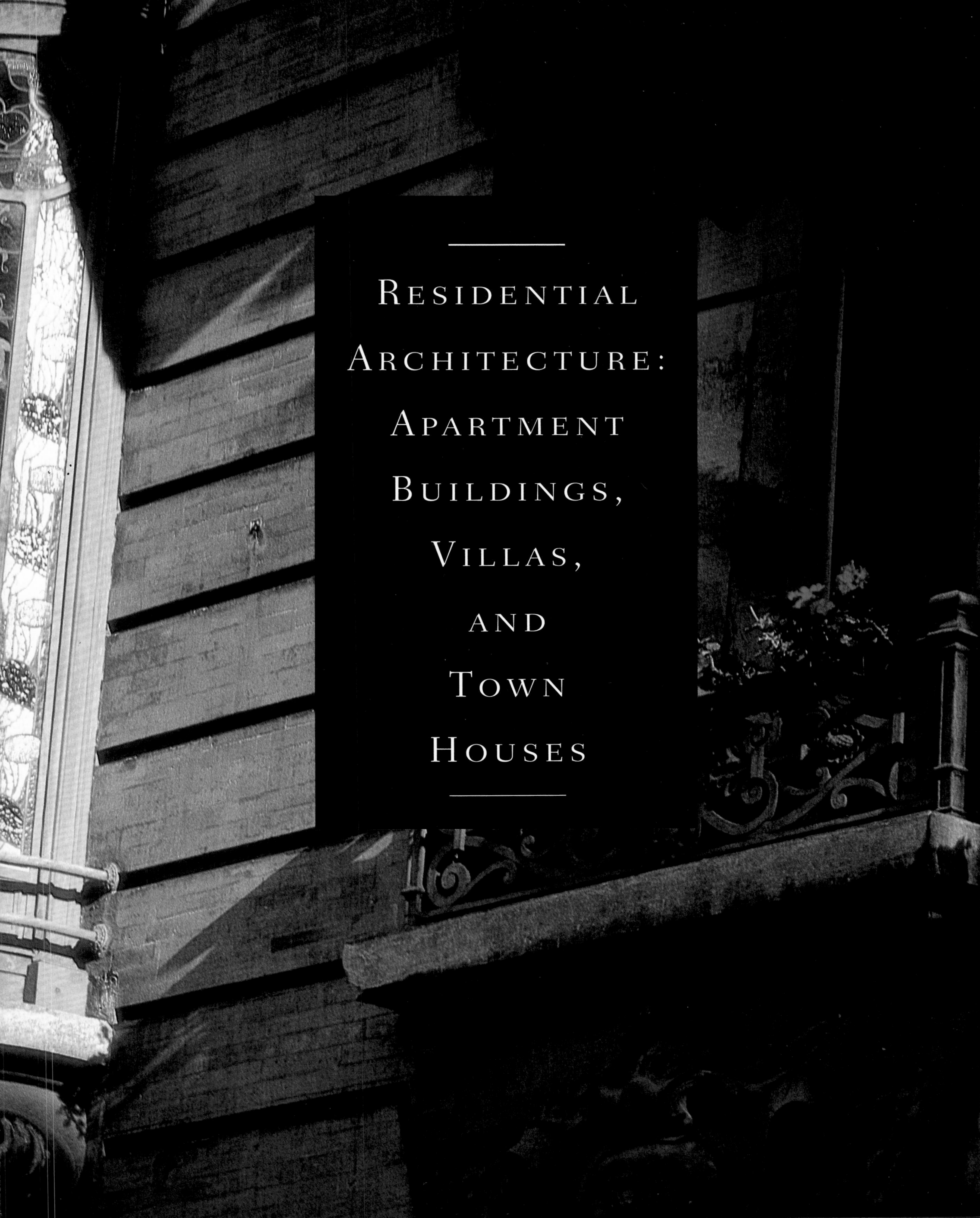

Residential Architecture: Apartment Buildings, Villas, and Town Houses

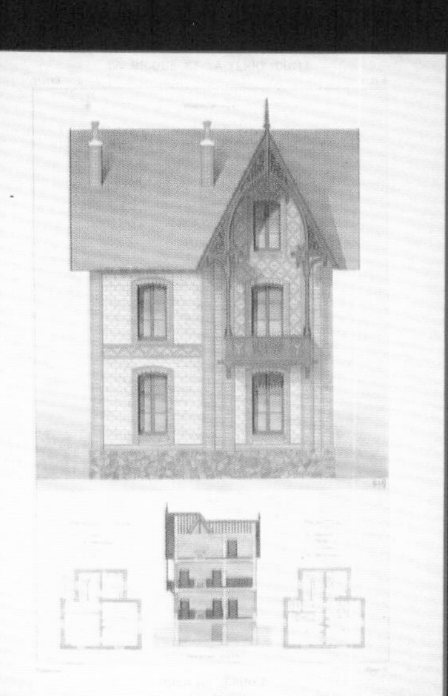

TOURNE-BRIDE
A
LAMORLAYE

Residential development was particularly prolific in nineteenth-century France. An enormous number of houses, apartment buildings, and *hôtels particuliers,* or town houses, were erected in this period, shaping much of the architectural landscape. The Industrial Revolution spurred the growth of the cities, in part because of the resulting demographic increase, but mainly because of the migration of the population from the countryside to the cities and suburbs, leading to a significant mixing of social classes. The rise of a large middle class brought about a great demand for homes of reasonable size and for rental apartments, which encouraged both a demand for the development of bedroom communities and at least partial restoration of the older centers of most French cities.

APARTMENT BUILDINGS AND THE EVOLUTION OF A BUILDING CODE

The typical nineteenth-century apartment building was, in fact, an eighteenth-century invention. In the earlier period, the range of residential construction included large, three-story houses with Mansard roofs; small, plaster-fronted apartment buildings, most often made up of four stories plus an attic; and fine stone homes, like the one Giovanni Niccolò Servandoni built in the 1770s in Place Saint-Sulpice in Paris. Buildings were thus of very different heights, as were the ceilings. The second and third floors generally had higher ceilings than the others, and the ground floor was sometimes rendered in a monumental manner, usually by integrating a mezzanine. The heterogeneous streetscapes that arose from the variety of buildings and the narrowness of the lots was regularized by a rigorous alignment to the lot line, which unified the street frontage. Paris was the laboratory in which urban paradigms that would prevail throughout the century were developed.

At the end of the eighteenth century, single-family houses began to disappear from the cities, replaced by vertical multiple dwellings. The rental building, intended to house several families and to earn income for the owner, became the basic unit in the denser urban fabric that accompanied the demographic surge in the big cities. The type was characterized chiefly by its internal organization. Whereas the earlier multiple dwellings arranged halls or rooms in open succession, without defining them by function, the new apartments adopted a more specific plan, which separated day spaces and night spaces, and distributed rooms from an entryway extended into a hallway.

The exteriors of apartment houses tended to follow a system of proportions that depended chiefly upon the nature of the streets on which they were built. Beginning in 1783, there was added to the

Chapter opening spread: A bow window in Toulouse, on Place de la Trinité. Nineteenth-century domestic architecture was characterized by the quest for luxury and comfort.

Page 28: Nine variations on the theme of the Picturesque villa, published by Pierre Chabat in Brique et terre cuite *magazine.*

Page 29: The Tourne-Bride villa in Lamorlaye, by Stephen Sauvestre, is characterized by its blend of different materials and its lively massing of volumes.

Opposite: On the Rue de Rivoli in Paris, a perfect example of a Neoclassical facade. The apartment building was erected in 1802, and its curved roof was added almost a century later, implementing the profile recently authorized by the building code.

earlier concept of the regularized street frontage the notion of the building's spatial envelope, which determined, on the basis of the width of the street, the volume into which the building was to be inscribed. The outline was determined by the height of the vertical facade and the angle or arc that described the slope of the roof. In Paris, the height of the facade plane was thus set at fifty-eight feet for roads wider than thirty-two feet, the angle of the roof at forty-five degrees, and the height of the ridge limited to seventy-four feet. These dimensions permitted buildings with a ground floor nearly thirty feet high, intended for commercial space, with five more stories above: the first of these a mezzanine, the second with a considerably higher ceiling, the third and fourth of approximately the same height, and the fifth, built under the roof, with a slightly lower ceiling. Maids' rooms, lit only by dormer windows, were usually constructed in the attics. On narrower streets, the height limits were proportionately lower, and the number of stories fewer.

The building codes that evolved later, even with the increasing height of buildings, did not vary much from the original guidelines. The 1859 code confirmed the 1783 guidelines when it raised the height of the street front to sixty-six feet for streets more than sixty-five feet wide. This comfortably allowed five-story buildings to be erected on the broad avenues. The next set of regulations, promulgated in 1882, made it possible to build higher on the wider streets, an arrangement reiterated in the 1902 code. Thus, the attic could comprise as many as three habitable stories rather than one. In this way, the architectural type of the apartment house remained quite consistent throughout the nineteenth century, even though the average width and height of buildings increased.

There was little building during the Empire, but the real-estate boom of 1823 to 1828, most noticeable in Paris, led to the construction of a great number of apartment houses. Along with new public buildings, these apartment houses, raising their spare and sober facades amid the typically disparate urban fabric, were concrete examples of the modernization of French cities. Examples in Paris were legion, many buildings following the lead of those on the Rue de Rivoli, designed by Charles Percier and Pierre-François-Léonard Fontaine in 1802. In the provinces, the fine apartment building constructed in 1839–42 in Fontenay-le-Comte in the Vendée to house the Passage de l'Industrie is a remarkable example, with its motif of Palladian windows above the entry porch and its limestone facade.

In the mid-1830s apartment buildings, still clearly under Neoclassical influence, began to feature more elaborate decoration, often inspired by the French Renaissance. Architects made the most of stucco and cast iron to devise economical but ornate ornament that tended to cover the entire facade. In the 1840s, a generation of buildings displayed the Picturesque aesthetic that was spreading as a reaction to the rigor of Neoclassicism. The technical capabilities to mold plaster and cast iron produced inexpensive moldings, window frames, balustrades, doors, and sculpted elements. Today, only its facade remains, but the famous Maison Dorée, built in 1839 on the Boulevard des Italiens in Paris, by the architect Lemaire and the sculptor Pierre-Louis Rouillard, was one of the first buildings to exhibit this change in style. The 1843 apartment house at 26 Place Saint-Georges displays a remarkable example of the type of sculpted decor that proliferated in the period, and that can still be seen on a number of buildings in the ninth arrondissement. Along similar lines, the Maison des Sangliers in Nîmes is a product of the decorative reaction that characterizes the period of Louis Philippe.

During the apartment-house boom, the urban private home, the *hôtel particulier,* a legacy of the classical tradition, survived, though it was often smaller and designed with simpler forms. The great private house, with its courtyard and garden, became rarer; in its place there arose in the 1820s the one- or two-story house with a porte cochere that opened directly onto the street. The multiplication of smaller homes on smaller lots required new solutions. The aristocratic *hôtel* of the ancien régime had been situated between a courtyard on the street and a garden in the back, but in the typical development of the 1820s the court disappeared or was combined with the garden. The house would be made smaller in order to retain a scrap of private garden in the back. Developed in the 1820s and inhabited at the time by so many artists that it was

A decorative motif dating from 1830 on the Maison des Sangliers in Nîmes. The clock implies a commercial presence in the building. Beginning in 1840, facades again became ornate.

nicknamed the New Athens, the Rue de la Tour-des-Dames in Paris displays a handsome collection of such houses. The two-story Hôtel Pourtalès, built in 1836 to designs by Félix Duban on Rue Tronchet in Paris, is laid out around a small court; the decoration of the facade is very delicate. A winner of the Grand Prix de Rome, Duban, along with Guillaume-Abel Blouet, Émile-Jacques Gilbert, and Pierre-François-Henri Labrouste, also of the Académie Française in Rome, was one of the premier practitioners of a Neoclassical style that was very much influenced by the Italian Renaissance.

VILLAS

The villa, a country or suburban primary residence, was entirely a nineteenth-century creation. It was born with the rise of the middle class, for whom it represented an alternative that was less expensive than the urban town house and more attractive than an apartment. The astounding proliferation of villas of every kind across the country shaped the suburbs of every French city in the nineteenth century. As César Daly aptly noted in 1864, in *L'Architecture privée sous Napoléon III*:

> *Our suburban architecture is that of a middle class that is generally rich, well-mannered, and enlightened. It could stand for the genius and character of modern civilization, just as the temples of Egypt and Greece, the baths and amphitheaters of Rome, and the cathedrals and châteaux of the Middle Ages help us to understand the civilizations preceding our own, and grasp their spirit.*

Villas drew on various traditions. They originated in French and English aristocratic country houses, to which one retired to enjoy the pleasures of the countryside, although these houses were often built near cities. The model of the resort or vacation home, however, like that proposed by Jacques-François Blondel in his *De la Distribution des maisons de plaisance* of 1737, was not really adaptable to the needs of the nineteenth-century middle class. Royal follies—whether the Petit Trianon or Richard Mique's 1780 thatch-roofed *hameau* in the park at Versailles, where Marie-Antoinette played shepherdess—were too specific to serve as models. It was common architectural practice to look to classical antiquity for solutions to architectural problems, but in this case there were

The Italianate villa of La Garenne-Lemot, near Clisson, adopted the style of the Picturesque villa quite literally. It was situated in delightful surroundings and complemented by outbuildings deliberately intended to evoke the Roman countryside.

no satisfactory models. The Roman villa had been a rural manor house geared to farming, and its architecture was ultimately very narrowly determined by functional considerations. The Italian landscape, however, depicted countless times by architects as well as by painters, suggested how to place a house in the landscape in a way that is both Sublime—because it evokes either the grandeur of natural space or the tragic quality of time, manifested by ruins—and Picturesque—because of the effects of massing, asymmetry, and irregular materials. In contrast to the Italian Renaissance villa, typified by Palladio, which was an imposing house in an agricultural setting, the Italian rural house provided a better model for the nineteenth-century suburban house. Its smaller scale made it economically accessible to the middle class, yet it still expressed an ideal of beauty and offered its owner the gratification of contact with nature, which was considered a symbol of social status. The estate of La Garenne-Lemore, built between 1805 and 1827 near Clisson, presents a Picturesque vision of an idealized relationship between the landscape and agriculture, whose buildings are literal expressions of Italian vernacular architecture. A park dotted with landscape follies, inspired chiefly by those of Tivoli, near Rome, adds the finishing touch to this Arcadia transplanted to the Nantes area.

Villas also borrowed from the Romantic architecture of landscape follies and from the local and exotic traditions such structures suggest. Among these eclectic stylistic models, some had more desirable connotations than others. The mountain chalet, for example, offered the advantage of being free of any reference to peasantry.

Until 1850, there was little difference between châteaux and the great country—or even suburban—villas, because the clientele was the same. As César Daly observed in 1864, the villa was

> *a new word for that class of structures that are elegant rather than vast, sought after by the well-off middle class. The meaning of the word* villa, *which even a few years ago was limited to the country residences of the upper middle class, has become wider, taking in both the higher and lower registers, absorbing, in the higher, the château, with some of its arrogance forsaken, and in the lower, the suburban residence, where a freer fancy reigns.*

Because the château was reserved for the elite, the villa came to be defined as a kind of miniature château that deliberately borrowed features of the château, but on a smaller scale, or else deformed them, sometimes to the point at which they became nonfunctional. For example, when a park is scaled back to a simple garden, it might become too small for strolling. Likewise, a bartizan or an ogival window could be enough to give the owner the illusion of living in a Gothic manor. Indeed, the fanciful Picturesque Neo-Gothic style endured longer among more modest houses than the châteaux, because it became associated with the general trend of eclecticism that characterized the newly developing suburbs and seaside resorts. The English influence was obvious, derived from the celebrated Fonthill Abbey, built in 1796 for the eccentric millionaire William Beckford, and from Horace Walpole's home, Strawberry Hill. The villa that J. Danjoy built in 1845 in the hamlet of Boileau in Paris exhibits features typical of the medieval Picturesque style in its decorative vocabulary, its asymmetrical layout, its wood-paneled, projecting bay, and its turret/stairtower.

Lyons's Rue Impériale, today Rue de la République, attests to the influence of the Haussmann model of wide boulevards throughout the big cities of France. The apartment buildings of the time were characterized by facades with shallow projections.

THE HAUSSMANN PLAN

The early years of the Second Empire witnessed a return to a certain architectural propriety, as well as an expansion of the stylistic repertoire applied to residential buildings. While the use of historical styles varied with the architect, for apartment houses the decorative treatment remained limited, and the facades tended to become simpler. Already under way in the last years of Louis Philippe's reign, this trend became more marked during the prefecture of Baron Georges-Eugène Haussmann, who exercised great control over the planning and redevelopment of Paris. Regulatory codes limited building projections into the public domain. As a result, facades became more planar, austere, and virtually unembellished except for balconies running along the so-called *piano nobile*—usually the second floor, or the third if there was a mezzanine—and the sixth floor. The balconies served to unify the streetscapes and enhance the vistas along the long thoroughfares that, as a result of Haussmann's urban plan, crossed the city and radiated from important intersections. As Victor Hugo wrote in *Les Années funestes*:

> *How fine! You can see from Pantin as far as Grenelle*
> *The old Paris is now just one endless street*
> *Stretching, elegant and fine as an I*
> *Saying, Rivoli! Rivoli! Rivoli!*

The numerous apartment houses built along the new boulevards were basically identical in their massing and design, the repetitive effect further emphasized by their regular widths, the even rhythm of window bays, the uniform use of limestone ashlar, and restrained ornamentation reduced to a few decorative elements, such as cornices, lintels, and balconies. A vertical rhythm that had allowed particular buildings to stand out was replaced by a homogeneous horizontal streetscape.

Famous engravings showing apartment houses in cross section, like Victor Texier's in his 1853 *Tableaux de Paris*, depict families of very different social conditions living under one roof. The size, ceiling height, and prestige of the apartments decreased with each story, from bottom to top. In the apartment house that Labrouste built in 1850 for the staff of the Bibliothèque Sainte-Geneviève, the director occupied the entire *piano nobile,* while the lower-level employees shared two or three apartments per floor on the upper stories.

This horizontal social stratification came to be replaced by a segregation by neighborhood and by type of building. In his survey of residential architecture, Daly distinguished three classes of rental buildings. The first comprised buildings with courtyards, gardens, coach houses, and stables. There were no shops on the ground floor, and the stairwell was decorated with some degree of ostentation. The apartments had large reception rooms on the street side, and private rooms, usually off a long hallway, on the courtyard side. The kitchen and servants' quarters were relegated to the very back of the apartment and were reached by a separate stairway. The second-class buildings had shops on the ground floor and less spacious rooms, but the apartments were laid out more or less like those in the first-class buildings. If the building did not comprise stables, there was no porte cochere. In the third class of building, the rooms were smaller, more crowded, and not as well arranged, and there were no service stairs. As Daly observed:

> *The outside appearance as well as the inside layout of a rental apartment should remain self-effacing, so to speak, answering only to the taste and needs common to the great mass of the people, and making an effort to satisfy these as much as possible. The general type, therefore, reflects but faintly the high concepts of art and the fancies of the imagination.*

The principles that emerged from the changes taking place in Paris were demonstrated in other French cities as well. In Lyons, the public works undertaken by the prefect Claude-Marius Vaïsse, such as the 1855 opening of Rue Impériale (today the Rue de la République), Rue de l'Impératrice, and Rue and Place Carnot, brought about the construction of a number of buildings. In Marseilles, the Rue Impériale was opened and developed along Haussmann's scheme, but with livelier architecture.

The typical urban town house began to exchange its private garden for a small garden in front. This set the house back a little from the street, isolating it in its lot, which gave it a monumental quality due less to its size, which was often small, than to its handsome situation framed in greenery.

Examples of such town houses are those built to plans by Jacques-Ignace Hittorff on Paris's Place de l'Étoile, and Labrouste's 1858 *hôtel* on Rue de Berry for the minister Achille-Marcus Fould. The layouts of the houses themselves, however, remained traditional, with reception rooms on the raised first floor, the family's private chambers on the second floor, and the ancillary rooms on the third. The necessary stables were relegated to the back of the lot, reached by a covered walkway, or underground, if the land was very expensive.

Freestanding town houses were exempt from the stylistic and regulatory restrictions that affected the apartment houses. Eclecticism could easily be given free rein—as long as the style remained within the conventions that the owner deemed fitting to his rank. In the Hôtel Vilgruy on Place François I, built in 1860, Labrouste abandoned the Louis XIII style of the Hôtel Fould for an eighteenth-century mode, which was embellished, however, with ornament in a contemporary spirit. The famous Pompeian house on Avenue Montaigne, which Alfred Normand built in 1868 for Prince Jérome Napoléon, was organized like an ancient Roman house around a central atrium and decorated in the appropriate manner. That house was demolished in 1891, but the Hôtel de la Païva at 25 Champs-Élysées is still standing, a testament to the opulence of the Second Empire. Païva, a celebrated courtesan of humble birth, had her young and wealthy lover, Comte Henckel von Donnersmarck, build her a sumptuous town house. The architect, Pierre Manguin, designed a fairly conventional Neo-Renaissance house, whose extraordinary interior decoration, carried out under the direction of Eugène Legrain, was partly inspired by the Château de Fontainebleau. There are marble sculptures by Jules Dalou and Albert-Ernest Carrier-Belleuse—in particular, an extraordinary mantel supported by two female figures—remounted paintings, and lots of giltwork; the showpiece is the onyx stairway.

Artists' studios were variations on the *hôtels particuliers*. They had few or no outbuildings or servants' areas; instead, the plan was organized around the double-height studio space itself, which was lit by a vast two-story window, usually with northern exposure. The house of the painter Jules Jollivet, in Paris's Cité Malesherbes, is one of the finest examples of this type of studio. Built in 1858 by the architect Antoine Jal, it is made up of four levels served by two stairways, one of them a service stairway. The painting studio is on the fourth floor, in the attic, while the garden-level space is occupied by the studio Jollivet used for painting on lava, his specialty. The artist's creations were directly applied to the facade, whose vigorous polychromy is utterly remarkable. Jollivet also owned an Italianate-style house, Villa Palissy, on the English Channel coast, whose exterior was entirely sheathed in terra cotta and glazed lava.

The custom arose of ceramists exhibiting their wares to passersby in this fashion, turning their homes into showcases. Glazed lava was employed this way on the facade of a ceramist's building constructed in 1867 at 16 Rue Fénélon, next door to the church of Saint-Vincent-de-Paul; its interior decoration also relies largely on this medium. A house built in Auneuil, in the Oise region, by a ceramist named Boulenger, goes further still: The interior and exterior alike are covered with different tiles, making the house a three-dimensional catalogue of the artist's creations.

PICTURESQUE HOMES

In nineteenth-century France private homes, more than apartment buildings, manifested the idea that architecture was not only solely a medium for the collective expression of social status and function, but a true artistic expression. Custom and convention informed the design of homes, which had to translate into built form the fundamental values of the social group that built them, while providing comfort as well. Thus, the ground floor was very often built over a cellar, both for reasons of hygiene and to raise the house onto a pedestal. The plan was symmetrical, with a flight of steps leading to a vestibule, off which, on either side of the axis, were the drawing room and dining room; the master bedrooms and washroom were on the second floor, and the children's rooms, servants' rooms, or both, on the third. Villas opened to the outside through their many windows, but also through overhanging elements such as balconies, bow windows, and terraces. A Mansard roof could accommodate an additional floor, and dormer windows usually provided opportunities for decorative motifs.

Within this coherent scheme, no type of building was less restrictive in terms of design than the nineteenth-century suburban house. There were no rules about lot lines, massing, or ceiling heights, and no limitations on building projections to inhibit the architects' imaginations, unlike the situation in the cities, where growth was strictly controlled by a host of regulations. Furthermore, architects could draw upon a repertoire of styles from every time and place. There were trends, of course, but for the most part the Neoclassical vocubulary coexisted easily with those of the Neo-Gothic and Neo-Renaissance modes, and countless vernacular elements continually enriched and enlivened the architectural language.

The picturesque seaside villas that the newly wealthy tradesmen built for themselves were more than signs of social and economic success, and more than functional shelters in which to spend vacations. Even though generally they were designed using a limited combination of elements, each home projected itself as unique, different from all others, through the imaginative richness of its architecture. Taken together, these houses formed communities that were homogeneous and at the same time utterly varied. Thus each homeowner, though conforming to a restrictive social model, nevertheless acted upon a desire to affirm his or her individuality. In this way, a house became an opportunity to relate the owner's personal history,

Residential design derived from the possibilities of construction materials as well as from the vast repertoire of styles.

Opposite: Les Dunes, a villa in Châtelallon-Plage, exhibits inventive wooden fretwork, an economical way to embellish gables.

Right: The Villa Belza in Biarritz, designed by Alphonse Bertrand in 1885, enjoys an exceptional location by the ocean. The theme of the corner turret was borrowed directly from the medieval architectural vocabulary.

The Picturesque style found many expressions in seaside villas.

Far left: A villa in Forges-les-Eaux.

Left: Roche-Ronde, a villa in Biarritz, by Alphonse Bertrand, 1884.

aspirations, local roots, travels abroad—in short, the summary of his or her life.

Members of the middle and lower middle classes certainly invested a great deal in their homes, but they always sought to maximize the relationship between cost and the effect obtained. Thus, structural elements such as the posts and beams, the masonry work, and the roof frame were always approached from both technical and ornamental points of view. Simple, inexpensive layouts, combined with mass-produced decorative elements, produced diverse and picturesque results. Naturally, the smaller scale of such houses and the multiplication of these effects over an entire neighborhood further emphasized the overall picturesqueness. This type of construction had the advantage of providing numerous options for every budget.

Unlike country châteaux, villas were adapted to the limited sites available in cities and the surrounding suburbs. The improvement of transportation systems had led to the development of outlying communities of private homes, used as both primary and secondary residences. The residential outskirts that burgeoned in the mid-nineteenth century represented, originally at least, attempts to join city and country, and to take advantage of the benefits of both. The transposition of the ideals of the aristocratic country house to the edge of the city, outside it but still accessible to it on a daily basis, arose from a desire for health and hygiene that the typical French city of the period could not easily satisfy, though it retained its central function as the site of commerce. Indeed, Haussmann's urban policy confirmed the city's status as the place where power was exercised and business was conducted in the collective interest—at least, as defined by the industrial middle class. In this context, the public buildings that housed the institutions common to society as a whole were symbolically foregrounded, both by their status as monuments and by their prominent placement on streets and avenues, according to a subtle hierarchy, whereas apartment buildings conformed to a rigorously imposed scheme, from which any architectural flourish was banned.

By contrast, the suburbs could exalt individuality by allowing the middle-class homeowner to turn his home and garden into a microcosm, in which he

Right: The reference to traditional half-timbering is given a twist with a profusion of fretwork.

Far right: The influence of exoticism, and particularly of the Neo-Moorish style, is apparent in La Tunisienne, a villa in Hyères.

could reign supreme—without subjects, perhaps, but in his own castle nonetheless. In 1877, Viollet-le-Duc gave a great deal of attention to the design of the private house, publishing a collection of model homes; he observed that "only the private home can inculcate the habit of being oneself."

The practice of parceling land into lots is an ancient one, but in the nineteenth century it became an essential means of urban development. Throughout the first half of the century, the division of vast aristocratic estates into lots, along with the opening of new roads by companies of real-estate speculators, resulted in the reconstruction of part of the center of Paris and the extension westward of new neighborhoods. Many such neighborhoods were laid out in the 1820s, but only really developed two or three decades later. A comparable phenomenon took place in the suburbs, except that there the building unit was the house, not the apartment building. A few developments on the west side of Paris are particularly worthy of note, such as the estate of the Château de Maisons, parceled into lots in 1833 by Jacques Laffitte, a banker. The articles and conditions of sale included rules intended to preserve the overall landscape; for example, it was forbidden to wall off the lots on the main thoroughfares. The architect Charles Duval built a number of villas there, such as 39 Avenue Albine, constructed for the singer Luigi Lablache.

The creation of Le Vésinet, also on the west side of Paris, in 1863, is paradigmatic. In 1856, Alphonse Pallu bought a government-owned forest, which he broke up into lots. He organized the town around a system of parks and tree-lined avenues, beautifully designed by an architect named Olive, and imposed easements upon the residents in order to maintain an aesthetic unity. The Paris–Saint Germain railway line largely made the development of Le Vésinet possible, and a train station, church, and other primary public buildings and shops made up the tiny downtown.

This type of speculative development was relatively rare, because real estate tended to be fragmented; most often, the suburbs developed spontaneously, incorporating small lots and forming residential sections around preexisting urban centers. Nogent-sur-Marne, for example, because of the railway line that reached it in 1850 and its privileged situation on the Marne River, offered a day trip for crowds of city residents desperate for greenery and fresh air. In this popular place for Sunday outings, architect G. Nachbaur, sometimes on his own, sometimes jointly with his sons, built a number of villas and apartment houses, including their own home, La Détente, at 3 Boulevard de la République, which exhibits a generous display of Picturesque architectural motifs: terra-cotta accents, wrought-iron elements, and millstone, an attractive yet inexpensive material that came to typify the suburban villa. Cities like Nogent are also interesting because they manifest the evolution of the typical suburban house, that simplified avatar of the middle-class villa, whose elements it attempts to replicate, just as the early villa tried to copy the château. In the twentieth century, the democratization of the private house also arose from a desire for social integration on the part of the working and lower-middle classes, expressed by ownership of a house that conformed ideologically and aesthetically to the residential style of the dominant class.

The middle class took up the aristocracy's practice of seasonal vacations away from home, and passed its summers at the seaside or at the spas. Here, too, the railway extended horizons. These resorts were ideal cities that had no utilitarian functions—there were no smokestacks, unlike in most of the big cities, including Paris. Such places projected a homogeneous, progressive, and positive image of society. As they were seasonal, their existence was cadenced by the migration patterns of a population ceaselessly seeking an eternal springtime, its wanderings—made possible by the railroad—leading it to re-create miniature landscapes where one could pass effortlessly from one period or country to another. These towns were, in effect, sites of experimental urban planning, in which the villa was the basic architectural element.

In these places, villas were required to project social status less than in locations nearer the cities, and were freer to exhibit ornamental flourishes that displayed the personal tastes of their owners. Whereas the middle-class suburban home of the Second Empire was often in the neo–Louis XIII style, which was respectable as well as economical, since it employed brick, in the 1880s architects began to abandon the conventions of historical quotation, borrowing liberally instead from vernacular sources. A new aesthetic took shape, one wholeheartedly committed to Picturesque effects, but drawing upon a much wider vocabulary than that of the previous generation. Without quite the whimsy of their counterparts across the English Channel, French houses drew a great deal upon British domestic architecture. Bow windows, which extend a sitting room outward and allow more light into the interior, entered domestic architecture in full force, both in private homes and apartment buildings. Because they were very often of wood or metal, providing a contrast in materials, and because they projected outward, bow windows enlivened the facades of buildings and broke up the compositional unity that respect for historical styles demanded. Asymmetry became the rule in the massing of architectural elements, such as large and elaborate roof profiles that bristled with dormers, half-timbered projecting staircases, and exuberantly projecting chimney stacks.

The desire to identify one's villa with a château, thereby appropriating the external signs of aristocratic ostentation, is obvious in the use of the turret motif in many villas. Today a hotel, the Villa Les Tourelles in Le Crotoy is named for its turrets. Likewise, the use of the Neo-Renaissance style in the Loire Valley refers explicitly to the local context. Among the many houses built in this mode are a house dating to 1845 at 37 Rue Briçonnet in Tours, and the Praslines Mazet house, on Rue du Général-Leclerc in Montargis, erected in 1920. Also in this style, the guardhouse of the Château de Chenonceau, dating to 1877, is in the tradition of Picturesque landscape garden buildings, whereas the *hôtel* at 116 Rue Béranger in Tours, built in 1884–85 to designs by Stephen Sauvestre, stands out for its Rationalist elegance. Henri Racine's 1889 development of small Neo-Gothic houses on Rue Léonard-de-Vinci in Tours is a testament to the endurance of the Picturesque tradition.

Reference to local styles was prevalent in almost every region, producing half-timbering on houses in Normandy, crow-stepped gables on the north coast, and wooden chalets in the mountain resort areas. But chalets were no less fashionable at the spas and seaside resorts, for example, at Vichy, where

This home in Auxerre looks more like a miniature château than an actual residence.

Napoléon III had several constructed for his own use, or at Le Touquet, where the first houses were made of wood. Wood was more than just an economical material. It was a metaphor for nature, transmitted by association with the primitive hut, which celebrated the life of the noble savage, and the English cottage, the domesticated version of the primordial shelter. Wood was also used for its decorative value, in half-timbering, gables, balcony supports, balustrades, and fretwork, an economical way to edge roofs. Many of the houses in Arcachon's "winter town" used wood as a means to blend the architecture into the splendid pine forest that makes the spot so charming. One example is the Péreire chalet, which was built for the resort's founder and torn down in 1959. Villa Marie, at 11 Allée Marie-Christine, exhibits very fine fretwork tracery. Analogously, the thatched roof, which was popular at resorts such as Le Touquet, gave the illusion of a rustic cottage. In the early twentieth century, wood began to be replaced by fake half-timbering, obtained by simply applying a coat of wood-colored plaster over cement. In Sologne, La Saulot, Auguste and Gustave Perret's remarkable 1908 hunting lodge, and one of their first projects, displays this variation on the Picturesque tradition, without compromising its overall Neo-Norman style.

From beyond national boundaries, exoticism serves as another fertile resource for the design of villas in resort towns. The architecture of remote countries provided specific elements, such as the veranda, imported from India, as well as entire house designs that were translated literally, lending the towns vivid Picturesque accents. Among the many examples of this trend are the Persian villa built in Trouville for the princesse de Sagan, which is remarkable for its brick decoration framing a set-back loggia; Trouville's Chinese pagoda, transported to Asnières in 1857; Le Havre's Chinese villa, built by an architect named Poupel in 1880; the 1892 Congo palace in Tourcoing, which no longer exists; Luchon's Swiss, Russian, and Persian chalets; the Indo-Troubadour "Englishman's Castle" above Nice, constructed for a colonel-archaeologist back from India; and the villa in Varengeville by Sir Edward Lutyens, the architect of New Delhi, who brought to the project a very personal expression of modernism.

The Mediterranean coast is dotted with exotic houses, especially "Oriental"—best described as Neo-Moorish—villas. After all, North Africa is only a night away by ship, and the port city of Marseilles has always absorbed influences from Africa and the East. Many of these Neo-Moorish villas were built by former colonials upon their return to France. Orientalism was an established Romantic current in the arts, made fashionable by painters such as Eugène Delacroix and Eugène-Samuel-Auguste Fromentin and by writers such as Théophile Gautier, Alexandre Dumas, and Gérard de Nerval. It received a further impetus during the Second Empire from poets such as Charles-Pierre Baudelaire. Michel Pacha, a former merchant marine officer who had served the Ottoman Empire for ten years, developed the resort town of Tamaris around 1880 and commissioned the architect Paul Page to build an institute of marine biology in an Orientalizing style. The same architect built himself a "beach hut" in the same style in Pierrefeu, north of Hyères. The latter town also boasts two particularly intriguing villas: in 1870–80, the architect Pierre Chapoulart built himself the Villa Algérienne on Avenue Beauregard—it was later rechristened the Villa Tunisienne—and then, in 1880, he built the Villa Mauresque, that is, the Moorish Villa, for Alexis Godillot, a local celebrity who had made his fortune supplying Napoleon's army with shoes. Helvetia, a villa near Ollioules, and Petite Afrique, near Beaulieu-sur-Mer, are other surviving examples of a phenomenon found all along the coast. Although their layouts tend to remain traditional, various characteristic features appear in the design of these villas: horseshoe arches, mosaic decoration, Moorish ornamental motifs, crenelated parapets masking tiled roofs, and minaretlike towers. Surrounding palm trees further contribute to the exotic atmosphere. The Neo-Moorish manner also appears in other regions of France. The tiny village of L'Herbe on the Bassin d'Arcachon, for example, includes a villa with a miniature golf course in this style, which is also true for the Villa Tunisienne in Vichy.

In most of the French resort towns styles mingled more or less haphazardly. Biarritz is a particularly remarkable case; the beauty of its location, its relatively well preserved buildings, and the range of their styles serve to make the town a veritable catalogue of fin-de-siècle eclectic architecture. Side by side with historicizing villas such as the Château Grammont of 1866, on Rue Saint-Martin, with its rather conventional brick-and-stone facade, or the more elaborately eclectic Château Boulard, on Rue du Maréchal-Foch, built by Louis-Joseph Duc in 1870, there are Neo-Gothic villas (Cyrano, of 1901, by the architect and Biarritz native Gustave Huguenin, on Avenue de l'Impératrice), Neo-Basque villas (Lou Bascou, of 1903, by Raymond Larrebat-Tudor, at the Hélianthe intersection), and even Anglicizing Neo-Norman villas (Château Françon, of 1882, by the English architect Ralph Selden Wornum). Though more prosaic than the villa that Henri Sauvage constructed in Nancy for the cabinetmaker Louis Majorelle, Natacha, a Biarritz villa designed by Sauvage in 1907, exhibits very interesting Art Nouveau decoration. Not far from Biarritz rises the curious château that was built in 1881 for the millionaire misanthrope Baron Albert de l'Espée. From the outside, it is a great stone mass perched atop a hill, but inside it is richly appointed with a Neo-Renaissance grand staircase and an enormous music room specially designed to house a huge organ.

The architecture of apartment buildings was often enlivened by decorative details. Here, a glazed terra-cotta motif on the Céramic Hôtel on Avenue de Wagram in Paris.

THE ART NOUVEAU EPISODE

Born in the 1890s, Art Nouveau, an art movement that took root in reaction to the dominant academic order, sought new sources of inspiration by turning to nature and freeing line in drawing. The Art Nouveau style fit perfectly into the eclectic rationale. Its explicit relationship to Neo-Gothic—through Viollet-le-Duc—merely confirmed its roots in the Picturesque movement. The finest Art Nouveau houses were designed by Hector Guimard, among them Henriette, of 1899–1900, a miniature château built in Sèvres (and now demolished), which was an extravagant stylistic exercise on the theme of the chalet; and the more sober Orgeval, of 1904–5, which illustrates the inventive ways in which millstone can be used.

The Villa Majorelle in Nancy is a masterpiece of Art Nouveau. Its composition and proportions, its details—such as gargoyles that combine medieval

The end of the century witnessed a renewal in architectural style. Art Nouveau sought inspiration in nature and in the exuberant mixture of materials.

Right, top and bottom: Mantels in the hôtel particulier *Bouctot-Vagniez in Amiens and in the Villa Majorelle in Nancy.*

Far right, top and bottom: A bow window and the entrance porch of Castel Béranger by Hector Guimard, on Rue La Fontaine in Paris.

and naturalistic features—and its largely preserved interior decoration make the house a showcase for the range of the cabinetmaker's talent. Majorelle's villa reveals the symbiosis sought by the practitioners of Art Nouveau between a strong Rationalist tradition—expressed in motifs such as the segmental stone arch, the metal consoles supporting the balconies, the clean rooflines, and the way the internal plan is articulated on the facade—and a genuine love of ornament that extended to the design of every element of the house, including the downpipes. This current is so richly illustrated in Nancy that a "School of Nancy" has been identified, and it is embodied in the city's unusual freestanding houses, especially in the Parc de Saurupt area, as well as in town houses and apartment and commercial buildings. For example, in 1903, Émile André designed at 92 Quai Claude-le-Lorrain two very fine attached town houses with Flamboyant Gothic–style gables, a horseshoe-arched window edged with blue glazed bricks, and butterfly-wing-shaped basement windows. Lucien Weissenberger's design sense was more restrained, as may be seen in the house built to his plans in 1903–4 at 24 Rue Lionnois; the house is quintessentially of the School of Nancy, its ornamental treatment recalling that of the furniture and other objects created by the movement's artists and craftspeople. The facade's decoration incorporates the thistle and pine motifs, symbols of the provinces of Alsace and Lorraine, which had been ceded to Germany in 1871. Other remarkable buildings designed by Weissenberger are the houses at 1 Boulevard Charles-V and 52 Cours Léopold. Other notable architects of the School of Nancy are Henri Gutton, Joseph Hornecker, Georges Biet, and Eugène Vallin; the latter, trained as a cabinetmaker, was responsible, with Biet, for a handsome building at 22 Rue de la Commanderie. Also important were the many greatly talented artisans whose stained-glass windows, wood paneling, painted wallpaper, and sculpted ornament enhanced Nancy's Art Nouveau architecture. The museum of the School of Nancy, on Rue du Sergent-Blandan, in a house built during the period, has a very fine collection of pieces in this style.

Art Nouveau houses are rare outside of Paris and Nancy, however, representing the exception rather than the rule. The style was too eccentric to be broadly popular, and too demanding in its pursuit of a universal formal perfection to have engendered even a pallid second generation. In the end, these houses were manifestos, built for idiosyncratic clients or by architects for their own use, such as the house that the architect Emmanuel Leray built on Rue de Viarmes in Rennes in 1906. Other houses built around 1900 show the influence of this style, even when they do not display its characteristic features. One such house is the Villa La Roche du Roi, which overlooks Aix-les-Bains and was built by Jules Pin in 1900. Its square plan is punctuated at each corner by a bulb-capped turret, and in the center by a tower surmounted by a dome shaped like an artillery shell. The thoroughly eclectic deco-

This town house, built in 1903 on the Quai Claude-le-Lorrain in Nancy, attests to the vitality of Art Nouveau in that city. The horseshoe-arched window, the naturalistic carving, and the butterfly-shaped basement windows are typical features of the style.

ration uninhibitedly mixes Romanesque, Gothic, Baroque, and Rococo motifs.

THE APARTMENT BUILDING AT CENTURY'S END

Apartment buildings were equally influenced by the Picturesque reaction at the end of the century. The rigors of the architecture built under Haussmann were beginning to pall; a decree of 1882 had already eased the regulations governing the street frontages. It permitted architectural projections if they employed lightweight materials, making possible the construction of bow windows in wood or metal. On the occasion of the opening of the Rue Réaumur, the Paris city council explicitly encouraged the development of new architectural effects, sponsoring in 1896 a contest for the facades to be built on that street. The goal, of course, was "to beautify Paris," with the stated desire, in the council's words, "to react against the monotony of the far too primitive style of these old houses, with their plain facades, to remove from the street the dishearteningly uniform appearance" that it had acquired under Haussmann's prefecture. In order to achieve "more picturesqueness, more artistic inventiveness," builders were allowed to consider the 1882 decree, which would not be ratified until 1902. The new codes permitted much higher roofs, as well as the convex roof profiles that produced the typical silhouette of the period; taller buildings at intersections, which meant that corner buildings could be given a monumental treatment; and bow windows of stone, which had a more solid appearance than those of wood and could thus be integrated completely into the design of the facade. The aim of this and other contests was simultaneously to defend eclecticism and to revive the architecture of rental buildings, while following a program that was both urbanistic and dictated by the requirements of immediate profitability: in other words, to go beyond the architectural doctrines that were the legacy of the Second Empire, while maintaining the context of a traditional city. The contest was only partially successful. In 1898, the first year in which it was juried, only fifty-three proposals were submitted for the nearly four hundred buildings constructed in Paris that year.

Alongside facades that look quite banal to us today, there are those that hold a particular interest because they reveal the profound terms of the era's architectural debate. While some architects merely attempted to inflate classical models, embellishing facades with sculpture, caryatids, projections, and attics with several stories, others engaged in a renewal of the architectural language by looking to floral and other plant imagery for inspiration, by deliberately using Picturesque motifs derived from vernacular styles and Far Eastern traditions, and by employing new or unusual materials. Guimard's 1898 Castel Béranger, for example, exhibits a successful combination of varied materials. Inspired by the Belgian architect Victor Horta's experiments, Guimard achieved a tour de force in designing an apartment building in the Parisian mold that was as Picturesque as any seaside home. Expanding upon the villa model, Guimard composed a collage of materials—limestone ashlar, millstone, bricks of different colors, and cast and wrought iron are juxtaposed on the facade—and architectural motifs, such as arched windows, loggias, stone and iron balconies, oriels, corbels, gables, and so on.

Other apartment houses display a similar pursuit of a new architectural language that attempted to find fresh influences and to compose plans and facades more freely without breaking entirely with tradition. When Art Nouveau buildings are most unconventional, it is sometimes due to their owners' personalities. Thus, the ceramist Alexandre Bigot, moved by the desire to advertise and promote his cast sandstone and to illustrate its architectural potential, commissioned two buildings in a row from Jules Lavirotte: the first, in 1901, at 29 Avenue Rapp and another, in 1902, at 34 Avenue de Wagram—today the Ceramic Hotel. The first has an ashlar base distinguished by a very beautiful

Metal was used in an expressive manner in this well-known Art Nouveau building on Rue Réaumur in Paris.

Reinforced concrete, which appeared at the turn of the century, at first was made to look like stone, as in this building on Rue Danton in Paris, by the Hennebique firm.

doorway adorned with female figures intertwined with ferns; the upper stories are of cement covered with cast sandstone panels imitating stone. Art Nouveau's Rationalist roots are evident in the great arch that supports the loggia on the top floor, a nonfunctional but spectacular gesture. Neo-Assyrian ox heads, a curious decorative motif, add a final touch to this unusual facade. The building on Avenue de Wagram is more sober, but its entire facade is sheathed with terra cotta. Similarly, a ceramist named Coilliot commissioned Guimard to design a town house in Lille with very distinct Gothic elements, especially the pointed equilateral arch that frames the facade. In Paris, Charles Klein also used terra cotta, at 9 Rue Claude-Chahu, for a highly unusual facade. Louis Duthoit, the son of Viollet-le-Duc's close collaborator Edmond-Armand-Marie Duthoit, built several apartment houses with terra-cotta ornament in Orléans between 1897 and 1904, including a series along Rue de la République, which had recently opened to connect the train station with the city center. The Hôtel Moderne, at number 37, recalls Lavirotte's Avenue Rapp building in Paris, constructed two years earlier.

SAUVAL
1638-1718

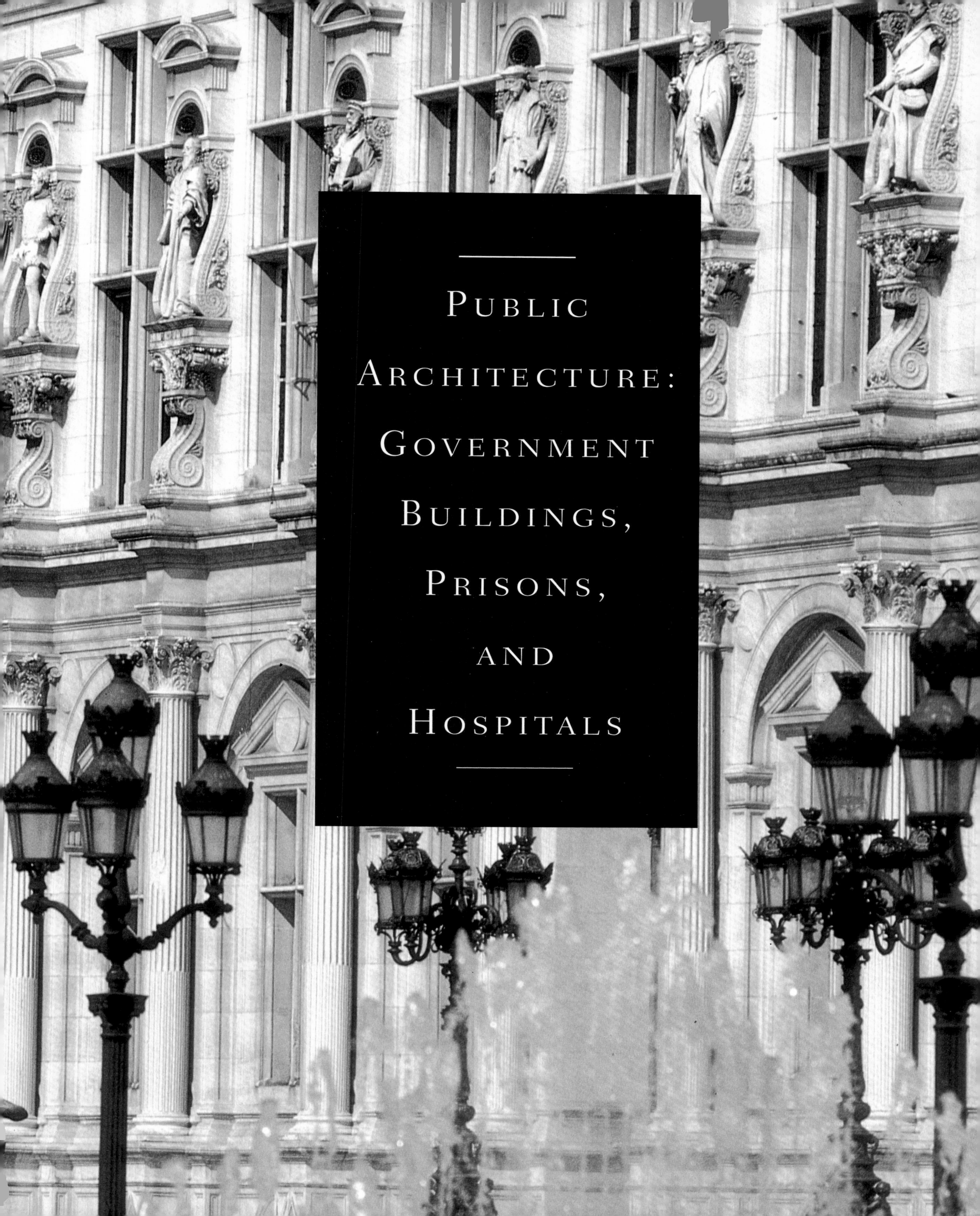

Public Architecture: Government Buildings, Prisons, and Hospitals

— CASERNE

— Ensemble

ÉLÉSTINS —

ent-projet) —

Dressé par l'architecte soussigné
Paris le 31 janvier 1877.

The origins of the modern idea of government in France may be traced far back in history, but it was already firmly established by the nineteenth century, independent of the fluctuations in political power and the revolutions that punctuated the century. Gradually, the idea of the state came to be embodied explicitly and systematically in an array of buildings, distributed throughout the country, which signaled the presence and power of the government, especially in the areas of administration and of the security and health of its citizens. The collective assumption of responsibility for the growing population and for new standards of sanitation and comfort gave rise to an unprecedented surge in construction and reconstruction. Serving as civil monuments, the public buildings of the era were shaped by fairly specific coventional programs and fit within a hierarchy according to purpose.

THE POWER OF THE STATE

Before the mid-nineteenth century, structures that represented the power of the state tended to be in a Neoclassical style. In 1808, Bernard Poyet gave the Palais Bourbon a Corinthian portico of colossal proportions that was designed to echo the portico of La Madeleine. The architecture of the Ministry of Foreign Affairs built by Charles Bonnard two years later was less austere, with an Italianate facade in which windows surmounted by semicircular arches alternated with engaged columns. Destroyed under the Commune, the building remained a constant reference for public architecture, a model of the resources available in the Italian classical mode.

In general, the most conservative Neoclassicism was used for building types requiring a certain decorum. This is particularly true for courthouses, which flourished in the period between 1820 and 1855. A style derived from the classical temple was applied almost routinely, with the row of columns in front becoming the inevitable symbol of the courthouse. Beyond the severity of the architecture, which was supposed to connote the rigor of justice, the explicit reference to antiquity and to Napoleonic Neoclassicism recalled the historical foundation and endurance of civil law, appropriately expressed by a majestic edifice. A courthouse was a temple to law.

Many of the courthouses built in the first half of the century seemed to have followed directly from *Précis des leçons d'architecture* by Jean-Nicolas-Louis Durand, an influential professor at the École Polytechnique. In 1809, he published a standard plan for a courthouse, comprising a front porch of columns supporting a pediment, behind which were arranged on either side of the central axis a series of great basilican halls surrounded by a portico. The front porch was approached by a flight of steps, which became as necessary an element of judicial architecture as the lobby or anteroom. Courthouses built along these lines between 1820 and 1850 are legion and can be found throughout France. In the Loire Valley, the courthouse of Orléans was built to plans by François Pagot in 1821–24; that of Tours, by Jean Jacquemin, in 1840–43; of Chartres, in 1844; of Blois, by Édouard Massé, in 1843–49; and of Châteauroux, by Louis Dauvergne, around 1850. The south of France is also rich in a great many buildings of this type: for example, in Périgueux, the courthouse is designed by Catoire; in Agen, by Jumelin; and in Nîmes, by Charles-Auguste Questel. The Marseilles courthouse, approved to be built in 1846 but completed only in 1862 to plans by Auguste Martin, systematically replicated the form of a Greek temple by presenting a facade of Ionic columns. The particularly austere facade of the Bordeaux courthouse, built to designs by Joseph-Adolphe Thiac in 1831–48, recalls the propylaea of ancient Greece.

Lyons's courthouse, built in 1835–47 by Louis-Pierre Baltard, breaks free of the Greek temple prototype; its long Corinthian colonnade evokes a sensation of genuine grandeur. Inside, the lobby, with its domes and rich decoration, is no less impressive. In a different style, the Chambéry courthouse, built in 1848–55 during the Sardinian occupation, has a square plan with a central courtyard after the fashion of Italian *palazzi*, from which it also took the red ocher color of its facade.

During the Second Empire, Neoclassicism began to lose its status as the only possible reference for public architecture. The abandonment of severe Neoclassicism is evident in the building of the Court of Assizes in the Paris courthouse, erected in 1857–68 by Louis-Joseph Duc. Athough the

Chapter opening spread: The city hall in Paris, a Renaissance-inspired expression of municipal power.

Preceding spread: Preliminary plan dated 1877 for the des Célestins barracks, by Marcellin Varcollier: a citadel within the city.

Opposite: The Nîmes courthouse illustrates a pervasive model borrowed from classical antiquity, which was used to signify the importance of the judicial system.

facade on Place Dauphine dutifully displays a row of Corinthian columns—the typical expression of the timelessness of justice—several elements of the design aim to give a less abstract picture of judicial architecture and to bring it closer to the civil architecture of the period: the absence of a pediment; the high, arched windows—in Duc's view, the image of a justice system that is active, matter-of-fact, and energetic; the rich decoration, with its allegorical figures representing prudence, truth, punishment, protection, strength, and equity; and the corbeled attic. The integration of judicial architecture into the eclectic aesthetic of the era is demonstrated by the commercial courthouse in Paris, built to plans by Antoine-Nicolas Bailly in 1860–64, the design of whose dome closely resembles that of Victor Baltard's church of Saint-Augustin. The Supreme Court of the Paris courthouse, also by Duc, borrowed a late French Renaissance style, less theatrical than the Court of Assizes, in keeping with the moderating role of a Supreme Court, as the critic Paul Sédille noted in 1879. Gustave Guérin's 1859–66 courthouse in Loches broke with the Neoclassical tradition with its Neo–Louis XIV style.

The endurance of the classical model, however, is evident in the Amiens courthouse. The earliest proposals, drawn up in 1860–63 by the local architect Jean Herbault, took as the building's model Henri Labrouste's Bibliothèque Nationale, with two stories on a square plan and facades punctuated by arched windows. However, the Council of Civil Buildings, represented by Jacques-Ignace Hittorff, enjoined Herbault to build the front and lateral facades with columned porches beneath a pediment. The pediment was not added to the building—inaugurated in 1869—until 1875–80, and this obvious addition gives the building an odd appearance.

MINISTRIES AND PREFECTURES

In France, ministries were customarily installed in former royal palaces or aristocratic *hôtels,* since these buildings were considered to have the prestige that the highest servants of the Republic deserved. This meant that relatively few ministries were built in the nineteenth century, and those that were, paradoxically, adopted the symbols of the absolute monarchy, most evident in the period of Louis XIV. In 1872, the Ministry of Finances was installed in the Louvre, which was partially renovated for the occasion by Hector-Martin Lefuel. The Ministry of War, by Louis Bouchot, and the Ministry of Agriculture, by Emmanuel Brune, professor of engineering at the École des Beaux-Arts, were both built in 1880 in the classical style of the seventeenth century.

By contrast, the prefectures represented a wide-open typological field, models for which usually

The grand staircase in the Marseilles prefecture, typical of the ceremonial formality of administrative buildings of the Second Empire.

The Versailles prefecture, built in 1862–67 to plans by Amédée Manuel, drew upon the classical canon to symbolize the dignity and power of the state.

ranged from those of the *grand siècle* of Louis XIV to the Neo-Renaissance, which was less pretentious and a more appropriate expression for an office of the local power. Indeed, the prefect's position was ambivalent: As the representative of the executive power in each of the country's ninety-five departments, and thus the virtual embodiment of the state, the prefect enjoyed considerable authority. But the prefect was also a functionary, one who had to keep an ear to the ground in the region and be accessible to the public, as well as host numerous balls and receptions. The prefects had been decreed in 1800. During the Empire they moved back into former provincial administrative offices and took up residence in former *hôtels particuliers* or converted church buildings, especially bishops' palaces. Only four new prefectures were built in this period, including the prefecture of La Roche-sur-Yon, a new town built in 1804–9 by the official engineer of bridges and roads, J. Cormier. In contrast, eight prefectures were built under the Restoration, evidence of the vigorous administrative effort of the time. The designs were most often by local architects, but carried out under the superintendence of the Council of Civil Buildings. For this reason, Alphonse de Gisors, inspector general of civil architecture, was commissioned to build the Ajaccio prefecture in 1826–42, after three designs were rejected by the Ministry of the Interior. Gisors would go on to design an insane asylum, barracks, and the town hall in Ajaccio. The prefecture of Angoulême was built by the local architect Paul Abadie—father of the architect of the church of the Sacré-Coeur—in 1823–34. Like other prefectures of the period, this one was a fairly sober edifice, conceived of as a simple *hôtel particulier* with a flight of steps flanked by columns. Although few people worked in the prefecture at that time, it was where the prefect lived and received visitors, and also where dignitaries visiting the department stayed. In Ajaccio, three times as much space was allotted to reception rooms as to offices.

The Second Empire witnessed an ambitious civil building program. No fewer than thirteen prefectures were erected during this time. The pomp with which these buildings were endowed confirmed the prefect's central role in local politics. Most of the prefectures reveal the influence of the grand architectural prototypes: palaces and royal châteaux. As Victor de Laprade sarcastically noted:

> *The littlest prefect, with no time to lose,*
> *Is determined to build the Louvre of loos.*
> *Proud if he leaves, when his mandate expires,*
> *A debt to his dept. as vast as the Empire's*

The Lille prefecture was built in 1865–72 by the departmental architect Charles Marteau, in the style of Versailles, with two wings forming a deep courtyard, at the back of which the principal entrance is signaled by a pavilion and a monumental staircase. In Poitiers, Alphonse Durand designed in 1864 a complex of brick and stone in the style of Louis XIII, comprising a main block and two wings arranged around a courtyard enclosed by iron gates. The same inspiration appears in the prefectures of Chaumont, Colmar, and Belfort, all built during the Second Empire. Lefuel's grand New Louvre (1852–57) also served as model for several prefectures, the most spectacular undoubtedly being that of Marseilles, built in 1861–67 at the direction of the prefect, Émile de Maupas. Auguste Martin, the departmental architect, composed a handsome, ornate facade with three slightly projecting pavilions with tiers of columns, the center one crowned with a dome—a design obviously taken from the Louvre's Cour Carrée. The interior is remarkable for its sumptuous decoration, designed by François-Joseph Nolan after Martin's forced resignation. In Grenoble in 1862, Questel drew up the plans for another great urban château, with angled wings and splendid interior decoration.

The administrative function of the prefectures increased during the Third Republic, overshadowing their ceremonial role. As a result, beginning in the 1870s building programs emphasized the prefect's and other offices, the archives, and the garages, at the expense of the reception rooms. Neo-Renaissance and even Neo-Gothic models replaced references to the *grand siècle* of Louis XIV, as expressions of an administration increasingly responsive to the citizenry. The Lyons prefecture, built in 1883–90 by Antonin Louvier, was typical of this development, though it retained an ornateness befitting a city of Lyons's importance. The prefecture of Bar-le-Duc, built in 1904–7 by Maurice

Royer, looks more like a town hall, whereas Quimper's prefecture, built two years later, is deliberately in the style of Louis XII, who annexed Brittany to France. Finally, the Limoges prefecture, built in 1897–1904 following a competition, to designs by Jules Godefroy, abandoned the symmetry that had characterized most programs, instead articulating several structures on a polygonal plan. The relative modesty of this configuration is tempered by the treatment of the principal facade, which displays a monumental sequence of paired columns flanked by a corner rotunda surmounted by a dome and a skylight, in the manner of department stores of the era.

The Poitiers city hall, one of the many Neo-Renaissance structures inspired by Paris's city hall.

CITY HALLS

More than ministries and prefectures, town and city halls were the most visible representation of the administrative network of the French government. Following the Revolution, the territory was divided into 40,000 communes, an act that superimposed a local administrative structure onto the existing network of towns and villages. In the smaller communes, the town hall—which often had the town school attached to it—symbolically integrated the rural communities into the national fabric and functioned as an important instrument of public service in the lives of the citizens. In the larger communes, the town hall was organized around a village hall and included a wedding hall and a council hall. The definitive advent of the Republic, following the vote on the famous Wallon amendment in 1875, which established the election of the president of the Republic by the Senate and the Chamber, obviously reinforced this system. The mayor and the teacher became, with respect to the priest, the representatives of secular authority, concerned with imposing Republican values in place of those defended by the Church.

The construction of city halls, expressions of local power and identity of the communes, began in the 1820s, a period in which mayors were still appointed by the powers that be, rather than elected. The city hall and library in Moulins, built in 1821–29 to plans by François Agnety, the departmental architect for Allier, is one of the finest examples of the prevailing Neoclassical style for municipal buildings. The principal facade, which contains the entrance to the city hall, has a pavilion featuring two tiers of columns and is crowned by the city's coat of arms. The rear facade, indicating the location of the library, is treated more soberly, in a style that recalls Rome's Farnese Palace. A courtyard with arcades on three sides occupies the center of the decidedly Italianate structure. Agnety used the same style for the hydropathy center in Vichy and the large seminary in Moulins, today a firehouse. Indeed, it was not uncommon for one architect to be granted exclusivity for a city's commissions for a fairly long period. And it is worth noting that communal and departmental architects not only designed new construction, but also conducted restorations and renovations of churches and châteaux.

Although mayors were still appointed from elected councils during the Second Empire, the town and city halls had already acquired a more important symbolic function. In Paris itself, the prefect Haussmann was installed in a city hall inherited from François I, to which a new building was added in 1837–46, by Étienne-Hippolyte Godde and Jean-Baptiste-Cicéron Lesueur, who respected the Renaissance style of the older structure. The style of Paris's Hôtel de Ville, drawn from Late Gothic and Renaissance sources, was well suited to this type of building, allowing an architecture that was still monumental though less austere than the Louis XIV style. The remarkable series of municipal buildings erected in each arrondissement of Paris under the Second Empire established the canon for this type of structure. Among these, the municipal building for the first arrondissement was built in 1857–61 as a pendant to the church of Saint-Germain-l'Auxerrois. Hittorff's design repeated the church's proportions and rose window, mixing Flamboyant Gothic elements with those inspired by the early Italian Renaissance. Poitiers's city hall, erected by A.-G. Guérinot in 1867–76, is a handsome example of a Renaissance-inspired composition that borrows from Philibert Delorme, especially in the banded columns of the main floor. The Tourcoing city hall, built by Charles Maillard in 1863–65, is another example of this florid style, which incorporates a profusion of decorative sculpture. For the Angoulême city hall, Paul Abadie—the architect of the church of Sacré-Coeur—used elements of medieval architecture, such as a machicolated belfry, to create a structure adapted to its own time; it is a reinterpretation of the medieval city hall, among the most apt architectural representations of civil society.

Despite the rapid spread of Neo-Renaissance models, references to local architectural traditions were common. The Wambrechies town hall was constructed in a regional Flemish style in 1868. In 1863–67, the architect Pellegrini designed the Chambéry town hall in a Piedmontese style, shortly after Savoy was returned to France.

The Paris Hôtel de Ville, burned down by the Commune in 1871, was rebuilt in a virtually identical manner, except larger, by Théodore Ballu and Pierre-Joseph-Édouard Deperthes, who extended the decorative repertoire of the design to include the early seventeenth century. Many of the city halls erected in France in these years were inspired by this fine structure, their compositions defined by a system of arched windows on the ground floor opening onto a formal hall, from which a grand staircase ascends to an awe-inspiring second-floor ballroom, which opens onto the facade through wide bays. Side pavilions housing the council chamber and the marriage hall frame the facade, punctuated in the center by a pediment that usually sports a clock and the city's coat of arms. A campanile rises above the building. Examples erected according to this model in the environs of Paris are the city halls of Suresnes; of Neuilly-sur-Seine, by Gaspard-Abraham André, in 1879–85; of Ivry; of Nogent-sur-Marne, by Victor Guillemin, in 1876–79; and in the provinces, the city halls of Limoges, by Alfred Leclerc, in 1879–83, and Tours, by Victor Laloux, in 1896–1904.

Even the Imperial Palace of Strasbourg, or Rhine Palace, built by Hermann Eggert in 1883–89 and intended to represent the political integration of Alsace-Lorraine into the German Empire, is in a Neo-Renaissance style that is more influenced by the precepts of the École des Beaux-Arts than by Pan-Germanism. It incorporates Italian elements—arched windows inscribed in a wall of rusticated stone, a classical pediment, and a monumental, rather baroque dome—and the sculptural program is also very elaborate. The building was prominently situated in the new town, opening onto a mall that is framed by an imposing complex of public structures. The other end of the mall is occupied by the university, built by the architect Otto Warth in a typical Beaux-Arts style. The French interpretation of Renaissance architecture is also evident in the many public buildings erected in Strasbourg by the Danish-born architect Skjold Neckelmann, who was educated in Vienna and at the École des Beaux-Arts in Paris: the local High Court (1882–92), the university library (1889–94), the new church of Saint-Pierre-le-Jeune (1889–93), and the law court (1894–98). The Neo-Gothic former post office, constructed in 1895, remains a stylistic exception in Strasbourg; enthusiasts of medieval architecture were so intimidated by the city's stunning cathedral that they avoided having their work compared with it.

By the end of the century, there were very few town halls that were not in the Parisian mode, so the architecture of the town hall and school of Euville is surprising. In the best Art Nouveau style, inspired by the School of Nancy, the complex serves as a manifesto for the famous Euville stone. This hard stone has been excavated since the sixteenth century from a nearby quarry and used extensively both in France and abroad, bringing so much prosperity to the town that a journalist in 1909 declared it "the richest in France." The municipality was thus able to commission a new town hall and school informed by its progressive

The monumentality of the Palais du Rhin in Strasbourg, built in 1889, represented the desire to integrate Alsace-Lorraine into the German Empire.

social policy: free medical care and a school open to the French and foreign quarriers. The greatest practitioners of the School of Nancy decorated the interior: the sculptures and entrance hall were by Eugène Vallin, the lamps by the Majorelle brothers, the stained glass by Jacques Gruber and E. Champigneulle, and the staircase by Edgar Brandt.

BARRACKS

Barracks are a simple type of building that obviously displays a specific function. It is not surprising that in the nineteenth century the very word *barracks* became synonymous with monotonous and severe-looking architecture.

The principles behind the design of barracks were already clearly enunciated by the beginning of the nineteenth century. As early as 1680, Sébastien de Vauban had established the model of a series of separate structures, each with its own staircase; this plan avoided the long hallways that allowed for too much movement and vibration in the building. The basic module is the barrack, of approximately 322 to 430 square feet; set end to end, these form long, rectangular buildings with windows at regular intervals. The first barracks on a square plan, with individual structures arranged around an interior courtyard, appeared in France at the end of the seventeenth century in the cities in the south.

The twenty years of almost uninterrupted war that marked the French Revolution and the Empire were hardly likely to have permitted the construction of new barracks, and the need for them was easily met by requisitioning many preexisting religious or aristocratic buildings. The infantry barracks at Chambéry were one of the very few new programs of the period. Built in 1804–10, they form a quadrilateral organized around a central courtyard that is lined with arcades. In the 1820s the national military was reorganized into a career army, made up of volunteers who served for long periods, and hence had to be properly housed. The numbers of soldiers remained quite high; the scale of the new construction required a certain standardization of plans and configurations, conformity to which was verified by a Fortifications Commission. Several types of solutions were proposed by various officers of the corps of engineers. In 1818, François-Nicolas-Benoît Haxo designed a model in which the barrack rooms were organized front to back, from facade to facade, each unit having its own staircase—a solution devised earlier by Vauban—and connected one to another by a covered portico on the ground floor. Colonel Emy improved upon this arrangement in 1822. Several infantry barracks were built on this model, such as the Caserne Bernadotte in Pau, whose well-composed facade is more than 557 feet long. The design that Belmas proposed the following year, on the other hand, organized each floor along a central corridor onto which the rooms opened directly. Some twenty barracks were built on this plan, including those of La Roche-sur-Yon in 1832, Lons-le-Saulnier in 1842, and Privas in 1855.

The cavalry barracks—called "quarters" as of 1824—posed specific problems due to the proximity of horses and men. The classic arrangement was to house the horses on the ground floor and the men on the floors above. A standard plan of 1843, providing the layouts and measurements to be applied to mixed-use buildings, arranged individual stables around a vast courtyard, with each building

The des Célestins barracks, built in 1896, conformed to the urban grid developed during the Second Empire to control the working-class neighborhoods in the eastern section of Paris.

assigned to a squadron. Several dozen quarters were erected along these lines, sometimes with the stables and residential blocks entirely separate, as at Tarascon, Lunéville, and Versailles-Satory. The increase in the value of land during the Second Empire led to a doubling of the depth of the stables, so that the horses were housed in four rows rather than two. A few police barracks were also built during this period, such as the one by Jean Jacquemin in Tours in 1845, built into the back of the courthouse, and Adolphe Thiac's barracks of 1850 in Bordeaux.

Architecturally, there are similarities between barracks and seminaries, the latter also intended to house communities of young men living according to similar disciplines of schedule and exercise. During the Restoration period a number of seminaries were built, such as those of La Rochelle, by Brossard, in 1825; Langes, by Amable Macquet, in 1838–46; Périgueux, by Catoire; the great structure of Lons-le-Saulnier, by Auguste Robert, who also built that city's barracks; and the small seminary of Tours, by Gustave Guérin, in 1849. The great seminary of Rennes by Henri Labrouste in 1854–72—today the Literature Department—returned to the traditions of convent architecture in its arrangement of four wings around a square courtyard bordered with a portico.

The Second Empire continued the military building programs of the preceding decades, but with a somewhat different function; barracks were established within cities themselves, especially Paris, in order to maintain public—no longer solely military—order. Thus, Paris came to be sectored according to a network of barracks built at strategic points, notably in the eastern and northern areas, which were hotbeds of uprisings, and near important structures, such as the city hall and the courthouse. These barracks usually occupied entire city blocks at the intersections of broad avenues, which permitted cavalry charges and the firing of cannons. The Caserne du Prince-Eugène, built in 1854–57 on Place du Château-d'Eau (today, Place de la République), Jean-Louis Grisart's 1857 Caserne des Petits-Pères, and Victor Calliat's 1862 Caserne de la Cité, which sits across from the courthouse and today houses the Paris police headquarters, are all examples of this policy. The decoration of these structures was treated with some degree of luxury, so that they might blend into the urban architectural fabric. The Caserne Saint-Charles in Marseilles, built in the heart of the city in 1860, is also typical of this treatment; with its majestic composition, pavilions with columns, and bulb-shaped roofs, it is a dramatic departure from the austere image usually associated with barracks.

The 1872 vote in France for compulsory military service—if drawn by lot—meant that many barracks would be required to house the additional troops. An administrative memorandum of July 14, 1874, defined a standard plan for infantry barracks, which was followed throughout the territory. The design of cavalry quarters, too, was specifically defined, instituting the separation between men and horses. The development of artillery brought about the construction of no fewer than 150 structures between 1875 and 1910, all of them with buildings arranged in a U shape around a courtyard opening onto the street, the same repetitive windows, and an almost total absence of symbolism in the decoration. New memoranda in 1889, and especially in 1907, following the establishment of mandatory military service, spurred the evolution

of barracks design. The plans were more splintered, the functions more dispersed, particularly for reasons of hygiene, and brick added a picturesque and colorful note to the typical facade design, as in Joseph-Antoine Bouvard's 1884 barracks on Rue Schomberg in Paris. The Caserne des Célestins on Boulevard Henri-IV, built in 1896 by Jacques Hermant for the Republican Guard, displays the monumentality prevalent in public buildings of a certain importance at the century's end. Its great arched doorway, in rusticated stone, was obviously inspired by the Italian Renaissance.

PRISONS

By the end of the seventeenth century, incarceration was the principal means to deal with crime in France. But to its former purposes of penalization, deterrence, and protecting the public were added new objectives of social regeneration. Prison was to instill in the inmates the principles of order, cleanliness, and physical and mental hygiene that they lacked. Prison architecture would participate in this program by translating into its plans not only supervisory controls, but also the task of reeducation that prison was supposed to provide. In 1771 the Englishman Jeremy Bentham had invented a panoptic system, which became literally central to most of the penal institutions of the nineteenth century. The layout was as follows: Six stories of cells were organized within a ring-shaped structure opening only to the inside; the guards' living quarters were in a central tower, from where the prisoners could be observed directly. The most practical variant of this system, which characterized most nineteenth-century prison architecture, has wings of cells radiating out from the central tower, from where the halls are observed down their length.

One of the earliest and most perfected applications of this design in France was the prison of Petite-Roquette in Paris, designed in 1825 by Hippolyte Lebas and built in 1831–36. It is laid out on a hexagonal plan, with six wings articulated around a central surveillance tower. For greater security, the wings were separated from the tower by open-air walkways. The prison was unfortunately destroyed in 1974. This system, used extensively in France, was developed in the United States by John Haviland, best known for the Eastern State Penitentiary (1823–35) in Philadelphia, the first prison planned with a radial cellular system. Built in 1843–50 to designs by Jean-François-Joseph Lecointe and Émile-Jacques Gilbert, and since demolished, the prison known as Mazas in Paris illustrates the panoptic precepts laid down by the Minister of the Interior in 1841. One section of the prison at Beaulieu, near Caen, built around 1845 by Harou-Romain fils, is another handsome example of this design. Four wings radiate out from a central tower. Each story of cells has a metal walkway around a covered court that is directly visible from the surveillance tower. The prison of Autun, built in 1847–56 by André Berthier, was also faithful to Bentham's original panoptic plan, its cells distributed around a glass-domed, circular hall. The women's prison in Rennes presents an original, hexagonal plan. Many prisons in France were built on the radial model: La Santé prison in Paris; the houses of detention in Châlons-sur-Marne and Évreux; and the Saint-Paul prison in Lyons by Antonin Louvier. There was also Mettray, the famous agricultural penal colony for children, in the Indre-et-Loire, built in 1839 by Abel Blouet, an architect specializing in the panoptic system. Mettray was born of the desire to reform minds through work, religious practice, and leading an orderly life within a community. The chapel, of course, has pride of place at the end of the compositional axis, on either side of which are distributed a series of identical small blocks.

It is obviously difficult to discern the plan of a prison from the outside, since the buildings are usually concealed by high walls. The appearance of prisons was also intended to convey the gravity and severity of their function, evoked through solid walls, massive stone blocks, and references to Egyptian and medieval architecture, such as battered pylons like those of Egyptian tombs and medieval crenellations and machicolations. The prison of Auxerre, for example, presents the image of a medieval dungeon.

At the end of the century, the panoptic layouts were replaced by comb plans, in which the cell blocks were all arranged perpendicular to a straight hall, a layout similar to that used for hospitals. The

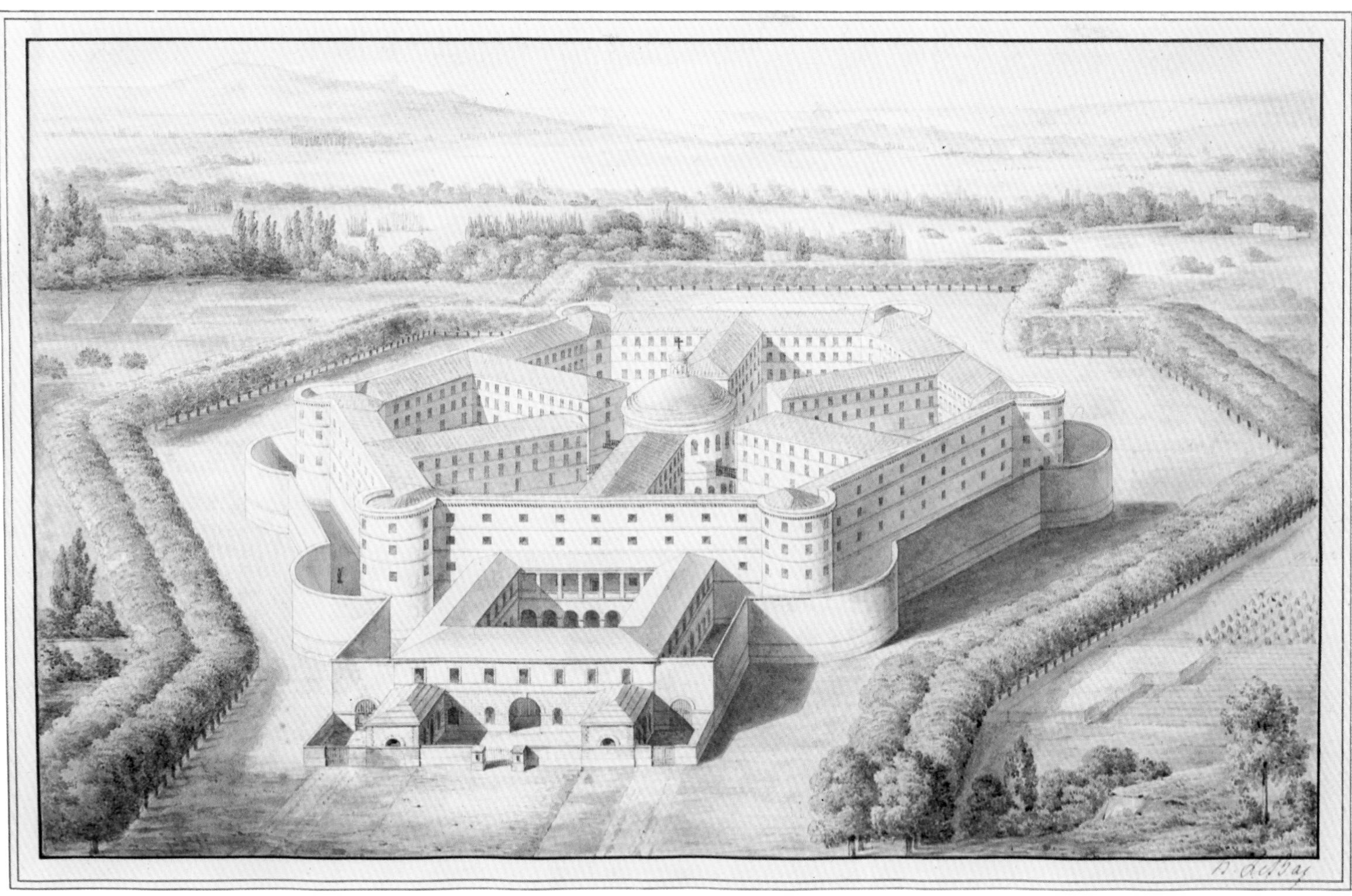

The Petite-Roquette prison in Paris, designed in 1826 by Hippolyte Lebas, was a paragon of the panoptic model used in most French prisons of the period. It was demolished in 1974.

prison in Fresnes, for example, of 1898, has cells built around an empty central area, and aligned on either side of the dining, bathing, and other common facilities.

HOSPITALS

Over the course of the eighteenth century, hospitals gradually became distinct from prisons as places to shelter or contain those whom society had abandoned. The program of medical institutions was influenced by new theories emerging from advancements in medical practice, hygiene, and the understanding of contagious diseases. Following the experiments of the late eighteenth century, especially those of Jacques-René Tenon, the first new principle to be applied was to classify the sick by illness and to segregate them in separate hospitals or blocks. Theories of hygiene were predicated upon a need for good ventilation, which would disperse illness-spreading miasmas. Architecturally, this meant planning the hospital in discrete blocks and placing wings far enough apart to ensure circulation of air and adequate sunlight.

In this way, architecture was expected to support medical practice by providing the conditions necessary to contain contagion. Even more, the austerity of the architecture was perceived to be concomitant with the seriousness of medical treatment. Any luxury in the construction would appear to be a diversion from the hospital's investment in its primary purpose, and thus be to the patient's detriment. The focus was on layout, comfort, and appropriate interior fittings. Decoration was to be reduced to a strict minimum, and the severity of the stylistic treatment was further emphasized by the repetitiveness of the window placement, with each window

EGO SUM RESURRECTIO ET VITA

Paris's Hôtel-Dieu hospital was cast in a Neoclassical style, yet its overall layout complied with concepts of the modern hospital.

corresponding to a bed. As the architectural theorist Jules Guadet wrote around 1900: "The hospital has but one aim, to try to cure, and everything must contribute to it. The architect must work toward it, just as the doctor does, and no less efficaciously." In this sense, hospitals may have been, at least in France, the first building type to follow an explicitly functionalist program, in the twentieth-century meaning of the term, in which architectonic qualities are determined by utilitarian considerations.

Theorized in the late seventeenth century by Bernard Poyet in his 1788 proposal for the renovation of the Hôtel-Dieu in Paris, the principle of a hospital as a building complex was first put into practice in the hospital in Bordeaux, designed by J. Burguet. Ten individual blocks are laid out on either side of a large central court, at one end of which sits the chapel. But the courts between the buildings are very narrow, and the single blocks are connected by a building, so that the whole interprets the hygienist ideal only imperfectly. The hospice of La Reconnaissance in Garches, built in 1836–46 from a design by Marie-Antoine Dalannoy and modified by Pierre Gauthier, comes closer to the ideal. In 1839 Gauthier designed the Lariboisière hospital, which was built in 1846–54. Eight small blocks on either side of a central court are connected by a ground-floor portico that allows in both air and light. The common buildings, including a chapel, are at the end of the esplanade. Heating and mechanical ventilation were meant to assure optimal comfort winter and summer, even though it was suspected that these systems favored the spread, rather than the dispersal, of germs. This was the first modern hospital.

The Hôtel-Dieu built by Jacques Gilbert and Stanislas Diet in 1864–76 clearly represents a step backward with respect to the hospital of Lariboisière. Although it remained faithful to the principle of small, independent blocks, it was built for a significantly larger patient population. Yet the Neoclassical architecture is attractive, with its rhythm of arcades set on two levels on either side of a central court. Even though it was completed in 1874, after Gilbert's death, the Hôtel-Dieu displays an approach that had been prevalent around 1850. Tenon hospital in Paris, inaugurated in 1878, better embodies the precepts of hygiene, with ample space between the blocks. It applied the Hôtel-Dieu's system of mechanical ventilation and ushered in the use of elevators to connect the floors and of an underground train to bring water to the entire complex.

In the late nineteenth century, the civil engineer Casimir Tollet, with somewhat naive enthusiasm, revived the theories of a century earlier, taking them to their logical extreme. For example, in 1872 he recommended that the rooms of the patients be oval, in order to facilitate the evacuation of stale air, "since upward movement was freed by the suppression of corners." Carefully smoothed plaster and rounded corners were also supposed to allow air to circulate more easily, and to keep dust from settling. This system, reprised the Rationalist theories of the Neo-Gothic architects of the period and replicated the forms of medieval hospitals, such as that in Beaune. It was applied in several hospitals both abroad and in France, such as the Bichat hospital in Paris, and hospitals in Saint-Denis, Le Havre, Épernay, Bourges, Le Mans, and Montpellier. The latter, completed in 1884, consists of single structures of one story over an open ground floor, which assured maximum air circulation. In 1894, Tollet published a reference work in which he evaluated his activity; the work conveys both the systematic quality of his research and the sometimes crackpot aspects of his theories.

The revolution caused by Pasteur's discoveries of the role of microorganisms in the spread and development of illness influenced the layouts of hospitals, as had the hygienist theories on ventilation. The architecture continued to remain secondary, and the dispersal of the buildings in small units facilitated antiseptic practices and the classification of the sick by disease. The hospitals, however, no longer required the health-giving properties of the countryside and so could return to the cities. A generation of institutions designed at the turn of the century evidence the integration of the multiblock hospitals into the cities, where they formed, in effect, small garden cities, such as, in Paris, the Bretonneau hospital, built by Paul Héneux (1895–1900); the Boucicaut hospital, by the Legros, father and son (1894–97); and the Rothschild hospital, by Lucien Bechman (1912–14). The use of colored brick and terra cotta that characterizes these last hospitals attests not only to the frequent application of these materials in the public architecture of the 1900s, but to the desire to give these hospitals a less severe appearance, as if it had become clear that austerity is not a condition of effectiveness.

INSANE ASYLUMS

The designs for insane asylums were very similar to those for hospitals. The primary functional consideration was the same: how to segregate the ill according to ailment. Specific treatments for psychiatric afflictions arose in the late eighteenth century, when asylums began to be differentiated from prisons and poorhouses. The principles of the modern asylum were posited only in 1818, in a report by the doctor Jean-Étienne-Dominique Esquirol, who recommended an open-air facility with segregated living quarters, in which patients would be categorized by sex and by twelve specific types of illness. The following year, in collaboration with the architect Hippolyte Lebas, Esquirol defined an ideal layout for such an institution. The residential quarters were arranged in a U shape around a central court that was oriented toward the common facilities and the administration building. The asylum of Saint-Yvon near Rouen, built in 1821–25 to plans by Jouannin and H.-C.-M. Grégoire; that of Marseilles, erected in 1838 by Michel Robert Penchaud; and especially the hospice of Charenton, built in 1838–45 by Jacques Gilbert, all illustrate these principles. The Marseilles asylum has been very much altered, but the other two institutions remain very interesting for their architecture. Saint-Yvon is remarkable for its rigorous Neoclassicism that recalls the work of Claude-Nicolas Ledoux, and Charenton for its Greek Revival architecture, no doubt influenced by Gilbert's long sojourn in Greece and Rome. The columned porticoes that connect or border the residential blocks are drawn from Pompeii's Soldiers' Field, while the chapel was inspired by the Parthenon. The setting for the monumental composition is equally magnificent, taking full advantage of its terraced site on a hillside overlooking the Marne River; the terrace plan is modeled on the systems of ramps at the villas of Frascati and the Temple of Fortuna Primigenia at Palestrina. The success of the architecture was acknowledged at the inauguration of the complex, which for half a century remained the paragon of its type. The critic César Daly wrote in 1852:

> *Charenton is better than an ordinary insane asylum; it is a type, a national experiment that is an object of study for everyone, nationals and foreigners, doctors, philanthropists, and architects, involved with this kind of asylum. Furthermore, it is a frank and faithful expression of the doctrines of the Rationalist school of architecture.*

A law passed in 1838 required every department to have a mental hospital. The result was a major campaign of adapting older structures and building new ones. Gradually, theories evolved, first favoring one-story structures, then multistory buildings. The living quarters were joined into a single group of buildings, and this made more imaginative designs possible, as may be seen at the asylum of Braqueville, near Toulouse, designed by Esquirol with Parchappe de Vimay, a great theoretician on asylums, and built by Pierre Esquié around 1860. Stylistically, the complexes of this period displayed recurring architectural motifs, such as connecting galleries and arcaded loggias, which gave the buildings, arranged as they were around a central court, an Italian Renaissance appearance.

Asylums for violent mentally ill patients were similar to prisons, on a smaller scale, following a panoptic design with separate courtyards for the patients' walks, as at the asylum of Yonne, in Auxerre, built in 1844–58, or the hospital of Sainte-Anne in Paris, built in 1861–67 by Questel, who also designed a striking chapel for the same institution.

The Charenton asylum by Jacques Gilbert is one of the nineteenth century's most beautiful Neoclassical buildings, splendidly situated on a hillside above the Marne River.

SAINT-ELOY
ECO

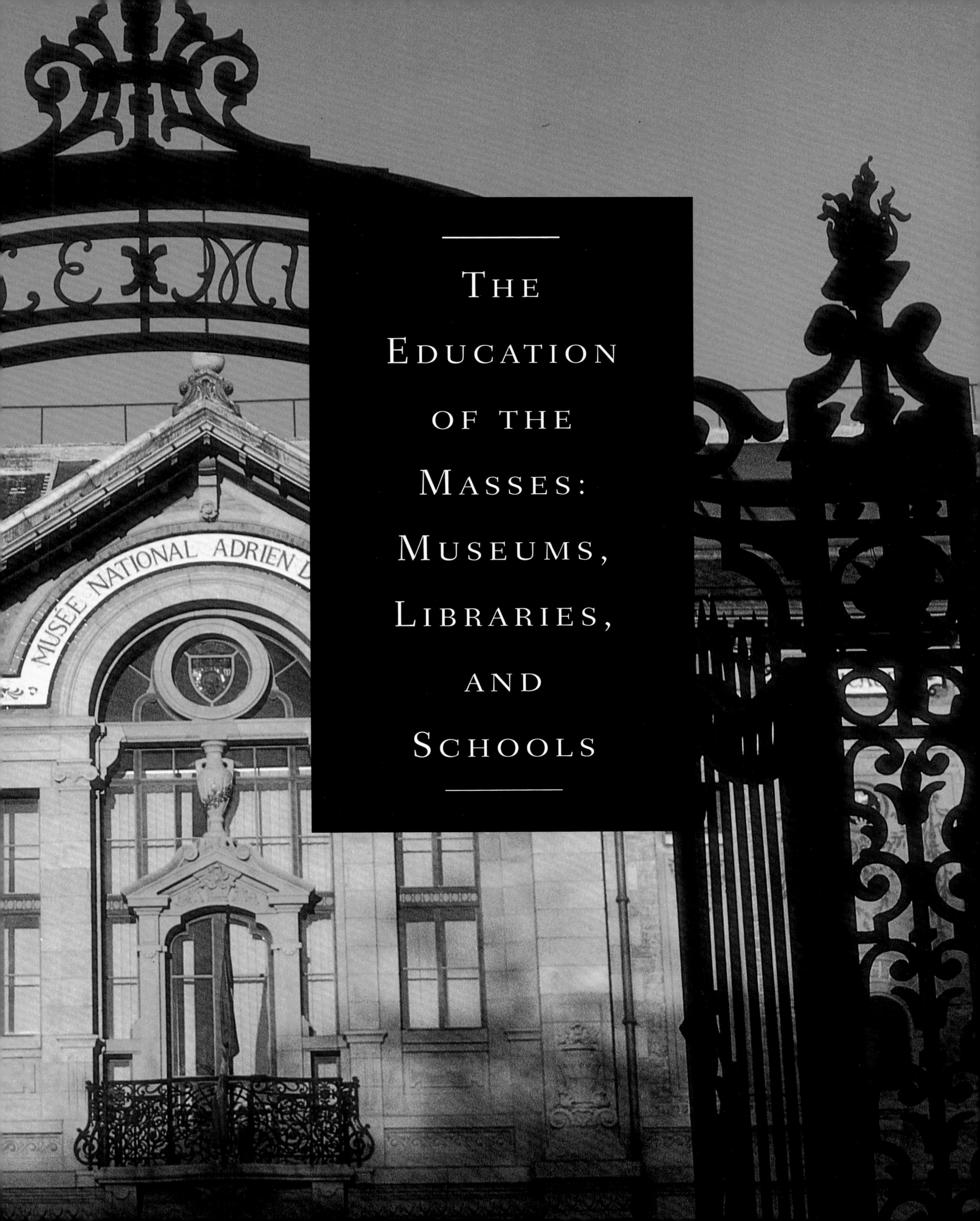

The Education of the Masses: Museums, Libraries, and Schools

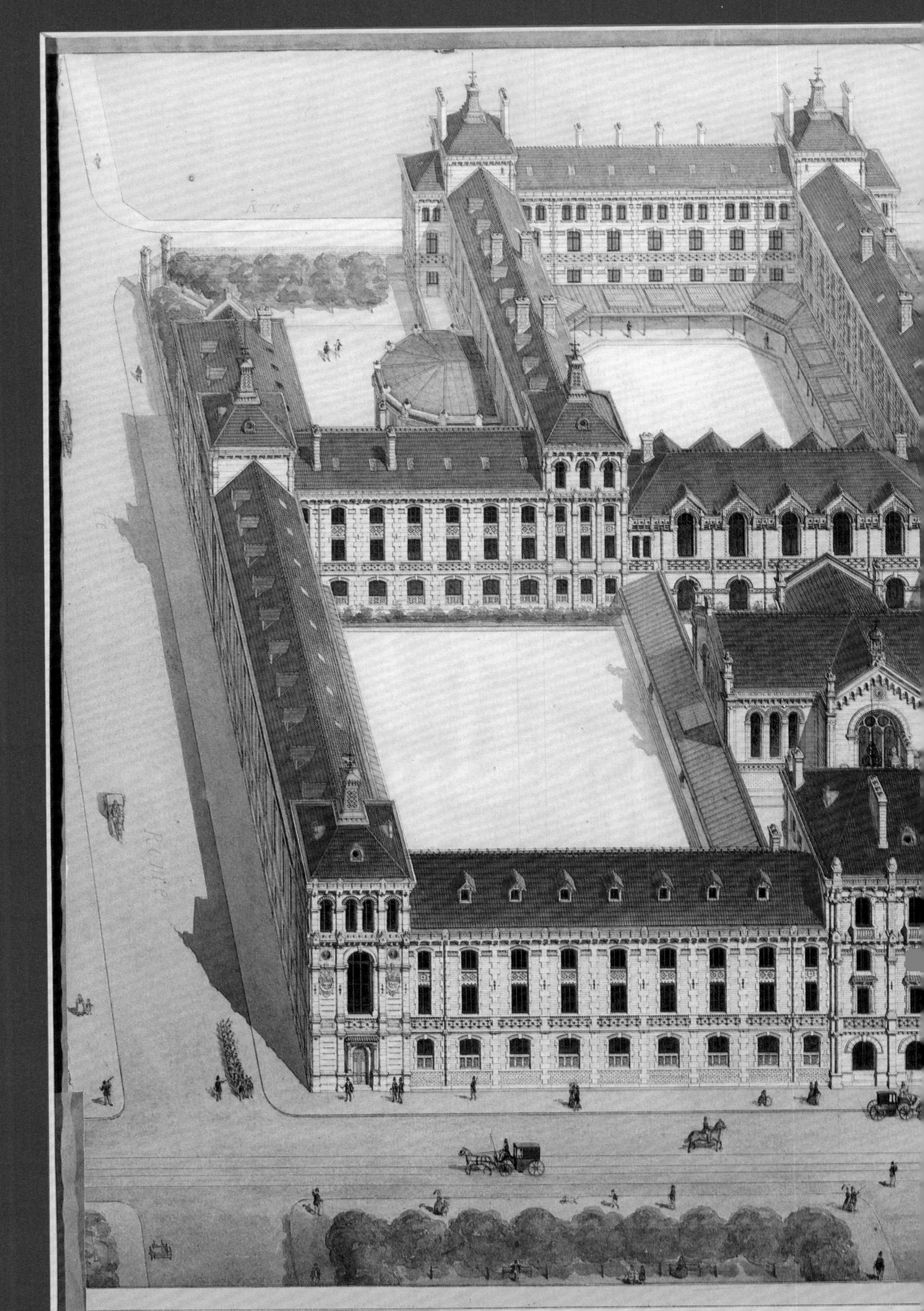

COLLÈGE CHAPTAL

Rue Goubeau

Architecte

Schools and museums, though less immediately associated with the image of the state, were nevertheless among the most important public buildings constructed in France in the nineteenth century. They expressed the era's vast educational mission and bore witness to the state's participation in economic and social progress. If schools and their teachers became essential fixtures of public life in even the smallest rural communities during the last quarter of the century, under the Third Republic, it was because the dissemination of knowledge was considered essential to social cohesiveness.

MUSEUMS

French museums of the nineteenth century had substantial symbolic value because they protected and displayed the cultural patrimony to an extraordinary degree, in order to expose it to the general public. As the repositories of the country's treasures, museums naturally enough became the ultimate monuments, as evidenced by the many designs for museums produced in academic competitions. For lack of funds, however, most of the earliest museums in France were installed in older buildings that were previously given over to other uses, quite often as convents. The Musée des Monuments Français, created in 1793 by Alexandre Lenoir from sculpture fragments saved from the ravages of the French Revolution, found a home in the convent of the Petits Augustins. The museum established under the National Convention was installed in the Louvre, which was renamed "the Palace of the Arts" for the occasion.

Despite the impetus that the Revolution gave to the idea of a public museum, the modern typology of the museum evolved abroad. Following the example of Munich's Glyptothek, built in 1816–30 to designs by Leo von Klenze, who was in part inspired by the published French Grand Prix projects of the era, several major museums were constructed in Germany—such as the Altes Museum (1823–30), by Karl Friedrich Schinkel—and in England—notably the British Museum (1823–47), by Robert Smirke—in the style of monumental Greek temples with imposing colonnades. For the Munich Pinakothek of 1826–33, Klenze abandoned this model in favor of an interpretation of the Italian *palazzo* of the High Renaissance, with a solid base surmounted by a main floor with arched windows and an attic; this building became the model for nineteenth-century museum architecture.

The museum of Picardy in Amiens was one of the first buildings in France to be constructed especially to house public collections. It was begun according to a design by Clément Parent, a specialist in châteaux, and then, after Parent resigned in 1855, it was completed by Arthur Diet, who had won the Grand Prix de Rome for a museum design. This ambitious edifice, with its stately proportions and elaborate ornamentation, borrowed its facade from the Louvre's Pavillon de l'Horloge, in particular the majestic dome that crowns the central block. The monumental staircase inside bears Diet's Greek Revival hallmark style with Renaissance elements, and the walls are decorated with frescoes by Pierre Puvis de Chavannes. The Salon de l'Empereur and the vaulted galleries derived from Raphael's Vatican Loggias are just as astonishing. The museum was finished in 1869; the central courtyard was not covered with a skylight until 1887. Grenoble's museum and library, designed by Questel and built in 1862–72, was also one of the first of its kind. The building, which has no interior court, takes up an entire city block. Great glass panels allow light into the interior. A lobby lit by three large arched windows in the facade joins the two parts of the program, the museum and the library. Questel skillfully translated Renaissance elements into the facade design—such as the mullioned windows surmounted by oculi that mark the lateral divisions of the building, a motif borrowed from Jean Goujon's Louvre—recomposing them to fit the program. In this way, he created a new image of the museum as an autonomous and immediately identifiable public building.

Museums of the Second Empire drew on various sources for their styles, usually Italian or French Renaissance. Often no one manner predominated, but the overall architectural richness, by convention, was meant to reflect the quality of the works on display inside. Marseilles's Palais Longchamp, built in 1862–69 to designs by Henri Espérandieu, celebrated the occasion of the arrival of the waters of the Durance River to the city; it housed two

Chapter opening spread: The Adrien Dubouché ceramics museum in Limoges.

Preceding spread: The Collège Chaptal in Paris, designed by Eugène Train in 1875, takes up an entire city block. The chapel occupies the center of the composition.

Opposite: Detail of an oculus at the Grenoble museum and library. The relief figures represent writing and reading.

museums, and the complex was executed with unbridled stylistic eclecticism. Applying an overall composition designed by the sculptor Auguste Bartholdi, Espérandieu sited two Renaissance-style wings, one containing the Musée des Beaux-Arts and the other the Musée d'Histoire Naturelle, around an imposing fountain fed by a water tower. A colonnade joins the two wings and forms a backdrop to this monumental arrangement. Contrasting with the Roman style of the wings are the heavy French-style roofs and the horseshoe-shaped staircase—inspired by Fontainebleau—that frames the central cascade, which is adorned with a sculptural group representing the Durance River. Gabriel-Jean-Antoine Davioud would later refer to this urban mise-en-scène in the Palais du Trocadéro that he built for the 1878 Exposition Universelle in Paris.

The Musée de Nantes, by C. Josso, is in an eighteenth-century style, and that of Bordeaux, built in 1875, follows the style of Louis XVI. Marseilles's Musée des Beaux-Arts, built in 1876 to designs by Espérandieu, reiterated the Italianate composition of the Palais des Études of Paris's École des Beaux-Arts. A *piano nobile* with arched windows rises from a base, but the ornamentation, inspired by the French Renaissance, is more florid than that of the model. Toulon's museum and library of 1887, by the architects Gaudensi and Allar, has a loggia borrowed explicitly from Palladio.

The principle of rooms receiving natural light from above, which had been tested at the Louvre in the late eighteenth century, became a technical given in museum architecture. The zoology gallery of the Muséum d'Histoire Naturelle in Paris, built in 1877–89 by Jules André, a student of Labrouste, concealed behind its monumental stone facade a vast, glass-roofed hall, surrounded by four floors of galleries supported on cast-iron columns. This breathtaking space once housed the museum's collection of stuffed and mounted animals. The building has been closed to the public since 1969 because of the poor condition of the glass ceiling and is currently undergoing a slow renovation. Ferdinand Dutert's 1894–95 paleontology gallery in the same museum provides another handsome example of a glass-roofed space, but instead of cast-iron columns there are cantilevered iron floors and balustrades. The design of the ironwork anticipates Art Nouveau in its naturalistic themes—lion-headed capitals, eagles at the keystones, thistles on the balustrades—and formal virtuosity.

And yet, at the end of the century there was a return to a heavier aesthetic in museum architecture, one that emphasized the monumental role assigned to these institutions. Lille's Palais des Beaux-Arts, built in 1895 by Édouard Bérard and Fernand Delmas, adopted seventeenth-century forms. Above the massive rusticated base rises a sequence of columns supporting alternating horizontal and curved pediments. Grand roofs and domes crown the structure. The Palais Galliera in Paris, built to designs by Paul Ginain in 1895–98 to house the private collection of the duchesse de Galliera, is a small building with scrupulously composed facades. It returns to the classical tradition, drawing on the Italian Renaissance in certain elements of the plan, notably in the curved forecourt bordered by porticoes.

The Grand Palais and the Petit Palais, built in Paris for the Exposition Universelle of 1900, are fully in the prevailing Neo-Baroque style of the time, with their colossal columns, their inflated domes, and their ornate and fairly substantial decoration. The Grand Palais contains the added surprise of its incredible glass ceiling. Four architects joined forces for the project: Albert Louvet, for the middle section; Alexi Deglane, for the front section;

MUSEE ET BIBLIOTHEQUE

Preceding pages: Left, top: The Grenoble museum and library is articulated in a fairly austere Neoclassical style. Left, bottom: Lille's Musée des Beaux-Arts displays seventeenth-century influences. Right: Marseilles's Palais Longchamp joins two museums around a monumental fountain.

Left: The reading room of Henri Labrouste's Bibliothèque Nationale, one of the masterpieces of the nineteenth century, has a vault of shallow domes with skylights.

Opposite: The Bibliothèque Sainte-Geneviève, also by Labrouste, was one of the first buildings in France in which the metal framing was exposed.

and Albert Thomas, for the rear section; while Charles Girault, the architect of the Petit Palais, was assigned to oversee the overall design. Aside from the technical virtuosity represented by the steel-framed glass ceiling—which was divided among three firms: Daydé et Pillé for the center section, Moisant-Laurent-Savey for the north section, and the Société des Ponts et Travaux en Fer for the south section—the decoration is remarkable. The wrought-iron floral ornamentation is thoroughly integrated into the structure, seeming to burst almost naturally from it. Because Louvet wanted to leave the structure of the central staircase exposed, he decorated it with metal volutes and foliage. These are not necessary as structural elements, but they express the architect's principle: "To consider the supports not just pillars but stems and branches of a robust vegetation that supports the platforms." The very credo of Art Nouveau.

LIBRARIES

Libraries, as a building type, closely resembled museums and were often associated with them. Like museums, libraries found their architectural origins in the painting- or book-lined galleries that were often attached to *hôtels particuliers* or to châteaux.

The Neoclassical library in Amiens, built by the architect Cheussey in 1823, was one of the few built in that period. The Bibliothèque Sainte-Geneviève, built to designs by Henri Labrouste between 1843 and 1850, marked a turning point in the evolution of the library. Labrouste had won the Prix de Rome in 1824, at twenty-three, and raised eyebrows with dispatches from Rome that the academy considered shamelessly impertinent, such as his attention to the technical and structural details of the ancient buildings he was studying, his social interpretation of their programs, and his frequent use of color in his re-creations. Upon his return to Paris in 1830, he opened an atelier that was one of the most respected in the city until it closed in 1856. Eight years later, he was named architect for the old Bibliothèque Sainte-Geneviève. This abbey library was ill suited to the heavy use it was receiving, and in 1839 Labrouste proposed that it be rebuilt. The funds were approved in 1843, after numerous studies.

The renovation of the old section was both simple and ingenious. The library was arranged on two levels, with the reading room on the second floor, where it would receive more natural light. The books were shelved on the ground floor and along the walls of the great hall. The need for fire prevention suggested the use of masonry and iron for the floors and metal supports for the roof. Labrouste's genius lay in exposing the cast-iron structure of the vault of the reading room, which was supported around the perimeter by the side walls, composed of arcaded bays, and a row of eighteen slender metal columns that bisects the space. The system was borrowed from that of the former refectory of the abbey of Saint-Martin-des-Champs, which was about to be converted to a library. Unlike Louis-Auguste Boileau in his design for the church of Saint-Eugène a few years later, Labrouste did not make literal copies of the columns, opting instead for fluted shafts with Composite capitals, in keeping with the Italian Renaissance style of the exterior of the building. The twin barrel vaults are supported by a double series of semicircular transverse ribs, connected at the median axis to the central row of columns. The arched ribs are articulated by iron filigree in a pattern of volutes and spiky tendrils.

In constrast with the airy, iron-framed interior, the library's exterior is very reminiscent of Italian cinquecento *palazzi*. The facade design recalls that of the Palais des Études at the École des Beaux-Arts of a few years earlier. Narrow arched windows punctuate the solid, unadorned stone walls of the base. A sculpted garland enlivens the transition to the upper floor, which is rhythmically composed of a series of inscribed arches framing lunette windows. Panels within the arches bear the names of hundreds of authors whose works were to be contained inside.

In 1854, shortly after the Bibliothèque Sainte-Geneviève was completed, Labrouste was named architect of the Bibliothèque Nationale, which had long been in need of renovation. The plans were completed in 1859, and the new reading room, with the multilevel stacks along Rue de Richelieu, was finished in 1868. While the exterior of the library is quite conventional, the reading room is rightly considered one of the finest architectural achievements of the nineteenth century. Labrouste designed it according to a very precise geometry. The square plan is puctuated by nine domes, each with a glass skylight, supported by metal semicircular arches and slender cast-iron columns. A clearly separate hemicycle extends around the room and acts as the transition to the stacks, which are accessed through a monumental doorway. Labrouste's two libraries share similar features: the shape and span of the arches, the design of the columns and their capitals, the white terra-cotta facing on the ceilings, and the naturalistic theme of the frescoes, as in the vestibule of Sainte-Geneviève, which refer to the garden of Akademos, traditionally a place of recollection and study.

The repeated decorative motifs in the design of the arches at the Bibliothèque Nationale, composed of Saint Andrew's crosses alternating with struts, is less inventive than at Sainte-Geneviève. Paint was used to emphasize the structural components of the ironwork, down to the rivet heads. Labrouste emphasized the structure as well in the overall design. Not only does the metal framing not rest on the side walls, but it is completely separate from them. The cast-iron columns are set in front of the pilasters that mark the bays of the side walls. Thus, the domed vaults, borne at only sixteen minimal points, seem to be floating above the mass of books lining the room. The spherical shape of the domes on pendentives, inspired by those in Brunelleschi's Ospedale degli Innocenti in Florence, allowed glass to be installed at the crowns, thereby letting in natural light from above. Derived from the Pantheon in Rome, this system had been applied on a smaller scale, for example, in 1823–26 in the side aisles of Hippolyte Lebas's Notre-Dame-de-Lorette and in the halls of certain *hôtels particuliers*. At the Bibliothèque Nationale the light color of the vaults, which compensates somewhat for the small size of the glazed openings, and the concentric patterns in the domes help to create the overall effect of a glass roof, a precursor of the many vast glass-ceilinged spaces to come. The stacks, located behind the reading room, are just as remarkable. Three levels of galleries with bookshelves are arranged around a central space. Everything is of metal, including the shelves and the gallery floors, whose metal gratings allow natural light to reach the lowest level.

The library was immediately recognized as a success by its contemporaries, as the engineer C. A. Opperman attested:

> *It is by means of initiatives such as this that modern architecture will emerge from the Greco-Roman routine that has held it in thrall for too long. It is obvious that the combination of iron and masonry, with earthenware and terra cotta, and with every other possible metal and material, is the truly characteristic feature of contemporary art.*

Ernest Lheureux's library of 1876–78 for the Faculté de Droit in Paris is explicitly in the mold of the Bibliothèque Nationale. Lheureux was a student of Labrouste and collaborated with him in the construction of the Collège Sainte-Barbe, which also had some very fine metal elements designed later by Lheureux himself (most notably the refectory roof of 1881–83). In the Faculté du Droit, Lheureux designed a magnificent tribute to the Rationalist ideas of Viollet-le-Duc by covering the space with a glass dome supported by ceiling beams placed in the corners of the reading room. Brick barrel vaults joined the glass dome and the stone walls. The glazed polychrome brick, gilt mosaic, and painted iron in gray and dark blue with touches of gold work together to produce, as a review of the time reported, "a harmony whose brilliant sweet-

The Palais des Études of the École des Beaux-Arts in Paris adopted the form of an Italianate palazzo. *Thirty-five years after the building was completed in 1839, the interior courtyard was covered with a glass roof to create an exhibition space for sculpture and models.*

ness is even further enhanced by the contrast with the pale monochrome walls entirely made of exposed stone." A second reading room designed along the same lines was built in 1880. This masterpiece was demolished in 1969.

UNIVERSITY BUILDINGS

The École des Beaux-Arts, created in 1816, was the first of the great educational institutions founded in the aftermath of the Empire. It was to be built on the site of Lenoir's Musée des Monuments Français, and some of the fragments in that museum were retained, including an archway from the Château de Gaillon. In 1819, François Debret began a Neoclassical structure organized around a courtyard, a project that Félix Duban took over in 1833, completely changing the building's appearance. The Études block, which was built in 1833–39, is an almost literal interpretation of a grand Italian Renaissance *palazzo*, with its arcaded ground floor, in the style of Bramante's Cancelleria; its *piano nobile*, in which arched windows alternate with engaged Corinthian columns; and its attic, complete with acroteria. Inside, a loggia surrounds a great rectangular open-air courtyard. Off the courtyard are an amphitheater, with a fresco by Delaroche, exhibition galleries, and a library, built in 1864.

The evolution of Duban's architectural references to include a more eclectic vocabulary is evident in the block that he built in 1860–62 on the Quai Malaquais. Although he retained the rigorous tripartite composition of the earlier structure, he endowed the attic with large oculi, which serve to accentuate the slightly protruding pavilion. In 1870, Ernest Coquart was commissioned to design a glass ceiling—which Duban had planned in 1856—for the courtyard of the Études building. As at the Bibliothèque Nationale, the metal structure is almost entirely separate from the existing masonry shell, resting instead on a series of slim cast-iron columns attached halfway up the inside walls. The care with which the metal-framed roof is treated and the very beautiful glass-covered court that results from it have made this complex an achievement of the highest order, surely an inspiration to the generations of architecture students that have passed through it.

Other mid-century educational structures referred to Italian sources, including Simon-Claude Constant-Dufeux's 1841–44 École du Dessin in Paris, whose Italianizing classicism might have inspired Labrouste's facade for the Bibliothèque Sainte-Geneviève, and Espérandieu's 1862 École des Beaux-Arts in Marseilles, which resembles Duban's Palais des Études but is less refined.

The mid-1870s saw the return of the fashion for great classical compositions, deemed more appropriate to the character of the university buildings. Higher education in France was undergoing a renewal in that era, addressing itself to a population of full-time students, not simply amateurs and dilettantes. Louis Liard, the future director of higher education at the Ministry of Public Education, noted in 1879:

> *Until the last few years, classes in the faculties of science and letters, at least in the provinces, were intended for the general public, an odd, constantly changing mix of very few scholars and writers, and the curious and idle. Hence these vast amphitheaters, open to all; hence, too, the absence of research laboratories, at most a few for the professors; few or no collections or libraries. Today, the faculties' teaching addresses a limited public; the com-*

mon efforts of the central administration, academic authority, and professors increasingly tend to group actual students around each professor's rostrum.

Under these conditions, the universities of the Third Republic sought to drape themselves in an ambivalent respectability by building in a classical style that was both monumental and pompous.

This new direction was marked by the initiation of several important projects. In Paris, Jean-Charles Laisné's École de Pharmacie and Lheureux's library for the Faculté du Droit were still in the Rationalist tradition defined by Viollet-le-Duc. But in 1878, when Léon Ginain designed the extension of the famous École de Médecine, originally built by Jacques Gondoin in 1769–75 and the very essence of eighteenth-century Neoclassicism, he fully respected his predecessor's achievement, but added an emphatic Greek-inspired flavor. The facade on the Boulevard Saint-Germain displays, along the entire length of its second floor, which contains the library, a sequence of monumental Ionic columns that recalls Duc's Palais de Justice.

In Bordeaux, Jean-Luc Pascal's 1879–88 Faculté de Médecine and Charles Durand's 1880–86 Faculté des Sciences et des Lettres are also faithful to the canons of classicism, with great orders of columns above a base. Similarly, in 1882, Pierre-Gérôme-Honoré Daumet, in designing Grenoble's Faculté du Droit, des Sciences et des Lettres, followed the most classical principles, with a rusticated base containing arched windows and, on the floors above, tiers of columns alternating with windows framed by moldings.

The building of the new Sorbonne in 1885 manifested the aspiration of the newly established Republic to develop excellent egalitarian education for its citizens.

The construction of the new Sorbonne, begun by Paul-Henri Nénot in 1885, marks the culmination of the Third Republic's architectural policy with respect to university buildings. Nénot had won the 1877 Grand Prix de Rome for "an Athenaeum in a capital city," and came in first out of a field of twenty-eight in the competition held for the renovation of the prestigious university that was to replace Richelieu's Sorbonne. The new structure would add a science department and a department of letters, the whole to be a definitive expression of the preeminent part played by the state in higher education. To counteract the moral order promoted by a reactionary aristocracy, the young Republic put into practice an educational program that emphasized the positivist values of science, but also explicitly referred to classical architectural thought. National unity was identified as the common thread linking absolute monarchy and the Republic. Thus, the Sorbonne was to be an homage to the *grand siècle* of Louis XIV, revised in the light of nineteenth-century Rationalism. The ambiguity and somewhat awkward tension of this position are visible in the composition of this vast structure. The final design of the facade, after numerous revisions, exhibits the monumental classicism of the Second Empire, with an arcaded base, a *piano nobile* marked with large Ionic and Attic orders, and an axial plan emphasized by two pavilions crowned with arched pediments. Aside from the great amphitheater decorated with a fresco by Puvis de Chavannes, the showpiece is the renovation of the court of honor, which Nénot composed around Jacques Lemercier's chapel. The court, in which Nénot reused existing motifs, such as the sundial in front of the chapel, is certainly grand, but it could have been conceived two centuries earlier. The Sorbonne's heterogeneous complex is unified somewhat by the austere facades on every side and the sumptuousness of its symbolic decoration. This project reflects how difficult it was in that period to devise an appropriate architectural typology for a university. The political and aesthetic ideologies were too contradictory and too far apart to permit a consensus.

The architectural eclecticism of Lille's late-nineteenth-century university buildings clearly illustrates the conflicts between aesthetic and ideological tendencies. The Neo-Gothic style that Louis Duthouquet employed for his 1885–1900 Université Catholique was, at the time, a deliberate reference to religious architecture. Carlos Batteur's 1886 Faculté des Sciences presents a composite Picturesque style, combining Ionic columns and friezes accented with colored terra-cotta tiles that evoke the theme of industry. Finally, the Neoclassicism of Alfred Mongy's Faculté des Lettres d'État, of 1892, represents an attempt to correlate architecture directly to the teaching of classical literature and the humanities.

SCHOOLS

Schools, more modest in program than universities, provided a far greater opportunity to define architectural typologies that expressed the progressive impulse underlying educational policies in nineteenth-century France.

While education was certainly not a nineteenth-century invention, it barely existed in the modern sense before the early part of the century. If significantly more attention was paid to the subject in the eighteenth century than earlier, it was due to Jean-Jacques Rousseau and the Encyclopedists. In fact, Rousseau's Declaration of the Rights of Man specified that "instruction is a universal need: Society must favor with all its strength the progress of reason and make instruction available to all citizens." The French *lycée,* or secondary school, system was established in 1802, and the state took over responsibility for the universities in 1806; but in the first decades of the century, primary education was provided principally by either religious communities or by so-called mutual improvement groups. A law passed in 1833 required each community to support at least a boys' school. The number of French students enrolled in school tripled between 1830 and 1840, rising from 1 million to more than 3 million, including girls. The latter were taken into account by an 1850 law, which established one girls' school for every community with more than eight hundred inhabitants. However, by 1869, only 40 percent of all ten-year-olds were enrolled in school, and in 1870 one-third of draftees were illiterate—which was identified as a factor in the French army's disastrous defeat in the Franco-Prussian War.

Despite the many small schoolhouses and nursery schools, most educational institutions made do with rudimentary accommodations, often in inherited buildings that had nothing to do with education. The few new schools tended to be in a modest Neoclassical style. The standardization of educational institutions went in tandem with the development of the school system. In 1832, an architect named Bouillon published the first designs of this kind, and the mutual-improvement structures resulting from the 1833 law relied heavily on them. In 1873, César Pompée published a collection of plans that was distributed throughout the subprefectures, foreshadowing the standardized designs that would be applied to French schools by century's end. These often incorporated the school—whether a single classroom or two rooms, divided between girls and boys—into the town hall; the architectural style proposed in the 1873 publication resembles that of the country train stations that were springing up throughout the country.

The idea of compulsory, free, and nonreligious education took root in France in the 1870s, becoming one of the driving forces of the Republic that was definitively established in 1875, since secularism was the primary mission of the republicans in the struggle against the monarchists and the conservatives. Public expenditures on education were quickly legislated, attesting to the national consensus that institutions were necessary to the exercise and maintenance of democracy. The larger goal was to guarantee the future of the Republic and of France by educating the population as a whole to value equality, civic responsibility, technical and social progress, and neutrality with respect to religious beliefs. The state retained responsibility for building most of the secondary schools, while individual communities paid for the new primary schools.

Regulations concerning the building of schools were published in 1880 to direct the outlay of the funds allocated for education. These very specific regulations addressed the use and size of rooms and their furnishings. Their application was overseen by a Committee of School Buildings, staffed by architects who demonstrated an allegiance to Viollet-le-Duc's Rationalist aesthetic. Among them were Félix Narjoux, Eugène Train—Viollet-le-Duc's son-in-law—and Antoine Buvard, all three official architects for the city of Paris, and all particularly distinguished for the schools they designed. In 1876–79, Narjoux built a school block on Rue Titon, in the eleventh arrondissement, whose style anticipated that of schools to come. Train designed the Collège Chaptal in Paris in 1863–75, which stood out among other *lycées* of its time because of its use of polychromy and of Romanesque and Italian references.

Groundbreaking legislation was passed in 1881 and 1882, mandating free, and later compulsory and secular, primary education. The architectural consequences of this vast and generous program were considerable. The 1886 publication of a basic architectural plan, which would remain practically unchanged for fifty years, confirmed the principal features of a primary school of this era: the separation of boys, girls, and nursery-school-age children, and a modular organization, with the classroom as a unit. The school thereby clearly declared itself a very specific public building of essentially local importance, easily identifiable by its basic unit—the classroom—and by its construction materials—red or yellow brick, often combined with stone. The *lycées,* too, once housed in former convents, acquired a greater monumentality, which was justified by their greater importance.

The Rationalist design of the Lycée Lakanal in Sceaux emphasizes the integral structural elements, such as the segmental and pointed window heads, as a means to enliven the facades.

The doctrinal orientation of the architects involved in the construction of school buildings explains the generally prevailing architectural choices. Verticality is stressed in the composition of the facade through the rhythm of piers separating the window bays into strong vertical elements, with brick spandrels between the floors. Rationalist prin-

ciples are followed in every aspect of the design: the application of materials according to their structural purpose; the articulation of structural details, such as visible metal wall anchors and segmentally arched lintels; and spare ornamentation. These tenets were applied to country and suburban schools alike, as well as to schools in cities and especially in Paris, where they could be as tall as five stories and sometimes resembled apartment buildings.

The Lycée Michelet in Vanves, on which construction began in 1862 from Duc's plans, displayed a uniform, fairly severe composition, but a series of *lycées* built after the Collège Chaptal sought to create a new image, predicated upon a more inventive use of materials. In the Lycée Buffon and the Lycée Molière in Paris, or the *lycées* of Grenoble and Montauban, Émile Vaudremer employed varied materials and Gothic-inspired motifs to enliven buildings whose plans were very simple and very much restricted by the program's requirements. The result, a subtle balance of Rationalism and the Picturesque, is typical of the educational institutions of the 1870s. As Louis-Charles Boileau wrote of the Lycée Buffon in 1889:

> *The type of architecture employed resembles that of the Gothic Rationalists, but with a noticeable difference. We are not here in the presence of a Gothicism impoverished to the point of looking like a style for a factory, which appears to be, for the students of the school of Viollet-le-Duc, the ideal modern architecture. The artist was able to create a delicate style that is neither Gothic nor Classical, something primitive, between Romanesque and twelfth century, that is personal to him. I am not saying that this style can go very far, but it suits utilitarian buildings nicely. . . . Terra cotta, bricks, stone, wood, mosaic, paint, the whole arsenal of inexpensive shapes and tones, derived from real and durable materials, is handled with very distinguished taste.*

The Lycée Lakanal in Sceaux, begun in 1882, is another of the best examples of the Rationalist tendencies predominating in that period. Anatole de Baudot, Viollet-le-Duc's most faithful disciple, was commissioned to design this *lycée,* the largest secondary school planned for the Paris area. Set in a park, its campuslike setting was in contrast to the arrangement of other *lycées* of the time. Everything about the project makes it a model of its kind: the elegance of the openings, whether the paired narrow windows of the dormitories or the wider windows of the classrooms; the artful play of the structural details and the polychrome brick and terra cotta; the visible use of iron for the structure of the floors and the gymnasiums; and the technical attention given to the sanitary facilities. In 1889, de Baudot built another *lycée,* in Tulle, in which he applied the same tenets, taking advantage of a site overlooking the valley of the Corrèze River to open up the buildings to the landscape, connecting them with covered walkways like the cloisters and arcades of the Middle Ages.

An architectural typology peculiar to the city of Paris began to take shape around this time, under the impetus of the Service d'Architecture de la Ville, which usually assigned the design of schools to architects connected with the city. More than three hundred primary schools were built in Paris between 1870 and 1914, and the strict control that the municipality exercised over the choice of principal contractors explains in part the near uniformity of these works. But, as Henri-Marcel Magne remarked in 1922: "Beginning in 1880, there were buildings being erected in the suburbs that followed new ideas, while Paris was still entrenched in its tired ashlar facades, all identically sad-looking, like barracks with their identical windows." The guidelines of the model regulations of March 11, 1899, recommended simple shapes and layouts, sober decoration, and the use of solid but simple materials that did not require expensive maintenance, "with funds allocated in a reasonable manner, so that they may achieve the greatest useful effect." These provisions, economical-minded but not very stimulating architecturally, aroused strong opinions. For example, Léon Riotor, secretary general of the Société Nationale de l'Art à l'École, founded in 1907, believed that "Paris must have the finest schools for the people, the healthiest, the best-lit, the most joyful, for art is the surest, the most powerful method of education." The school of yesteryear was "filthy, dilapidated, ramshackle"; the new one "will shape taste through its decor, initiate children to the beauty of lines, colors, shapes, movements, and sounds," as Magne added a few years later. It is evident that physical health and moral elevation were thus closely associated, with perhaps excessive faith in the pedagogical virtue of aesthetics. The principle of repetitive, identical classrooms inhibited architectural variety. At century's end, architects attempted to enliven the overall designs of *lycées* by addressing the ancillary elements of the program, such as the gymnasium, the director's residence, and the drawing classrooms. Julien Guadet, professor of theory at the École des Beaux-Arts, considered Jules Bouvard's 1890–93 school on Rue Saint-Lambert in Paris, for example, to be "an almost theoretical composition."

Louis Bonnier, director of the Service d'Architecture de la Ville de Paris, sponsored a municipal policy that sought to redefine the neighborhoods' public buildings. In 1902–12, Bonnier, an architect himself, designed a school complex in the Grenelle area that stands out as a paragon. The school, on Rue Sextius-Michel, rigorously translated the program into a plan that is perfectly logical, but that effortlessly uses Picturesque architectural elements to both articulate and unify a series of different volumes: a ground floor that opens up to the

The school on Paris's Rue Sextius-Michel, designed by Louis Bonnier, went beyond the rigorous typology imposed upon primary schools by incorporating polychrome brick and highlighting ancillary elements of the program, such as the entrance porch.

outside through glassed-in bays, classrooms that receive daylight through large windows, thus avoiding the "barracks look," small windows in the halls, and deeply overhanging roofs. Brick lent itself naturally to the building's rhetoric of construction, but Bonnier exploited more than its architectural and ornamental qualities, which are clearly visible in the great arches that close off the ground-floor gymnasium. He took the Rationalism a little further: lines incised in the cement lintels reveal their internal armature; the structural joints are marked by mosaic motifs; the wood is blue or red, depending upon whether it was sawed or turned; the pipes are blue for water, red for gas, green for waste, and so on. The Rue Sextius-Michel school prefigures twentieth-century modernism in several ways: by its isolated placement, the deliberate pursuit of light and transparency, the facade's straightforward expression of the plan, and the reasoned use of color and materials. And yet, the school retains many qualities of the nineteenth-century architectural tradition: the integration of the structure into the streetscape, the symbolic expression of its nature as a public building, a sense of ornamentation, the use of various and rich shapes and materials, and a high standard of construction.

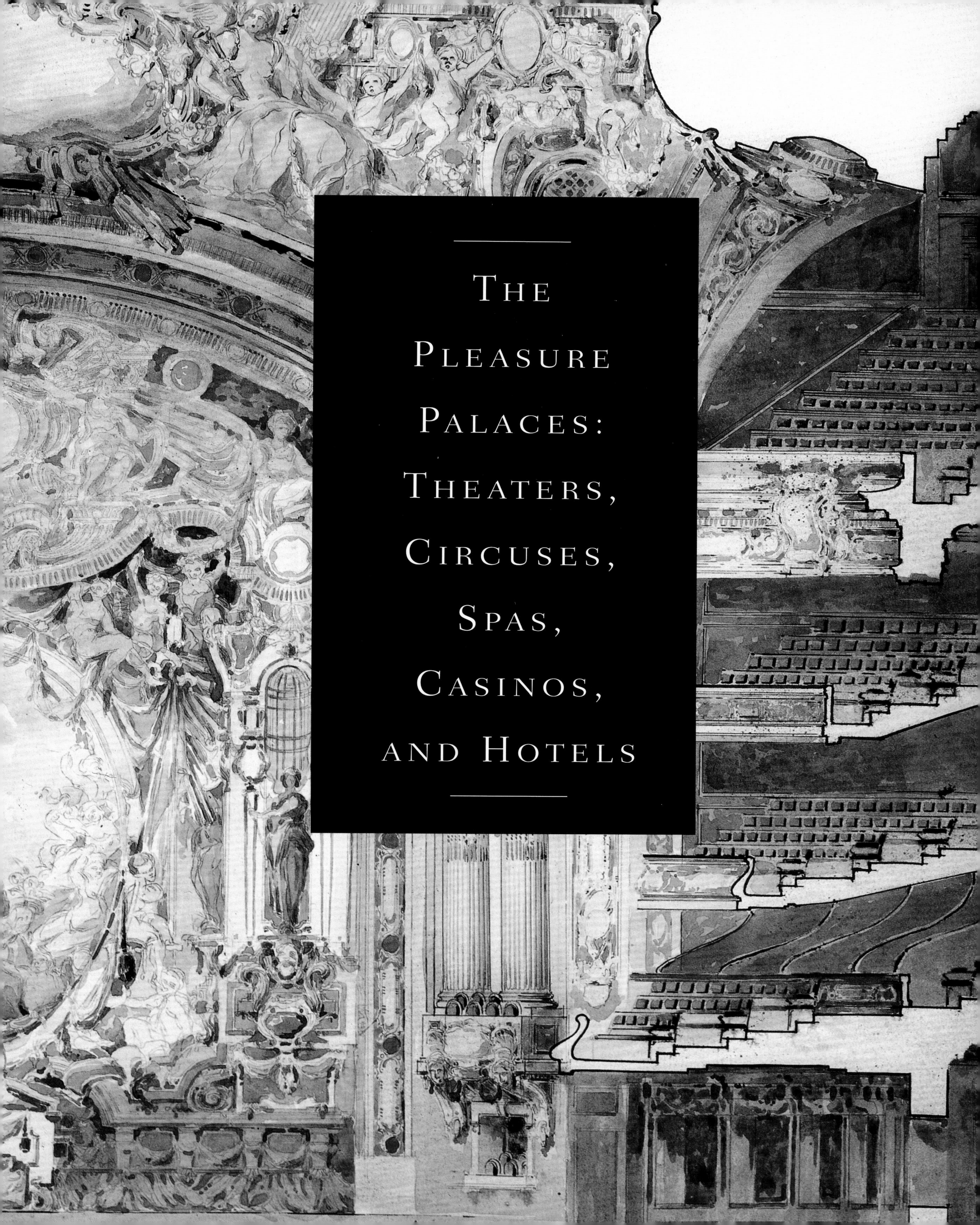

The Pleasure Palaces: Theaters, Circuses, Spas, Casinos, and Hotels

THEATRE DE REIMS
MUSIQUE
AUBER
CORNEILLE
MOZART
MOLIERE
ROSSINI
COMEDIE
1867-1873
PREMIER PRIX AU CONCOURS EN 1866

AGENCE
1870

In a century in which the distribution of wealth became more democratic, more people had access to pleasures formerly reserved for the elite. In France this phenomenon stimulated the proliferation of structures built specifically for entertainment and for the refreshment of mind and body. Theaters, opera houses, casinos, and hotels sprang up in the cities' most prestigious sections. The ostentation that characterized these projects added a festive ambience to the public space. Their elaborate decoration and monumental scale often combined to make each building a spectacle in its own right, serving as a natural extension of the entertainment available within and a conspicuous affirmation of the desirable lifestyle of the newly rich classes. Thus, the pleasure palaces of the nineteenth century flaunted their theatrical image as both an exhibitionistic and insolent parade of wealth and an invitation to share its fruits.

THEATER IN SOCIETY

The primary type of leisure architecture was the performance space, especially the theater. In the late eighteenth century, theater architecture had abandoned the Italian tradition for an austere form of Neoclassicism, a revision made evident by two buildings that would remain important points of reference: Bordeaux's Grand Théâtre, designed by Victor Louis and built in 1773–80, and the Théâtre-Français in Paris—later the Théâtre de l'Odéon, now the Théâtre de France—designed by Marie-Joseph Peyre and Charles de Wailly and built in 1767–70. Both present monumental facades with majestic colonnades but no pediments, porticoes on the sides, and large entrances that draw attention to the lobby and grand staircase. In its basic plan, this model was replicated throughout the nineteenth century, but with an expansion of the stage, which became clearly visible from the outside. The style of theaters, however, moved toward a more Baroque-inspired expression. The colonnades were often combined with arcades that opened up the building to the streetscape, and the theater became an essential element in the urban configuration. Likewise, the theater became a space whose social function largely overlapped its mere artistic purpose. The important role of theaters is apparent from the beginning of the century onward, in the tradition illustrated in the eighteenth century by Claude-Nicolas Ledoux in Besançon and so handsomely embodied in the Bordeaux theater.

Chapter opening spread: The design for the opulent interior of a theater by Boille, around 1905.

Preceding pages: Left: The influence of the Paris Opéra is unmistakable at Alphonse Gosset's Théâtre de Reims of 1863. Right: Paris's Théâtre de Vaudeville of 1876, designed by Auguste Magne, is integrated into the urban streetscape.

Above: The foyer of Rennes's Grand Théâtre occupies a majestic Neoclassical rotunda.

Several major theaters were built in France during the Restoration of 1814 to 1830, a period in which theater and opera were extraordinarily popular. The famous Boulevard du Crime, home to many theaters and various kinds of performance spaces, was one of the highlights of Paris nightlife.

The first important nineteenth-century theater in Paris was the opera house designed by François Debret on Rue Le Peletier. The assassination of the duc de Berry on the steps of the old opera house on Rue Richelieu had sounded the death knell for that hall. The new building, which was constructed in only a few months, presented a fine facade on the narrow Rue Le Peletier, with an arcade on the ground floor and Palladian-style windows on the floor above. One could reach the boulevard directly through the Passage de l'Opéra. Other theaters in Paris and in the provinces generally displayed designs along this theme: ground-floor arcades opened onto a gallery from which one entered the lobby; the second floor had large arched windows that allowed daylight into the foyer; there were end pavilions, sometimes decorated with statues; and the auditorium was Italian in style, in the form of either a hemicycle or a horseshoe. In Paris, the architect Guerchy's Théâtre du Gymnase, Huvé and

Guerchy's Salle Ventadour—today converted into an annex of the Banque de France—and Hittorff and Lecointe's Théâtre de l'Ambigu, all built during the Restoration, adopted these configurations, adapting them to the site. In order to reduce the frequent risk of fire, the roof frames of these theaters are of metal and terra cotta, and from 1829 on, all were gaslit. Catoire's theater in Périgueux is in the austere Neoclassical style so dear to that architect, and thus presents a restrained interpretation of the prevailing compositional devices. In contrast, Lyons's grand theater, built in 1826–42 to plans by Chenavard, Pollet, and Dardel, is on a scale befitting a large city. It rises like an independent monument, its finely wrought facade continuing uniformly around the sides.

The architectural style of theaters followed the general evolution of architecture, displaying, at mid-century, a change of direction toward a more ornate manner, one more open to various influences and free from the narrow constraints of Neoclassical norms. Léon Feuchère's Théâtre d'Avignon, built in the 1840s, was ahead of its time. The architecture itself is very theatrical, focused on a richly ornamented pavilion with an Italian Renaissance–inspired portico, above which an arcaded niche forms a loggia. But even as the architecture became more expansive, the political powers of the Second Empire were taking back the theatrical institutions themselves. A number of theaters considered "uncontrollable" were destroyed, censorship increased, and opera and other spectacular performances were encouraged over melodrama. As Camille Doucet, head of the Division des Théâtres, wrote to his minister:

> *The workingmen are very fond of the theaters that present melodramas, but no matter what we do, what influence we attempt to bring to bear on the Directors and playwrights to keep these plays on a more or less decent path, we never succeed, and the people nearly always find bad teachings and bad examples in melodramas.*

The building that ultimately embodied the era's architectural development and established an enduring new aesthetic was, of course, the Paris Opéra, built in 1862–75. The desire of Napoléon III to endow the capital with a prestigious monument could have found no better project. Opera itself, the most refined of all the performing arts, provided the perfect site for the conspicuous display of well-off citizens—one has only to reread Balzac to be convinced—and for an architectural program in which decoration could flourish unconstrained by anything except financial considerations. The surviving Neoclassical principle of isolating great public buildings placed the Opéra on a sort of urban pedestal, thereby consecrating its status as a public monument and reinforcing the grandeur of the work, one in which sculpture and, on the inside, painting served to enhance the architecture. Charles Garnier understood all this perfectly, bringing to the Paris Opéra all his talent as an architect, as well as his ability to blend decorative elements into a unified whole, which is one of the fundamental features of nineteenth-century architectural achievement.

The Paris Opéra was also a monument of primary importance in the transformation of Paris during the Second Empire. Its development profoundly affected that of the surrounding area. The Avenue de l'Opéra was built across the old street pattern, extending out from the axis of the principal facade toward the Louvre, thereby affirming, in the classical tradition, the connection between the center of worldly and cultural life and the royal residence. In the ensuing years, the renovation of many cities would be characterized by the planning of new avenues on axis with opera houses and theaters, confirming the privileged status of the theater in public life. While the proponents of Romanticism in the 1830s considered the cathedral to be the ultimate symbolic monument, two generations later, the opera house would replace it as the highest achievement of the collective genius. Théophile Gautier was identifying this shift when—with an entirely Romantic emphasis—he wrote of the opera house as "civilization's worldly cathedral," which offered an analogous locus of emotion and mystery. Although secular spectacle replaced sacred ritual, one remains awed by architecture's achievement of the Sublime.

For the design of the Paris Opéra Charles Garnier was selected out of 171 candidates in a

CHOREGRAPHIE
ACADEMIE NATIONALE DE MUSIQUE
POESIE LYRIQUE

Charles Garnier's Paris Opéra is a stunning masterpiece of nineteenth-century French architecture. The complex sequence of formal spaces, including the foyer, the grand staircase, and the auditorium, is clearly visible in the section drawing. The exterior epitomizes the synthesis of classical references and the nineteenth-century taste for opulence.

competition held in 1860. Like all the brilliant architects who had passed through the École des Beaux-Arts, he favored an axial plan. The entrance hall was placed along the longitudinal axis, with the foyer above. The grand staircase, the auditorium, the stage, and the business offices are all clearly legible from the outside as a result of the play of volumes and roofs that state their presence, an effect made technically feasible through the use of iron in the framework. In Guadet's view, "in a composition whose imagination seduces you, that you believe to be a brilliant fantasy, reason explains and justifies everything." But Garnier refused to use metal to advance an architectural aesthetic, relegating it to a purely utilitarian role, signaling the limits of his interpretation of Rationalism. For him, architectural elements had primarily a plastic value. The lyrical and sensual architectural environment, with its gilt and its arabesques, demonstrates the gradual shift of his style toward a liberated Neo-Baroque manner. Garnier expressed his masterful ability to achieve dramatic spatial effects by devising a progression of different volumes with varying sizes and ceiling heights. The Opéra also combines different styles: the principal facade is composed of a monumental Italian Renaissance order, while the back of the building, where the business offices are, is treated in a French seventeenth-century style. In this way, Garnier achieved a synthesis of the Romantic, the Rational, and the Neo-Baroque.

The Paris Opéra immediately became the model for all theaters built in France between 1860 and 1900. They adopted Garnier's revised Italian style, with ground-floor arcades, second-floor loggias with Palladian-style windows that emphasize the importance of the foyer, and exuberant decoration. The Théâtre de Reims, for example, built in 1873 to designs by Alphonse Gosset, was explicitly inspired by the Paris opera house, then still under construction. It is notable for its opulent symbolic ornamentation on the theme of music and the lyric arts.

Gabriel Davioud's two theaters of 1859–62 on the Place du Châtelet in Paris exhibit further the influence of Garnier's model. The first of the two theaters, known as the Théâtre du Cirque Impérial, was designed for fairy-tale plays and military performances for a general audience, the second, for opera. Together with the Théâtre de la Gaieté, along the Square des Arts et Métiers, these theaters were supposed to replace the seven theaters, which Haussmann referred to as "forgotten fleapits," that had been torn down when the Boulevard du Temple and the Place de la République were rebuilt. Strictly in the Haussmann mold, the two theaters' principal facades were their most expressive elements. The lateral facades, especially those facing the quai and therefore visible from afar, were integrated with the facades of the apartment houses that were attached to the theaters, an arrangement intended to offset the construction costs. Auguste Magne's Théâtre du Vaudeville was also incorporated into an apartment block, the only sign of its role as a public building being the treatment of the rotunda on the corner.

Feuchère and Carpentier's 1862 theater in Toulon had an open loggia that was treated with a certain emphasis. The central bays are flanked by projecting wings with niches containing statues. The auditorium is marked on the exterior by a pediment, energetically overflowing at the top of the building. Gaspard André's Théâtre des Célestins of 1873–77, in Lyons, was also designed with a loggia, in which a tier of Corinthian columns anchors large Palladian-style windows, as on Garnier's opera. The very ornate attic partially masks a traditional hull-shaped roof. The theater in Montpellier, designed by Joseph Cassien-Bernard and built in 1884–98, also closely resembles this model, except for the treatment of the base, which has rectangular bays instead of arches and a sloped roof.

CIRCUSES

Another type of building that addressed the public's hunger for spectacle, though more modestly and in smaller numbers, was the circus, whose cylindrical shape was inherited from the scenic panoramas that had appeared in France in 1800. Invented by an Irishman, Robert Barker, these panoramas quickly became extremely popular—the first one in Paris was built on Boulevard Montmartre—as crowds thronged to see vast cylindrical paintings depicting city views, famous landscapes, or battle scenes. The

A sketch for Jacques-Ignace Hittorff's Cirque Impérial.

panoramas, which in a sense prefigured both photography and cinema, were popular throughout the nineteenth century.

The Cirque d'Été on the Champs-Élysées, built by Jacques-Ignace Hittorff in 1838–42—the first circus built in Paris—looked very much like a panorama, with the same circular plan, blind walls, and raised lantern to diffuse the light, though inside there were bleachers against the walls, rather than a viewing area in the center, as in the panoramas. The close relationship between the two building types is evidenced by the conversion of panoramas to circuses and vice versa. For example, Garnier's 1882 Panorama Français on Rue Saint-Honoré was later turned into a circus.

The constraints of the plan leave the architect little freedom except in the decoration. Hittorff was inspired by drawings he had made of Sicilian temples between 1822 and 1824. He promoted the use of polychromy as based on historical precedent, maintaining that the ancients had heightened "with color and painted ornaments, not only the interiors of their temples, but also the outside walls of their cellas, their columns, architraves, metopes, cornices, pediments, and even the tiles on their roofs." The Cirque d'Été no longer exists, but the Cirque Marigny, built by Garnier in 1881, was converted into a theater in 1892. Hittorff's 1852 Cirque d'Hiver, on Boulevard du Temple, reiterates the architecture of the Cirque d'Été, but with a much more restrained polychromy.

Most of the circuses built in France followed the model that Hittorff perfected in Paris. The Reims circus, built in 1865 by the city architect Narcisse Brunette, combines stone and brick in a fairly sober classical composition. Amiens also has a handsome circus, its roof supported by female figures in metal. The circus of Châlons-sur-Marne, built in 1899 by Louis Gillet, is in a classic polygonal shape but is unusual in that it is made of reinforced concrete, although the trusses supporting the roof are metal. On the facade, two clown heads burst out of a hoop, as if the wall were as thin as a sheet of paper. Above the entrance, the transom is decorated with a sculptural group taken directly from the Chantilly stables.

Paris's Cirque d'Hiver, also by Hittorff, is one of the best examples of a building devised for the exhibition of horsemanship.

SPAS

The very raison d'être of seaside resort towns and spas, where life seemed to be devoted entirely to the satisfaction of luxurious appetites and pleasures, lent itself perfectly to the exaltation of architectural fantasy. Here, there was no rigorous principle to which one had to submit, as with hospitals or schools, no public dignity to be respected, except what the insolence of wealth demanded, no tradition to be followed. After all, what did a spa or seaside resort have to offer? A casino, baths, a grand hotel, and villas, all in a beautiful setting, to which one came for regeneration.

Spas were certainly not a nineteenth-century invention. From the Roman thermal baths onward, the tradition of bathing in springs persisted throughout the centuries, emerging more markedly during the Renaissance, but without inspiring a specific architectural expression. Of the few hydropathy establishments built in the late eighteenth century, the only one that survives was built in 1762–68 by an engineer, Jean Querret, in Luxeuil, Franche-Comté. This Neoclassical complex of pink Vosges sandstone could have been constructed eighty years later. Until 1850, in fact, the architecture of baths remained within the parameters of classical antiquity, retaining the window configuration of Roman thermal baths and the general form of a basilica, but without attaining the monumental scale of Rome's Terme di Caracalla and others of its type. Néris-les-Bains, whose first stone was laid in 1826, is one of the finer bath structures of this period, while the baths of Bagnères-de-Luchon, built in 1848–52 by Edmond Chambert, are still very much in the Neoclassical style; with its axial plan, Doric colonnades, and so-called thermal windows derived from Roman prototypes, the building is practically a replica of an ancient complex. The same spirit informs the baths at Mont-Dore, built by Louis Ledru in 1817.

At mid-century, spa architecture began to adopt the image of the château—or rather, of the palace—which suited the opulence of the era's newly developing resorts. The Second Empire saw the decisive growth of these towns and their burgeoning architectural programs, largely made possible through the arrival of the railroads.

Spa architecture gradually liberated itself from its Neoclassical heritage as the fashion for such resorts increased, requiring the construction of establishments large enough to accommodate crowds of people coming to take the waters. Although there was always a compromise, usually a skillful one, between the Roman model and regional features—because it was desirable to emphasize the virtues of the local springs—it was never at the expense of a degree of opulence. The Royat baths, built in 1852–56 by Agis Ledru, a winner of the Grand Prix de Rome, still shows the determining influence of the imagery of classical baths, with a central block derived directly from the basilica of Constantine in Rome. A few years later, in 1876–77, Ledru expanded the baths of La Bourboule by adding new, functional wings grouped around a domed central pavilion.

The development of hydropathy resulted in an increased number of baths and spas. Traffic was through a vast lobby, which served as both an entrance hall and a place to meet and socialize, and thus exhibited elaborate decoration. The baths of Mont-Dore, renovated in 1890–94 by J. Camut, have gone through a number of changes, but the second-floor waiting room is in its original condition, with a vaulted navelike space supported by transverse ribs. The voussoirs of the arches alternate between white limestone and gray andesite lava, which gives the space a Romanesque-Moorish appearance and recalls the churches of Auvergne. The overall effect is heightened by the colors of the marble floor and by the green porphyry engaged columns. The César spring has pride of place in an apse at one end, as if in an Early Christian basilica. The baths of Bourbon-l'Archambauld, built in 1881–88 to designs by Charles Le Coeur, is equally notable for the polychromy of its main hall. A pattern of ceramic tiles in shades of blue and green gives the place a strange, almost underwater feeling. The exterior also employs polychrome

Opposite, top: The baths at Bourbon-l'Archambauld are organized around a light-filled navelike space.

Opposite, bottom, and right: The baths at Mont-Dore are designed with references to Early Christian and Romanesque architecture. The design is executed with several types of colored stone in addition to metal, which is left exposed to show its utilitarian nature.

brick, a traditional material in the north of the Bourbonnais. In Châtelguyon, the baths by G. Redon use the same composition as those of Royat: a central block with three arches, flanked by two wings. It was renovated in 1906 by B. Chaussemiche in a regionalist Romanesque style; its showpiece is the great hall, which is lined with red marble Corinthian columns and has a handsome coffered ceiling. In Vittel, the 1905 hall became a glass-roofed atrium.

A local style was often adopted in order to situate a town's identity as a spa in an ongoing temporal context, but exotic features produced more picturesque results. Architects often favored the Moorish style, because it easily evoked the Orient, as it was idealized in literature, from Gustave Flaubert to Charles-Pierre Baudelaire, and in painting, from Jean-Auguste-Dominique Ingres to Eugène Delacroix, where refined pleasure is associated specifically with bathing. This style also evoked the traditional Oriental bathhouses and lent itself to the application of colored terra cotta and mosaic, which contributed to a festive appearance. The baths of Salies-de-Béarn is a splendid example of this Orientalizing vein. It was built in 1857 and, though partially renovated, retains its original design inside and out. The earliest baths in Deauville and Vittel and the Hépar spring in Vichy also adopted a Moorish style.

If the architecture of resorts consistently incorporated exotic styles, it was not only a means to extend the boundaries of eclecticism but also a way to signal that these towns were microcosms—symbolic concentrations—of what the world had to offer the nineteenth-century bourgeoisie. Dream cities were erected around hydropathy establishments and, later, casinos; the architecture created a holiday atmosphere, in which life followed a fantasy schedule determined by the timetable of one's cure, the hours of the gaming room, or curtain time. In between, leisure time was spent strolling down covered walks, by the sea, or in the park. These towns were also designed to be sites of communion with nature. If the sea or a lake offered no distant horizon facing a row of eclectic facades, a park provided the essential element of nature within an urban context. In Vichy, for example, the entire town was built around a park—the center of which is occupied by the casino. Covered walks, skylights, and glass canopies mediated the interrelationship between nature and architecture, allowing light to bathe interiors as well as exteriors, and permitting plants within the buildings. The transparency that metal and glass made possible addressed a desire for light and air, which was accentuated by florid decorative motifs intended to express nature's bloom.

Baths remained a popular outlet for eclecticism because they provided a program that accommodat-

Above, left: The baths at Salies-de-Béarn.

Above: A detail of the terra-cotta decoration at Bourbon-l'Archambauld. The hygienic quality and decorative potential of glazed tile made it a material of choice for bath architecture.

ed the nineteenth-century ideal of encompassing in a single work the sometimes contradictory essence of things: history and fashion, body and spirit, nature and architecture. Baths and hydropathy establishments recurred regularly as subjects of competitions at the École des Beaux-Arts—forty-seven times between 1819 and 1914. They were always the object of grand compositions with classical references often highlighted by restrained polychromy, but by the end of the century baths engendered an exuberant architecture almost entirely free of academic constraints, where references to Rome mingled with references to Constantinople, by way of Egypt and China. Paul Bigot's winning project for the Prix de Rome in 1900 was in this freewheeling vein, all the more so since the complex he created incorporated both baths and a casino, the two pillars of spa refreshment, as the magazine *La Construction moderne* observed:

> *What have we here? A "hydropathy establishment," with the obligatory "casino": a physical cure and a lift for the spirits, or at least the brain; the god of the Waters and the demon of gambling; the nymph of the springs and the nymph of baccarat. There are thus two kinds of buildings, very distinct and very distant; on the one hand, the spa factory or cookery; on the other hand, at some remove from the first, the ones where one goes to forget the daily drudgery of taking a cure, to think only of the—no less refreshing—pleasures of gossiping, flirting, billiards, and cards; balls, concerts, theater, and so on and so on.*

By the turn of the century, the architecture of spa towns was as magnificent as that of the univeral expositions. There were recurring themes, such as gigantic domed structures with large thermal windows, flanked by minaret-style towers, as at the 1902 baths at Évian (discontinued as baths in 1983) and at Vichy, where the gilded dome built in 1900–03 by Charles Le Coeur and Lucien Woog recalls the mosques of Iran.

The interior decoration of these buildings allowed fantasy even more play, often reveling in images or allegories of water. The female figure is consistently associated with water, from the frescoes at Bagnères-de-Luchon by a student of Ingres, Romain Cazes, whose female figures refer to nearby places and the springs feeding the baths, to Vichy's symbolic frescoes on the theme of baths by Alphonse Osbert, recalling the manner of Puvis de Chavannes. Medical symbols are also prevalent, especially those associated with Mercury and his attributes, such as the caduceus.

CASINOS

Casinos, indispensable complements to the baths, were often the most important structures in resorts. They were more than just gaming establishments. As defined by the architect Gustave Rives, who specialized in opulent eclecticism, the casino was

> *located in the most agreeable site of a seaside resort, it combines all the amusements that the urban leisure class cannot do without, even when seeking rest and health . . . it must be close to the best section of the bathing beach, or else to the baths. . . . It is a somewhat more intimate place than a theater, but in the end it is a kind of open-admission club.*

The casino had evolved far from its etymological meaning of a small Italian-style country house, being derived rather from an English tradition. The first structures that suited the definition of a casino appeared at the end of the eighteenth century. *Vauxhalls*, an English import, as the name suggests, combined ballrooms, concert halls, and gaming rooms, as well as restaurants and cafés. In Paris in 1796, three were built simultaneously: the Vauxhall d'Été, the Vauxhall d'Hiver, and the Colisée on the Champs-Élysées. The program of the *vauxhall* thus went far beyond the mere function of a gaming house; likewise, casinos would include these various functions throughout the century. Thus, a casino had to be made up of three parts: a hall for parties with contiguous rooms, a café/restaurant with billiard and smoking rooms, and a club that included the gaming rooms. In some cases, casinos even had writing rooms, reading rooms, libraries, and fencing rooms.

It was not until the end of the century that casinos came into their own in the plans of spas and resort towns. The first casinos in these towns were frequently modest, provisional, wooden structures, built in the earliest stages of development of these places, whose rapid growth usually led to hurried reconstruction or phased extensions. Arcachon's Moorish-style casino, built of wood in 1865, is one example. It burned to the ground a century later.

The casino at Trouville was extended several times. The one in Vichy, originally built by Charles Badger in 1865, was also enlarged. The central nucleus, with a theater and a contiguous hall for parties, was retained, though renovated more than once, and two lateral wings were added, along with a circular glass canopy over the entrance. In 1900, Charles Le Coeur built a new theater, connected to the old casino by a block containing a great hall, the original theater having been turned into the gaming room. Today, an elegant glass canopy shelters the entrance. In Vittel, the resort sprang from the earth fully formed, when, between 1882 and 1884, Charles Garnier built the train station, baths, casino, hotel, and church.

The styles of the casinos tended to vary between a fairly pompous classicism, with entrance loggias and prominent roofs identifying the shapes of the principal halls, and a Moorish mode, offering an invitation to travel beyond real time to exotic realms where money ceases to mean anything. Georges Dejean's 1898 casino at Néris-les-Bains, which adopted the layout of Garnier's casino at Vittel, is an attractive instance of the former manner. A Moorish style was used to handsome effect at the casinos of Arcachon, Hendaye, Menton, and in the gaming room of the casino at Monte Carlo, designed by Dutrou in 1872. The casino built on a pier in Nice, after the manner of the English piers, opened in 1884 and was expanded in 1890. The Orientalizing profile of the roof expresses the casino's urbanity and worldliness.

In the early twentieth century, as the popularity of gambling increased, the number of gaming houses multiplied. Vichy, for example, had six gaming houses at that time. Architecture abandoned classical and Moorish models for sometimes extravagant expressions. In the words of the architect Émile Guillot in 1912:

Vichy's casino includes a handsome theater, a restaurant, reception rooms, and gaming rooms, offering various forms of entertainment to spa visitors.

Today's casinos are the buildings that perhaps best satisfy the tastes, both refined and avid for new forms, of our generation, which is increasingly taken with artistic ideals. In olden times, in fact, it was only in churches, cathedrals, and the châteaux of princes that architectural magnificence and beauty were given free rein; today, the gaze of amateurs, connoisseurs, and artists—whose number is legion, though they once were but a modest host—have turned toward less mystical and special places, places that are open freely to all.

The casino in Évian, built by Albert Hébrard in 1911–13, is topped by an enormous dome of reinforced concrete, inspired by the Byzantine church of Hagia Sophia in what was then Constantinople (now Istanbul). The casino in Enghien, designed by the architect Autant and an engineer named Cottancin, and which was destroyed by fire seven years later, was in the shape of a ship, complete with masts and poop, and with its prow on the lake.

Inside, the decoration of casinos was always ostentatious, in keeping with the sums of money circulating on the tables. As one observer noted: "The decoration of the casino must be informed by the purpose of the establishment, gay and harmonious in its lines and colors, while enamels, fabrics, ceramics, mosaics, visible woods, marbles, and gilt are so many precious aids for the architect." The gaming room at Monte Carlo, redone in 1898 by Henri Schmit, following Garnier's extension of the main block in 1878–79, is a paragon of this aesthetic. Every inch of surface is covered with gilt, paint, and marble, the whole in a style evoking the era of Louis XIV. Its glass cupola rests on pendentives representing the four seasons. Garnier's theater—with an allegorical decor that is a show in itself—is as successful as his Paris Opéra. At Aix-les-Bains, the great hall of the Casino du Grand Cercle, built in 1883, lost some of its original splendor after its pillars and metal arches were covered with staff in 1937, but its vaults are still covered with Antonio Salviati's mosaics of gold mixed with shades of green and pink, which diffuse an otherworldly light.

THE GRAND HOTELS

In the development of resorts in the nineteenth century, the grand hotel was an indispensable complement to the casino. The rich clientele that squandered their fortunes at the gaming tables could stay only at establishments appropriate to their status. The development of the luxury hotel in the nineteenth century was a response to the desire of a cosmopolitan clientele that enjoyed going from town to town, according to the seasons, and was willing to pay to flaunt an aristocratic way of life. These hotels differed from their predecessors by their size, often several hundred rooms; in this regard they followed the image of the American hotels, which instituted the formula in the 1830s. The scale of these establishments allowed for common rooms that were often splendidly decorated. The first hotels of this kind appeared in France at the beginning of the Second Empire. They were often connected to railroad stations, and they offered a range of specialized rooms, such as restaurants, smoking rooms, reading rooms, billiards rooms, gaming rooms, and ladies' lounges. The comfort of the sleeping rooms often left something to be desired, especially in the area of sanitary facilities.

The Grand Hôtel du Louvre, built across from the Louvre in 1855 to designs by Alfred Armand, Auguste Pellechet, Jacques-Ignace Hittorff, and Charles Rohault de Fleury for the 1855 Exposition Universelle, is one of the earliest examples. It had seven hundred rooms and three glass-ceilinged lobbies. There were shops on the ground floor, and a grand staircase led to the second floor and its grand salon and dining room, each more than 130 feet long. The hotel was gradually turned into a department store. The Grand Hôtel on Boulevard des Capucines, which Armand designed in 1862 across from the Opéra, also had seven hundred rooms. The Hôtel Continental was built for the 1878 Exposition Universelle. These palatial structures all had grand skylight-covered salons or halls, a feature that would become standard in the hotel program. By the end of the century, the glass-ceilinged grand salon replaced smaller lounges, concentrating the public life of the hotel into a single space that was decorated as luxuriously as the private rooms. The skylights that appeared in grand

The casino theater of Monte Carlo is a masterpiece of its kind, notable for its exuberant ornamentation. Charles Garnier fashioned the theater in a style reminiscent of his design for the Paris Opéra. The themes of music and the lyric arts are represented in numerous statues and other elements both inside and out.

hotels and restaurants not only lit interiors, they also produced a phantasmagorical play of light reflected in mirrors, creating the illusion of a world without limits, in which life unfolded amid the gleam of gold and finery.

At the turn of the twentieth century, most of the luxury hotels in Paris were on the Rue de Rivoli, near the Opéra and the Gare Saint-Lazare, and on the Champs-Élysées. Some ten great hotels were built near the Champs-Élysées during this period, among them, the Élysées-Palace, designed by Georges Chedanne in 1898; the Mercédès, by Chedanne in 1903; the Majestic, by Sibien in 1905; the Astoria, by Rives in 1907; the Carlton, by Humbert in 1909; and the Claridge, by Lefebvre and Duhayon in 1914. All but one of these hotels have been altered and transformed into offices or apartments. Only the Majestic, today the Centre de Conférences Internationales, has retained most of its decoration.

Every seaside resort had its grand hotel, as well as countless hotels of every degree of luxury, their accommodations ranging from royal suite to bachelor's single. One of the oldest is the Hôtel du Palais in Biarritz, which was originally built in 1854 to designs by Charles Durand for the empress Eugénie and which, in her honor, followed an E-shaped plan. The resorts on the English Channel coast, which were early tourist towns, also boast attractive hotels; one of the oldest of these is surely Trouville's Hôtel des Roches-Noires, built in 1868. In Deauville, a resort begun in 1859 by the duc de Morny, the Hôtel Normandy, designed by Théo Petit and built in 1911–12, is contiguous to Georges Wybo's casino of 1912. In 1855, the town of Cabourg was parceled into lots according to a fan-shaped plan, the center of which is occupied by a casino. Its Grand Hôtel was built in 1862 and renovated in 1892 in a Renaissance Revival style. Other resorts have their luxury hotels, such as the Grand Hôtel at Houlgate and the Westminster at Le Touquet.

The hotels built at the spas were similar in appearance, although they lacked the majestic site of the seashore. Aix-les-Bains still has several magnificent hotels, today converted into apartment buildings: the Splendide (1881–84); the Hôtel de l'Europe, which includes a series of rental villas, where Queen Victoria stayed several times; the Regina Hôtel Bernascon (1900, by Jules Pin); and the Excelsior (1906, by Alfred Olivet). In the center of town, the Grand Hôtel, built to plans by Pellegrini in 1853–54, is remarkable for its glass-roofed atrium, surrounded by galleries in the Italianate style, a theme taken from the local architecture. In the Hôtel Métropole, built in 1883–84 by Le Faure and Garriguenc, the atrium became a covered pedestrian thoroughfare. In Évian, the Hôtel Royal, designed by Albert Hébrard in 1909, confirmed the importance of that spa.

Two luxury hotels were erected near the casino at Monte Carlo. The Hermitage, designed by Monaco-born Jean Marquet in 1890, boasts a superb winter garden. The Hôtel de Paris, aptly enough, recalls Parisian architecture of the Second Empire, in particular the Grand Hôtel on the Boulevard des Capucines. Begun by Dutrou in 1866, it was redone several times, first by Schmit in 1897, then by Édouard Niermans in 1908. The hall and the Empire salon display two remarkable interiors. In Cannes, the Hôtel du Parc, built in 1893, is now an apartment house with a fine park, as its name implies. The Hôtel Carlton, which opened in 1911, still stands on the Croisette, its eclectic facade flanked by two small corner turrets that are capped by bulb-shaped domes. Menton's Hôtel d'Orient more discreetly incorporated turrets into its Moorish design. In the same city, the Riviera Palace, built in 1898, today an apartment building, presents an interesting decorative scheme of enam-

Opposite, top: The grand Hôtel du Palais in Biarritz was originally built for the empress Eugénie, in 1854.

Opposite, bottom: Today, the former Hôtel du Parc in Cannes, like so many other grand hotels of the nineteenth century, has been converted to apartments.

eled terra cotta and painted panels displaying the city's coat of arms. The lobby still retains its original decor, including Ionic capitals and a frieze with painted Cupid motifs. At one time, the Riviera also had a theater with a convertible dome, so that the auditorium could be in the open air. Abandoned by the wealthy clientele of crowned heads that used to winter on the Mediterranean, many of the hotels on the coast no longer serve their original purpose.

The Negresco in Nice is one of the last great luxury hotels of the Belle Époque. It was designed in 1909 by Édouard Niermans, an architect who made his name with brasseries, theaters, and hotels. He was responsible for the designs of the Moulin Rouge, the Casino de Paris, the Théâtre des Capucines and the Théâtre Marigny, the Hôtel de Paris in Monte Carlo, and other grand hotels in Ostende and Madrid. The Negresco was erected on the Promenade des Anglais at a time when buildings on the waterfront were considered undesirable. In its first years, the hotel offered lower rates for rooms facing the sea. But from 1913, when it opened, it was the ultimate in comfort—it had electric lighting, central heating from radiators, mail distributed by pneumatic tubes, and telephones—as well as luxury. A plethora of stuccowork and sumptuous, classical-style marbles adorn the salons and what was once the dining room, which open off an elliptical hall girdled by a colonnade and covered by a skylight.

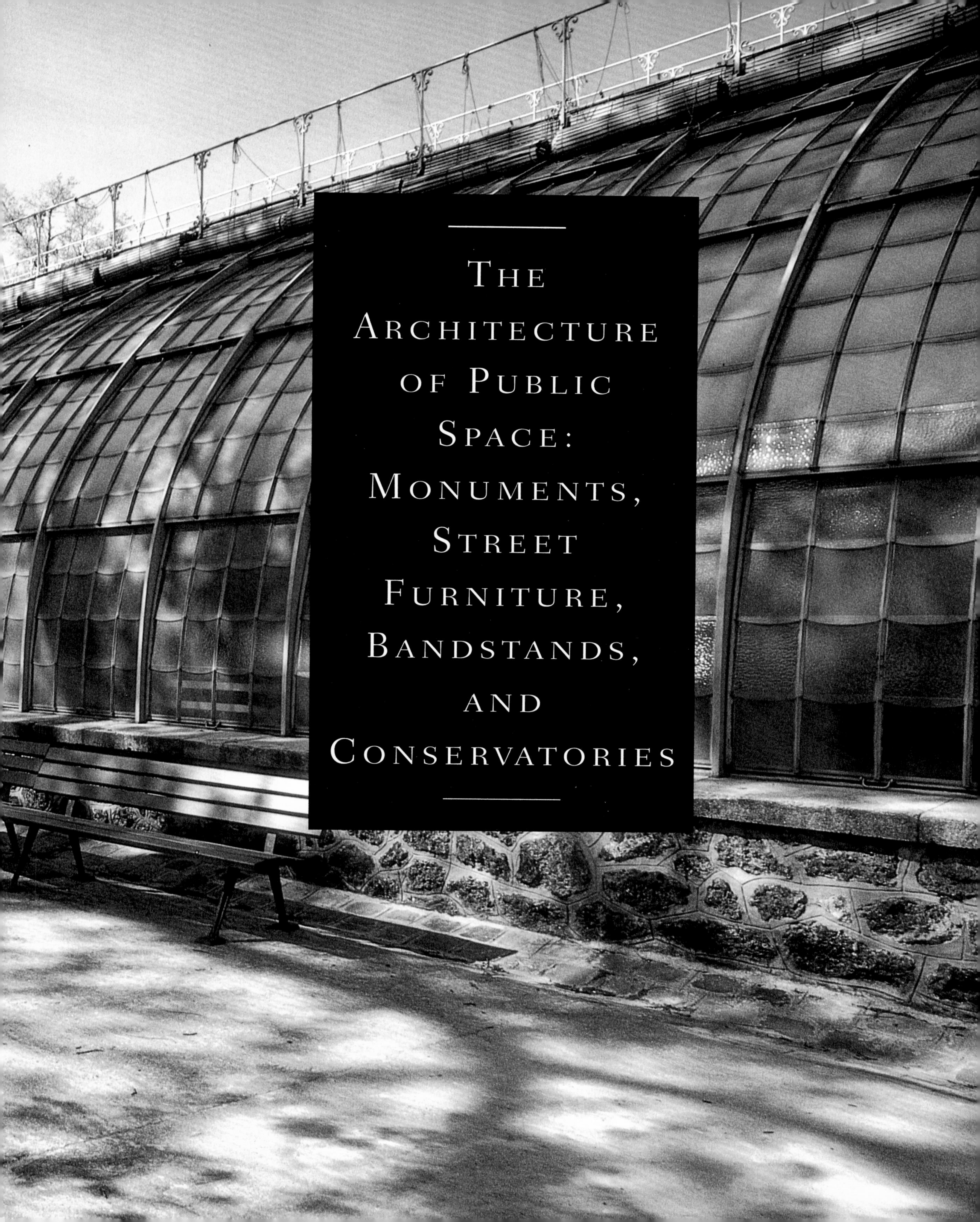

The Architecture of Public Space: Monuments, Street Furniture, Bandstands, and Conservatories

Public space, in all its aspects, was tremendously important in nineteenth-century cities. As private life became increasingly family-centered and society was stratified into various classes, public spaces, where the working and middle classes met, became the melting pot of collective identity. Architects and planners in France during the nineteenth century were preoccupied with defining such spaces in a way that would be both homogeneous and universal. In Paris, rich and poor neighborhoods received the same elements of urban comfort—park benches, for example, were the same all over the capital. Beginning in the 1840s, specific types of so-called street furniture were installed throughout the country, with myriad stylistic variations: lampposts, benches, public toilets, bandstands, and so on.

In counterpoint to these ubiquitous elements, the art of the monument was gaining attention, its purpose to remind passersby that society as a whole was represented in the collective space. Monuments, as well as the monumentality of public buildings, including apartment buildings, manifested a desire to bring together a social body in France that was still deeply divided. Common references in the form of monuments were meant to provide landmarks of consensus drawn from the classical language of architecture and history.

MONUMENTS

The nineteenth century loved history, and this is particularly apparent in France. The cult of great men that was a legacy of the classical tradition gradually gave way to the practice of commemoration, which nurtured a national identity that was expressed by more than the sovereign alone. Monuments celebrated the heroes of French history, episodes of wars, and civic, moral, and didactic values. Monuments were intended to be instruments of education for the people. Of course, the political meaning of monuments changed with time. They were entirely identified with Napoleon in the early years of the century, then marked by the growth of capitalism and the revolutions, and finally, beginning in the 1870s, designed to celebrate the French Republic. Increasing material

Chapter opening spread: The large Auteuil greenhouse in Paris's Bois de Boulogne.

Preceding pages: An 1806 design by Alavoine for a monumental statue in the form of an elephant, which was to be erected in the Place de la Bastille. Only a life-size model was finally installed.

Opposite, top: The Eiffel Tower, the quintessential monument of the century, marked the triumph of the engineer's craft when it was completed in 1889.

Opposite, bottom: Design for a monument to Léon-Michel Gambetta, on the Pont de la Concorde, by Henri Nénot.

progress throughout the nineteenth century meant new subjects for public statues that redeployed the allegorical and symbolic vocabulary of antiquity to celebrate virtues associated with the evolution of society and newly acquired wealth. Greco-Roman mythology remained the sculptors' source of symbols and forms.

The cult of monuments was accompanied by the increasing monumentalism of architecture over the course of the century. The curriculum of the École des Beaux-Arts tended to transform every building into a vast composition that acquired an individual symbolic value from its size and layout. Architecture's monumentality was brought to bear on the design of urban space. The new thoroughfares were laid on axis with monumental structures; the Boulevard de Strasbourg, for example, is exactly on the axis of the Gare de l'Est. Apartment houses became monumental, too. Their specific placement in the streetscape could dictate a particular ornamental treatment. Thus, apartment houses on corners might have rotundas whose roofs were visible from afar. Fountains played a special part in the urban organization, perhaps occupying the space of an entire apartment house. Gabriel Davioud's fountain of 1856–60 on the Place Saint-Michel, for example, rises five stories. Its expensive materials and decorations are evidence of the monumental value that was attributed to this kind of structure during the period.

The most important monuments erected early in the nineteenth century bore Napoleon's imprint. The celebration of military victories motivated the construction of the Colonne Vendôme in 1806–10, from the bronze of the cannons taken at Austerlitz; the Arc de Triomphe du Carrousel, designed in 1806 by Charles Percier and Pierre-François-Léonard Fontaine after the arch of Septimius Severus in Rome; and the Arc de Triomphe de l'Étoile, designed by Jean-François-Thérèse Chalgrin in the same year. The latter was completed thirty years later, after a long interruption. Originally planned to celebrate the victory at Austerlitz, its program was expanded in 1833, becoming a commemoration of all the wars of the revolutionary period and of Napoleon's time. An elephant, of bronze melted down from cannons captured from the Spanish, was planned for the Place de la Bastille. After several variations on the theme, a life-size model of the project, designed by Jean-Antoine Alavoine, was erected in 1810, but the monument itself was never built.

The tone of public monuments in France changed under the Restoration of the Bourbon monarchy. The most telling monument of this period is the Chapelle Expiatoire built in 1816–20 to designs by Hippolyte Le Bas and Pierre-François-Léonard Fontaine in the cemetery of the Madeleine, on Rue d'Anjou, on the spot where Louis XVI and Marie Antoinette were buried following their execution in 1793. The Napoleonic saga continued to inspire important monuments after 1830. The return of the emperor's ashes in 1840, for example, was the occasion for a large-scale project. Louis-Tullius-Joachim Visconti won the competition held for the design of Napoleon's large tomb in the church of Saint-Louis des Invalides. The raising on the Place de la Concorde of the Luxor obelisk, a gift to Louis Philippe from Mahmud II, was also commemorative, a memorial to Napoleon's Egyptian campaigns. The obelisk was installed under the direction of an engineer named Lebas, on October 25, 1836, before a considerable crowd. The Colonne de Juillet on the Place de la Bastille was erected in 1833–40, above the vault containing the remains of the victims of the 1830 revolution. A winged Mercury, a frequent symbol of commerce in the 1820s, stands on a globe atop the column. Bearing a torch and a broken chain, he stands for freedom. The creation of the Commission des Monuments Historiques in 1837 gave new meaning to the term *monument,* which came to encompass the medieval churches and châteaux that were considered the foundation of France's national identity.

During the Second Empire, although republican commemorations were out of favor, nationalism was still an essential component of monumental art. Many statues were made of Vercingetorix, including one, twenty-three feet high, that in 1865 was placed at the summit of Mont Auxois, at the supposed site of Alésia, where the Gallic leader valiantly, if unsuccessfully, resisted Julius Caesar. In Clermont-Ferrand Auguste Bartholdi portrayed Vercingetorix on a rearing horse, brandishing his sword; the statue was not cast until 1903.

Economic and social progress was another frequent subject for monuments. One such example is Jean-Baptiste Carpeaux's *France Carrying Light to the World and Protecting Agriculture and the Sciences,* raised in 1866 at the Louvre's Pavilion Flore. This sculptural group reintroduced the theme of light, which in the classical period had stood for religious faith, but during the Enlightenment came to represent humanity's progress. Sculptors also dwelled a great deal upon figures from the Old and New Testaments. More than fifty-two feet in height, J. Bonnassieux's statue of the Virgin in Le Puy, of 1857–60, is perched atop a volcanic peak, from which it gazes down at the surrounding countryside. Its nationalist content lies in the bronze of which it is cast, which came from cannons captured from the enemy during the Crimean War.

Following the war of 1870 and the fall of the Second Empire, republican values gradually came to the fore. To commemorate the defense of Belfort, the most heroic episode of the war of 1870, Bartholdi set a gigantic stone lion—"awakening in fury and springing at the first shouted alarm"—by the citadel. The statue was inaugurated in 1876, as was a one-quarter replica on the Place Denfert-Rochereau in Paris. The colossal size of the Belfort lion attests to the ambition to address the French people collectively, now that they had the authority to confer legitimate power. Bartholdi's *Statue of Liberty* is in the same political vein, inspired by the idea of giving the United States a statue to celebrate its independence. Financed by a French subscription and made in Paris, the statue was finally raised in New York Harbor in 1886. The quarter-size model was cast in bronze and placed on the Île des Cygnes in Paris.

With the advent of the French Republic in 1875 came the need to identify institutions by their architecture and statuary. After 1870, more statues were made of Joan of Arc than of any other figure because she symbolized the province of Lorraine, which had been lost to Germany. Beginning in the late 1880s, however, the Republic itself provided the subject for many monumental statues. In 1883, the Morice brothers erected a colossal statue of the Republic in the eponymous square, and in 1889 Jules Dalou made a plaster model of the *Triumph of the Republic* for the Place de la Nation. The centenary of the French Revolution provided the occasion for a vast commemorative movement that combined the glorification of progress with a nationalist celebration of the Republic.

The Eiffel Tower also arose out of this commemorative context. It was the highlight of the Exposition Universelle of 1889, and should be seen as its contemporaries saw it: a colossal attraction as ambitious as the challenges that the nineteenth century had set for itself, a spectacular tribute to the idea of material progress and, consequently, of social progress. An individual and collective achievement, the Eiffel Tower was a theatrical performance of technology. Against the grand backdrop of the exposition, itself an extravagant display of images and objects gloriously recounting the century, the tower spoke loudly and clearly of human genius. It expressed itself with a kind of monumentality previously reserved for the realm of the sacred. But if the tower miniaturized the spires of the cathedrals, it was to exalt rational intelligence by raising a sublime monument to it, one with no other function than to render abstraction visible. Iron, an industrial product, was both the ultimate modern material—obviously malleable by the laws of science—and a symbol of the new forms brought about by technological progress. Eiffel's achievement was that of Jules Verne's dream—mastery over nature and the elements.

STREET FURNITURE

The nineteenth-century glorification of progress went hand in hand with the distribution of material prosperity, of which the increasing elaboration of public thoroughfares was a tangible sign. At first, street furniture was site-specific; soon after, it was distributed in small or middling quantities through manufacturers' catalogues. Cast iron was employed from around 1815 onward for its strength and its capacity to be molded, especially for various kinds of everyday objects, such as lampstands, bench supports, and drinking fountains. During the Second Empire, Adolphe Alphand, director of the

The glass canopy at the Porte Dauphine Métro stop in Paris is one of the surviving examples of Hector Guimard's famous Art Nouveau designs.

Service des Promenades et Plantations de Paris, and Jean-Antoine Davioud, chief architect of the same office, who designed and commissioned a host of city kiosks and other stands, encouraged the development of more complex furniture that used metal in all its forms, along with materials such as wood and terra cotta. The designers were responsible for a repertoire of many kinds of specialized kiosks and other structures, such as public toilets—*pissotières* and *vespasiennes*—newsstands, flower stands, bandstands, and shelters of every sort, which were sometimes grouped as ensembles along the street. These kiosks contributed greatly to the definition of public spaces, by both their intrinsic qualities and their placement.

The basic elements of metal street furniture, lampposts, and public benches were certainly not nineteenth-century inventions. In the late eighteenth century, Paris already had eight thousand street lamps, but they were usually attached to the walls of houses. The appearance of the first free-standing lighting fixtures was a function of the development of gas lighting, which was introduced experimentally in Paris in 1817, in the Passage Montesquieu, and gradually replaced oil lamps between 1830 and 1870. In 1831, Paris had 69 gas lamps and 12,941 oil lamps; in 1848, 2,608 gas lamps and 8,600 oil lamps; in 1870, 20,766 gas lamps and 971 oil lamps. Beginning in 1865, the so-called Oudry model generally replaced the earlier lampposts, designed in the 1830s, but other elements remained the same, except that the base was made of cast iron and not stone. More luxurious designs, with as many as five branches, were employed for the monumental urban sites, such as the lampposts that Hittorff designed in 1836 for the Place de la Concorde. Cast-iron lamps continue to be used in various forms to the present day, though they were superceded in 1922 when electric lighting appeared, allowing for more powerful bulbs set on higher steel posts.

Public benches with cast-iron legs and crossbars also came into general use during the Second Empire, with two types predominating. One had a curved profile, with wooden slats, while the other had a straight back and supports that might be shaped like tree branches, or, in the center of the city, might be more architectural and formal, with the city's coat of arms in a cartouche.

By the late nineteenth century, there was a great variety among the kiosks on the streets and in the parks of Paris. Many were of wood, sometimes with pressed zinc decorations, like the newsstands by Grant et Cie, which numbered some four hundred in 1900. The Morris column was created in 1868 by the company of the same name as a support for announcements of theatrical performances. In 1871, Richard Wallace offered the city of Paris fifty bronzed-iron fountains, each with a basin sheltered by a dome borne by four caryatids. In 1876, fifty-four were installed; there were seventy-three extant in 1961, of which fifty-one were large models.

The famous iron entrances to the Paris Métro completely changed the stylistic vocabulary of the material. They were designed by Hector Guimard in 1900, the result of a direct commission by Adrien Bénard, the enlightened director of the Compagnie du Chemin de Fer Métropolitain de Paris. The cast-iron floral arabesques that still blossom at the entrances to the Metro are among the most spectacular expressions of Art Nouveau—all the more reason to regret the destruction of several of Guimard's kiosks, in particular those in the Place de l'Étoile and the Place de la Bastille. The glass shelters above the Abbesses and Porte Dauphine stations survive, as do about one hundred simple entrances.

BANDSTANDS

Inspired by garden follies, and in particular by the beloved gazebos characteristic of Picturesque gardens, bandstands became especially popular after 1848, thanks to Carl Wilhelm's invention of the *orphéon.* Originally these were male choral societies, but they came to include instruments. A great number of popular orchestras sprang up all over France, a phenomenon that coincided with official recognition of music as a subject of instruction for the masses and a form of cultural expression and intellectual progress. Before 1848, the performance of music outdoors was limited to military fanfares, but in July of that year outdoor concerts were authorized, "on the condition that these gatherings take place in places identified beforehand and such that they may easily be surrounded by the police in case of the appearance of disturbances." In part because of the popularity of waltzes during the Second Empire, covered bandstands, such as the "Concert Musard" reinstalled in the Champs-Élysées, multiplied throughout the public parks of Paris and other French cities. In the absence of an inventory, which would be difficult to determine, the number of metal bandstands built in France may be estimated at some five hundred, many of which were later torn down or abandoned. More specifically, twenty-three bandstands of this type still exist in the Midi-Pyrénées region, as well as six wooden ones, more or less evenly distributed throughout the area. There are also four metal bandstands and four wooden ones in the Poitou-Charentes region, where at least seventeen have been torn down.

The basic typology of the bandstand was easily defined: a light roof over a base. The roof both shelters the musicians in case of rain and acts as a sounding board. The supporting shafts are few and thin, so that the audience's view is unobstructed on all sides. The platform is raised on a masonry base, which provides space below for storing chairs and aids visibility. Many bandstands were built of wood, but the great majority employed cast-iron columns with iron or cast-iron brackets, often with delicately ornate volutes, supporting a light metal roof. The degree of detail was often a function of the importance of the city or the site, but the recreational

nature of bandstand architecture was always expressed by exuberant decoration that frequently included the lyre as an emblematic motif.

It is difficult to trace the stylistic evolution of the bandstand. The great majority of surviving bandstands appear to have been built between 1890 and 1914, probably because of the increasing popularity of military bands in that period. Many bandstands were built from standard plans published in architectural journals. The care given to these structures is evident, for example, in the bandstands in Parthenay, in the Deux-Sèvres department, built around 1900. The cast-iron columns were made by Jouffray et Cie, a foundry in Orléans, and are decorated with channels and rings. Above the capitals, the column heads are joined by wrought-iron arches with complex filigree. The bandstand is topped by an elaborate metal lantern, which bears a lightning rod decorated with a lyre. The original lamps, however, have disappeared. Only the metal chains from which they were suspended remain, attached to the middle of each arch.

The decoration of bandstands gave free rein to their designers' fancies, but within defined boundaries. Nevertheless, certain examples stand out as being particularly inventive, such as Louis Hourlier's 1880 bandstand in Cannes, whose columns lean outward, like the cast-iron struts that Viollet-le-Duc recommended in his *Entretiens sur l'architecture*. Another example is the very elaborate bandstand in the park in Nancy, whose roof arches, which are shaped like basket handles, recall the Louis XV style of the nearby Place Stanislas.

Bandstands were often associated with covered walkways in France's resort towns and spas. In Vichy, for example, more than 765 yards of covered walks, designed by Charles Le Coeur and the ironworker Émile Robert and intricately decorated with punched-iron foliage, cross the Parc des Sources. In Vittel, Félix Nachon's walkway of 1897–1905 was unfortunately clad in concrete in 1930.

Hundreds of bandstands were built throughout France in the nineteenth century, in a variety of styles.

Above: A bandstand in Nancy, in a Rococo style.

Opposite: A bandstand in Cannes, notable for its canted columns.

Right: A bandstand in Parthenay, with delicate spandrels and festoons.

CONSERVATORIES

The architectural styles of street furniture frequently employed motifs from nature, whether in the bench supports shaped like tree branches or the ivy garlands draped around lampposts. Indeed, the merging of nature and architecture was essential to nineteenth-century urban planning. The century's legacy of countless rows of trees and sumptuous public parks are evidence of more than a mere desire to embellish city landscapes. They were also an antidote to the increasing industrialization of the country and the resulting expansion of the cities. The incorporation of nature at the heart of the city resolved the conflict between a Rousseauesque desire for freedom that was associated with nature and the anxiety produced by living in the completely artificial environment of modern society.

As a result, public and private conservatories and winter gardens multiplied from the 1840s onward. They reflect the desire to create an easily accessible microcosm of nature, in which its exuberance and variety could be encapsulated. In the iron-and-glass conservatory, a symbiosis of technology and nature was expressed perfectly by the effects of transparency and weightlessness.

The years from 1835 to 1850 were notable for a generation of very modern-looking public conservatories, characterized by a spare geometry, arched roofs, and decoration that was reduced to the articulation of metal cames holding the panes of glass in place. The conquest of light allowed by the systematic use of metal for every part of the building simultaneously satisfied the gardeners, who were concerned with the plants' well-being, and the visitors, who savored the exhilaration of being in a tropical paradise tamed under the European sky, in structures that were no longer reserved for a privileged few.

The great conservatory of the Jardin des Plantes in Paris, built to designs by Charles Rohault de Fleury in 1834–36, is one of the finest examples of its generation. A graduate of the École Polytechnique and the son of the man who built Paris's remarkable Passage du Saumon, the architect visited England in 1833 and brought back technical information about conservatories, especially on their heating systems. Upon his return, he developed a design with two symmetrical wings, with curved profiles of iron and glass springing from a low masonry wall, from two parallelepiped pavilions. Rohault had not only carefully worked out the proportions of the whole, but had also designed subtle and elegant details, such as the cast-iron pilasters, thirty-six feet high, adorned with lions' heads. He considered that "the variety of the shapes of the large and small roofs and the long, curved greenhouses, by projecting onto each other transparent masses, produces picturesque perspectival effects, to which the sun adds a remarkable effect." The complex included a huge iron monkey cage about fifty-nine feet across. Rohault's project was only partially completed, due to lack of funding. The wing was redesigned in 1846, completed by a handsome facade with a loggia, and then reworked again in 1855 to include a great hall whose vaulted ceiling was supported by ringed trusses.

The Jardin d'Hiver on the Champs-Élysées in Paris was in the same formal mold, but instead of a studied cultivation of exotic plants this winter garden displayed the delights of an endlessly blossoming springtime. As one observer noted, "A covered garden is not a purely horticultural building, but rather a fantastic building dedicated to pleasure, in which horticulture is merely one more occasion for, one more element of enchantment." The architect for this drawing-room-cum-greenhouse was Hector Horeau, who in 1847 also designed the Jardin d'Hiver in Lyons, a winter garden with a frame made entirely of wood, except for the wrought-iron garlands that fill the spandrels. The Paris winter garden, replacing an earlier wooden greenhouse, was a superb metal-framed structure built in 1847 at what is today Rue Marignan. The glass roof was supported by wrought-iron trusses more than sixty-two feet long, which rested upon twin iron columns nearly thirty feet high, connected at the top by iron arches. The interior space was in the shape of a Latin cross and organized around parterres, paths, fountains, and statues, creating a garden in which balls and concerts were held. As Victor Hugo described the space, following a ball:

> *Upon entering, the eye was stopped by the effulgence of a flood of light; through this light, one distinguished all sorts of magnificent flowers and strange trees, with the foliage and shapes of the tropics and the Floridas. . . . Indeed, the only virginal thing in that place was the forest. The prettiest women and the*

Integrating nature and architecture, the Champs-Élysées winter garden, built in 1848, prefigured the great iron-and-glass structures that would appear in the second half of the nineteenth century.

> *most beautiful girls in Paris were whirling in this brilliant illumination like a swarm of bees in a honeycomb.*

With the initial success of the Jardin d'Hiver, other projects were proposed for neighboring sites, chief among them Rigolet's 1852 design for the Carré Marigny and Maureal's of 1853.

The economic prosperity of the Second Empire favored the construction of many private hothouses, many of them quite large, as well as numerous winter gardens. While unremarkable technically, these luxury structures—visible signs of wealth—are notable for their refined details, elegance, and carefully conceived proportions. They are especially interesting for the way they integrate the decoration into the details of the construction, demonstrating the iron worker's art rather than the engineer's. Many of these greenhouses were built by specialized firms that began selling through catalogues in 1855. The most important manufacturers of the time were: Guillot-Pelletier, founded in Orléans in 1853; Schwartz et Meurer, which had taken over two firms, Dormois and Bergerot, and which produced many items in addition to greenhouses; and Izambert. The popularity of these structures was partly due to the world's fairs of the era, which presented palaces that resembled enormous conservatories and later served for horticultural shows. Four small greenhouses were exhibited at the fair in 1855; eighteen in 1867; twenty-one in 1878; and twenty-five in 1889. The largest conservatory at the 1867 Exposition Universelle, by Dormois, was more than 120 feet wide and more than sixty-five feet high. It was destroyed by a storm at the end of the fair. Of the many conservatories built privately during this period, one of the most important was the complex built at the Château de Ferrières near Paris around 1859 for James de Rothschild. It was designed by English architect Joseph Paxton, a specialist in iron-and-glass construction who was famous for a large conservatory at Chatsworth and the immense Crystal Palace of the 1851 Great Exhibition in London. From Edmond About's work in Osny in 1878 to Gaston Menier's at La Malnoue in 1905, there was widespread taste for monumental, dome-shaped conservatories.

The construction of public gardens in the provinces, modeled after those developed in Paris under Haussmann, gave rise to a number of greenhouses, some of them of considerable size. The most important were the greenhouse in Bordeaux, by Charles Burguet, built in 1856 and demolished in 1930; those of the Jardin du Thabor in Rennes, by Jean-Baptiste Martenot, built in 1862–63 and altered in 1950; and those in Strasbourg, by Hermann Eggert, of 1877–82. All of these structures exhibit the same plan: an arched nave abutting a stone gallery, punctuated by three glass pavilions, that at the center being the greenhouse for tropical plants. The complex in Lyons's Parc de la Tête d'Or, built by the architect Domenget in 1877–82, is one of the most monumental, with five attached pavilions; the largest of these has an ogival vaulted roof and is nearly seventy feet in height. This pavilion was unfortunately renovated in 1972, with infelicitous, heavy-handed details, such as segmental instead of curved arches. Deserving of mention are other, more modest greenhouses with only one central pavilion, such as those in Montpellier, by Bésiné and Schwartz et Meurer, of 1860; Nancy, by Michaux, of about 1870; Tarbes, by the firm of Saint-Eloy, of 1881; and Nantes, by Guillot-Pelletier, of 1895.

The conservatories built between 1845 and 1880 tended to adopt a heavier style than those of the preceding generation. It is not unusual to find them incorporated into eclectic masonry structures, with the metal elements treated in a fanciful manner. Two buildings that no longer exist today were examples of this trend: the Neo-Byzantine Palais Rameau of 1878 in Lille, by Mourcou and Contamine, and the Jardin d'Acclimatation of 1890–93, in the Bois de Boulogne, by Émile Bertrand.

The greenhouses built and the spas and the public winter gardens at the turn of the century often employed stylized plant imagery and Art Nouveau

Left, top and bottom: Details of the Nantes conservatory and the Auteuil greenhouse. The rhythm of the metal armature creates a lightweight lattice effect. The wrought- and punched-iron decoration evokes the plant life contained within.

Opposite, top: The greenhouses of Lyons's Tête d'Or park comprise one of the most important complexes of its type in France.

Opposite, bottom: The conservatory of the Nantes public park displays a well-balanced composition.

motifs, as did glass architecture found in restaurants and hotels. In Paris, for example, Rougeot, Chartier, Julien, Lucas-Carton, and Maxim's had stained-glass ceilings that contributed to the seductive appeal of the interiors. Charles-Albert Gauthier's double greenhouse, built for the Exposition Universelle of 1900, was more traditionally decorated, but well within fin-de-siècle taste, with protruding honeycomblike cells and lacy filigree. On the inside, the vault—a series of pointed equilateral arches—was made entirely of iron, including the trelliswork posts that replaced the traditional cast-iron columns. The conservatory was torn down in 1909. The new hothouse for the Auteuil Fleuriste, constructed two years earlier by Schwartz-Haumont from plans by the architect Formigé, revived the classic layout of a domed pavilion with vaulted wings on either side, but in a very spare, formal style that restricted the ornamentation to the cornice line. Pau's Palmarium, built by Émile Bertrand in 1896–1900, contrasted its glass hall, supported by astounding columns that rise into branchlike ribs, with two very academic stone pavilions that house a theater and a casino.

The history of monumental iron conservatories in France ends where it began, in the Jardin des Plantes. Rohault de Fleury's greenhouses, damaged by Prussian bombs in 1871, were repaired in 1874. The unfinished wing was completed in 1882–89 from Édouard André's plans, which were very similar to Rohault's of 1854. The result, with arched panels in the glass roof, though very attractive, was severely criticized by contemporary horticulturists as impractical. Rohault's greenhouses were rebuilt some years later, in 1907, by the architect Blavatte, to plans so faithful to his predecessor's that the later greenhouses were often mistaken for the original ones. However, only the foundations and the base wall were retained. As for André's structures, they were replaced in 1934 with a new building, whose heaviness merely emphasizes the elegance of Blavatte's work.

The large hothouse of the Jardin des Plantes in Paris was rebuilt in 1907 on the model of Rohault de Fleury's 1836 greenhouses.

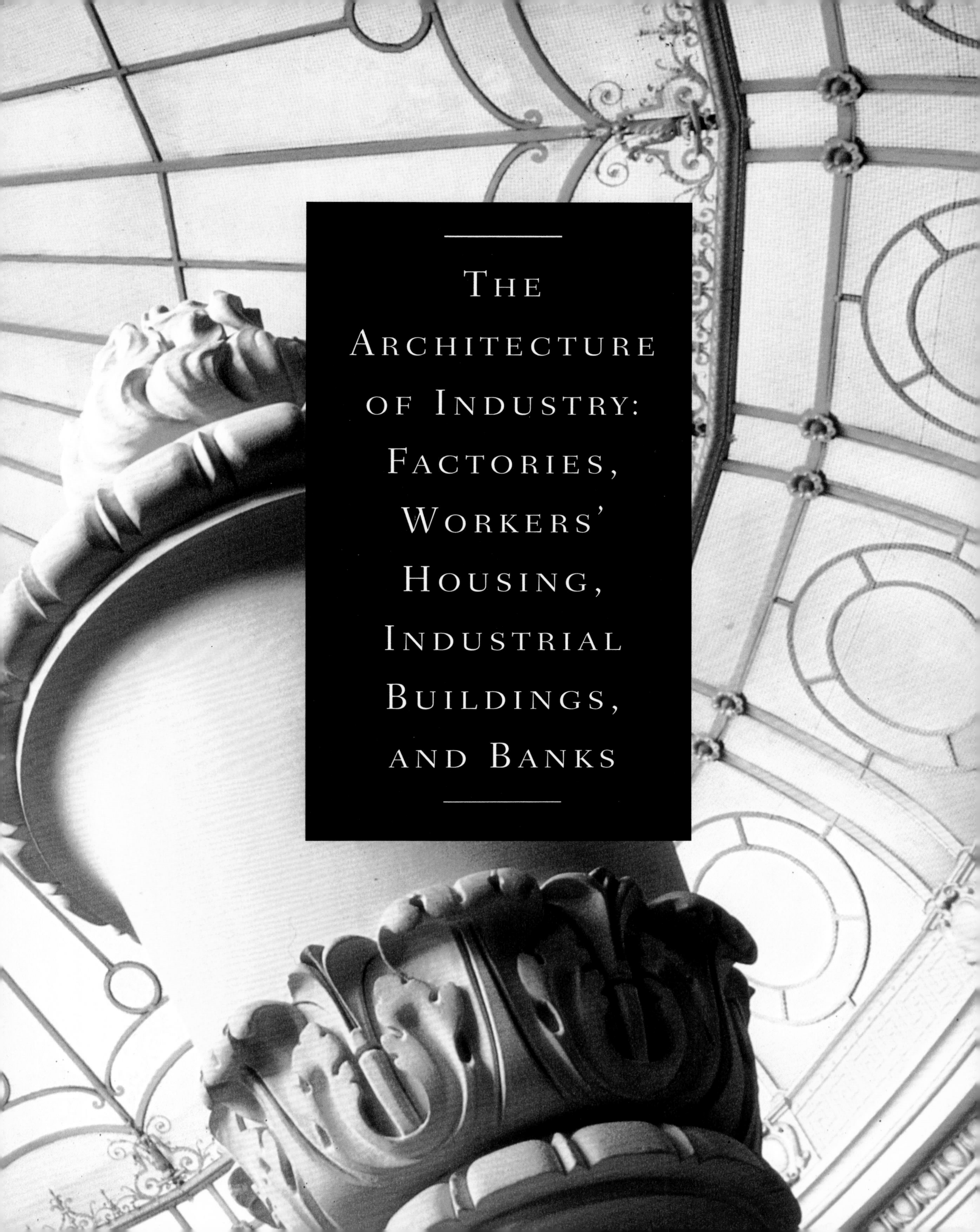

The Architecture of Industry: Factories, Workers' Housing, Industrial Buildings, and Banks

COMPTOIR D'ESCOMPTE
DE PARIS

Industrial development, first in Great Britain, then on the European continent, inevitably spurred utilitarian architecture in the nineteenth century. Factory design evolved in response to the new requirements of production, in particular, the increased space needed for machinery and for the transmission of power. Yet, in France, architecture lagged behind the advances of industry, which frequently made do with converted old buildings, especially convents. The growth of industrial sites was often a matter of successive additions and conversions of existing buildings. Economy was the determining factor, and few manufacturers could afford to display their ambition in the architectural expression of their factories. Thus, even though metal architecture was very closely associated with the development of the nineteenth-century iron and steel industry, structures built specifically for industrial purposes tended to employ traditional materials.

AN ECONOMICAL ARCHITECTURE

Until around 1860, industrial buildings were commonly and summarily composed of load-bearing masonry walls that supported wooden roofs. The architecture was usually modest, subordinated to the needs of production. The prevailing style was an austere Neoclassicism. The unpretentious facades were enlivened with minimal elements, such as arched windows, and, more rarely, with cornices, pilasters, and pediments. However, there were notable exceptions. Among them, the Lainé warehouses in Bordeaux, built in 1820 and named for their engineer, are notable for fine vaulted ceilings that shape a large central space. The site has been converted into a cultural center and performance hall.

Multistory mills appeared in England in the late eighteenth century. The configuration allowed the motor power of a mill or steam engine to be distributed easily by means of shafts running beneath the floors of each level. Made of wood, these structures were serious fire hazards, all the more so because of the presence of flammable materials such as cotton, linen, and oil. As a result, during the same period in England, framing of cast-iron columns and beams began to be used in order to reduce the risk of fire. Iron beams soon became standard in the English textile works of the first half of the nineteenth century. However, because of the significantly higher costs of all-metal structural elements, often the posts were still of wood, though they might be reinforced and protected by a sheath of iron. This type of mixed construction, using stone, iron, and wood, was also common in French spinning mills and factories in the first half of the century, such as those built in Alsace for Koechlin, Heilman Frères, Schlumberger-Grosjean, Dollfus-Huhguenin, and Husseren-Wesserling.

Metal was also used to good effect in the great multistory docks built during this period in the major English ports, such as London and Liverpool. One of the few structures to follow this architectural current in France was a gasworks built in 1833 in Lyons-Perrache, near the station of the Saint-Étienne–Lyons railway line that had been inaugurated the previous year. The gasworks had cast-iron beams and a corrugated-iron roof—probably one of the first uses in France of the latter material.

Chapter opening spread: The glass dome of the Crédit Lyonnais headquarters in Paris.

Page 122, top: The Paris stock market, a temple to money, shown at the time it was completed, around 1825.

Page 122, bottom: Detail of the ironwork and brick decoration at the Menier factory in Noisiel, designed in 1871 by Jules Saulnier.

Page 123: The monumental facade of the Comptoir National d'Escompte, of 1882, designed by Édouard Corroyer, expressed the growing importance of that banking establishment.

Left: The combination of brick and metal at the Lys reservoir in Tourcoing is typical of nineteenth-century industrial structures.

THE USE OF IRON

Around 1850, cast-iron columns were just beginning to be employed in industrial buildings, which usually had wood floors and roof frames and masonry exterior walls. The cost of metal was still high, compared with that of traditional materials—an argument for this kind of utilitarian construction—and machinery and other equipment were not yet bulky enough to require very large, unobstructed spaces. The great advantage of metal was thought to be its fireproof quality. The first industrial structure in France with an all-metal roof frame was a customs warehouse in Paris, built in 1851. Built at about the same time, the warehouse where the iron of the Forges de la Providence was stored, on the Quai de Jemmapes in Paris, also had a roof frame made entirely of metal. It was consciously designed as an impressive demonstration of the possibilities of the new material, an advertisement for the forge. During the Second Empire, many industrial buildings combined iron and wood in floors and roofs, but relatively few had roofs only of metal, and those that did concealed them behind conventional facades.

In the 1860s, at the government's initiative, a few large factories returned in their designs to the grand architecture of the eighteenth century. The architect Laudin's 1863 Manufacture Impériale de Sèvres, for example, has a classical composition, with sculptures on its pilasters and pediments. While production took place in other structures behind it, the principal building was assigned the function of commercial representation, which the architecture had to fulfill with a luxury as great as that of the porcelains and ceramics produced by the factory. The architecture of the cannon foundry of Bourges, of 1865–75, is very attractive and frankly classical, its central court surrounded by low buildings with arched windows and punctuated by pavilions with pediments that are decorated with symbolic sculpture. The Manufacture Nationale d'Armes in Saint-Étienne, of 1866, exhibits a similar arrangement, although with a more urban layout.

In this period there appeared an element that would quickly become standard in industrial architecture: the sawtooth roof. This was constructed asymmetrically in two sections; only the north-facing section was of glass, so that the workrooms received consistent natural light, but not direct sunlight. This feature seems to have been introduced in France in the early 1860s, and a decade or so earlier in England. When the woolens firm of Rime et Renard in Orléans rebuilt its workrooms from the ground up in 1868–71, it adopted metal roofs of this design.

Two important Second Empire buildings demonstrated the achievement of industrial architecture. An 1860 trade agreement between France and Great Britain abolished tariffs on metallurgical products and so obliged French producers to improve their plants. Schneider et Cie in Le Creusot commissioned a new ironworks that covered nearly thirty acres and combined puddling furnaces, forging presses, and rolling mills. A vast space almost four hundred yards long and more than one hundred yards wide was built to house everything. The entire framework was made of metal, with rows of cast-iron columns supporting a triangular roof of rolled iron. The room terminated at both ends in large glassed gables. This spectacular structure, which was inaugurated in 1867, served two purposes. First, it joined under a single roof several complementary activities, within a space that was as unencumbered as possible by its supports, and was thus one of the first buildings in France to establish the formula of the modern factory. Its second function was to present an architectural manifesto of the firm's power and its desire to be modern.

The second landmark structure of this period was the mill for Menier, a chocolatier in Noisiel. Built across a branch of the Marne River on the site of a mill made in wooden sections around 1840 and later enlarged, it displays a visible skeleton of iron members filled in with colored bricks that compose alternating patterns of cacao flowers and the initial *M* for Menier. The whole is remarkable for openness of the exposed structure, braced with Saint Andrew's crosses, and for its vigorous decorative motifs, which are altogether exceptional for this kind of building. The architect, Jules Saulnier, who had designed sections of the factory in the 1860s, apparently formulated in 1869 an initial, traditional masonry design for the mill. After 1870 he amended the design to include a metal structure, which was built in 1872–77 by a metal-construction firm founded in 1868 by Armand Moisant. In his description of the project, Saulnier related that "M. Menier liked the novelty of the idea. This building was the most important one of the works, because of its position, size, and purpose: He did not object to the expense and was determined to decorate it with a luxury unusual in industrial architecture." Adapting the combination of brick and iron employed in Victor Baltard's Les Halles, the central covered market in Paris, begun in 1853, the mill in Noisiel initiated a rich tradition of iron bracing that would find expression over the following decades in countless industrial buildings, usually in summary form but quite often in the same decorative spirit, and all the more graceful because the structural elements so easily lend themselves to it.

After 1870, metal roofing eventually became standard in industrial buildings, in part because of the increasing availability of rolled steel, sections of which could be riveted together. Roof design underwent numerous variations, but within a circumscribed range. Financial considerations determined the roof profiles, though no single type predominated, and the spans remained modest. Sawtoothed roofs were common in France by 1880. However ordinary, these roofs could still permit spectacular spans when industrial requirements called for them. For example, the Aix-en-Provence match factory, built in 1906 to house the new continuous-feed phosphorous-match machine, is a handsome example of elegant utilitarian architecture, whose roof has a raised central monitor like that on Les Halles in Paris. Today, the building houses the Méjanes library.

THE CHÂTEAUX OF INDUSTRY

Toward the end of the century, representation of company image became important in factory design. Some factories were treated as veritable châteaux, with crenelated towers and machicolations, thereby confirming not only the leading role of industry in the modern world, but also the new social status of the captains of industry, who aspired to replace the feudal lords in the territories they ruled.

Opposite, top: The Menier chocolate factory in Noisiel, on the east side of Paris, was built in 1872. This famous structure combines Rationalist elements, such as iron crossbars, with the decorative fancy of colored brick.

Opposite, bottom: This former match factory in Aix-en-Provence today houses the Bibliothèque Méjannes. It is a stunning example of the adaptability of nineteenth-century industrial structures to creative reuse.

Right: The belfry of the Castellane champagne factory in Épernay attests to the sumptuousness considered appropriate to the architecture of such establishments. The belfry contains a water tower.

Factories were often designed to look like castles. The Motte-Bossut spinning mill in Roubaix, of 1883, is a large, five-story red brick structure, its floors supported by cast-iron columns, as in the English factories, and its exterior decorated with a small tower and a monumental chimney, both festooned with machicolations. The annexes, also of red brick, are in a classical style, with pilasters and pediments. Several factories in the same area applied this combination of a utilitarian plan—levels supported by metal columns—a monumental exterior resembling a château, and a reference to local architectural tradition in the use of red brick: the former Wallaert Frères spinning mill on Rue Jean-Jaurès in Lille, built in 1898–1906; the Leblan factory in Lille, today a housing complex; and the former Lamartine cotton mill in Hellemmes. One architectural element in particular tends to appear frequently in the urban factories, which are usually enclosed by high walls, and that is the entrance porch, the factory's most visible feature, which functions as the public facade. The entrance to the former Thiriez Frères spinning mill in Loos-les-Lille, designed by Émile Vandenberg in 1894–96, is typical.

The champagne manufacturers also manifested the desire of the leading industrialists to show the signs of their power and prestige. Mindful of the elitist appeal of their product, the owners commissioned industrial structures that had an aristocratic air congruent with the image of luxury that champagne was expected to convey. These buildings became, in effect, architectural displays of the firms' commercial ambitions. The Pomméry buildings of 1873 in Reims, designed by Charles Gozier and Alphonse Gosset—architect of the Reims theater—included Tudoresque towers and high, crenelated walls with red brick quoins and blue-gray paint. The appearance of the complex also suggests Pomméry's efforts to enter the English market. The application of the Gothic Revival style, so popular in England, was considered to be an appropriate image to convey to the faithful clientele across the Channel. The Castellane factory in Épernay is even more spectacular. The architect, Marius Toudoire, famous for the Gare de Lyon in Paris, arranged a series of buildings along the railway that runs through the factory complex. Overlooking the complex is a water tower in the shape of a monumental campanile, identical to that of the Gare de Lyon. The principal facade was also designed to look like a train station, with a main courtyard for receiving important visitors to the establishment. Colored faience on the attic spells out the names of distant places, the destinations of the precious bottles.

WORKERS' HOUSING

The industrial projects of the nineteenth century extended into workers' towns, built to provide employees with affordable housing. The factories engendered new neighborhoods, just as medieval boroughs clustered around castles. The earliest housing units constructed specifically for workers were designed like barracks. In Le Creusot, for example, home of Schneider, a major ironworks, a structure for machinists was built around 1845. It was nearly 330 feet long and had 130 rooms on four levels. The so-called Miners' Combe, built by the ironworks of Manby and Wilson in 1826, had abandoned the barracks model some twenty years earlier. Its two-story structures included self-contained flats, each with its own entrance and attached

The Pommery champagne factory in Reims is distinguished by an architectural image that was inspired by the Elizabethan style—an homage to the company's British clientele.

mudroom, where the miners could wash before going into their homes. There were no common spaces, not even common staircases or landings where one might encounter one's neighbors, a layout that was supposed to assure social peace.

The phalanstery in Guise, on the other hand, was designed specifically with collective space in mind, and thus stands out because of its ideological roots. In 1859, Jean-Baptiste Godin, inspired by Charles Fourier's 1822 *Traité de l'association domestique agricole,* commissioned housing complexes adjacent to the factory that made his cast-iron stoves. Fourier had proposed the "phalanstery" as a means to provide a fair distribution of capital and work, because it would give workers the "equivalents of wealth": a home, education, social security, amusements. For Fourier, small, autonomous communities, focused around a kind of château, would provide a balance between work and pleasure. Beyond the city and its conflicts, the phalanstery could flourish, a communal society with a carefully regulated way of life and shared common services. This gregarious palace, its architectural definition paradoxically based upon the classical palace, would allow the proletariat to find "social happiness" in a dignified, healthy, and balanced lifestyle. The Guise "familistery" applied the overall plan recommended by Fourier, with a château comprising three blocks, a day-care center, a school, a theater, and separate shops. It is most noteworthy for its interior. The residential quarters are reached from balconies around a large glass-roofed courtyard, a central place that was supposed to encourage social life; it was a symbol of progress—air, space, and light—but also an instrument of supervision and indoctrination. Weekly lectures were held on morality and the system of participation, and there were dances on Sunday and annual holidays in honor of work and childhood. Émile Zola, staying in a phalanstery as preparation for a future novel, asked himself: "Order, rules, mechanicalism, comfort. But what of the wish for adventure, the risks of the free, adventurous life?" Cité Napoléon, on Rue de Rochechouart in Paris, built in 1851 by Gabriel Veugny, is an urban adaptation of Fourierist design, with common landings beneath a glass roof. But a quasi-military regimentation—for example, the residents were forbidden to go out after ten at night—discouraged applicants, and the experiment proved a glaring failure.

The "familistery" in Guise is one of the more successful attempts made in the nineteenth century to provide workers—in this case, those at the Godin cast-iron stove factory—with a communal living environment, complete with everything considered necessary for their well-being.

The workers' colony in Mulhouse was undoubtedly one of the most successful of its kind in France, and was often imitated. It was sponsored by the Mulhouse Society for Workers' Cities, founded by Jean Dolfus, the mayor and a major industrialist. More than one thousand houses were built between 1854 and 1888 from plans by Émile Müller. The basic design was a four-family house with four private gardens, one for each unit. The workers could one day own their homes, a factor that was considered particularly beneficial to the morale—and the morality—of the workers: "Anyone can appreciate how much the hope of owning one's home causes a man to be more hardworking, frugal, and steady, and how much more active and interesting his life becomes," wrote the social critic Jules Siegfried in 1877. Similarly, the Association of Coal Mines of Blanzy, near Montceau-les-Mines, recognized in 1878 that the firm,

> *in order to attach its workers to the coal-bearing land, by stimulating in them the sense of economy and love of property, sells parcels of land to those who distinguish themselves by their good behavior . . . and at the same time advances them money to help them build a home. The worker raised to the condition of homeowner becomes frugal and steady; he works courageously, and ceases going to taverns; from that day forth society has gained a friend to the social order!*

Several colonies, most of them consisting of two- or four-family houses, were built for the region's laborers and miners.

Unlike group housing, which bred promiscuity and trouble, individual houses appeared to assure the virtues of hygiene and social integration. Yet, the few private initiatives in the area of workers' housing were prompted not solely by interest in the social well-being of workers but by the industrialists' concern with keeping and controlling the labor they needed for their enterprises. The Pumpmen's housing estate built by Schneider et Cie around 1860 was made up of twelve one-story houses along the lines of those of the Mulhouse colony. There followed the Villedieu development, of 1865, comprising eighty single-family homes, whose kitchens were in attached sheds, a solution replicated in the Saint-Eugène colony of 1875. Schneider et Cie completed only eight percent of the housing at Le Creusot between 1850 and 1875, even though the workshops expanded significantly. The workers' colony at the Aniche mines, built in 1872 to plans by the architect Meurant, is practically a catalogue of the various kinds of residential groupings: single-family homes, rows of attached houses, and two-, three-, and four-unit houses, each with its own little garden. The whole is thoughtfully composed, as evidenced by the symmetry in the distribution of the blocks and the views at the end of the streets. The housing estate developed in Tours in 1871 by Alfred Mame, a publisher who specialized in religious books, presents an urban context—it is made up of single-family homes organized around a great rectangular square that is planted with trees.

The workers' colony of Noisiel, constructed in the 1880s, was informed by a paternalistic spirit that sought to guarantee the workers' well-being. It adopted the concept of flats developed in Mulhouse, offering small, identical, attached brick houses around a village center, complete with a town hall—the mayor was, of course, the owner of the factory, Émile Menier—two cafés, so that sworn enemies could avoid each other, and a company store selling the products of the farms that the firm owned in the surrounding countryside. At the top of the hillside on which the estate was built, Menier constructed a home for the elderly, with a cemetery behind it. The Fourierists' utopia of communal self-sufficiency became, in Noisiel, an instrument for wholly subjugating the workers to the company's needs.

The early twentieth century witnessed a gradual transition from the explicit paternalism of the first workers' colonies to a policy of public housing under the aegis of the state or the large municipalities, such as Paris. These efforts remained somewhat timid before World War I. A number of foundations also sponsored proposals for affordable city housing for workers. Apartment buildings and developments providing low-cost housing were constructed in Paris and its immediate environs by the Société Philanthropique, the Société Française des Habitations à Bon Marché, founded in 1889, and the Groupe des Maisons Ouvrières. The projects built by the Rothschild Foundation stand out for their quality and their ambition. The complex constructed on the Rue de Prague in Paris in 1905 under the direction of Henri Provensal occupies a city block; it has an interior courtyard and provided common services, such as a day-care center and a bathhouse. Its architectural design, which relied principally on brick, was economical but varied its effects to provide interest. It inspired the city of Paris's own programs of low-cost housing, which began in 1913 but did not reach their full capacity until after World War I.

The overall plan of the Guise workers' housing was inspired by the Château de Versailles, but the facades were treated with brick, an inexpensive material, as was characteristic of industrial architecture.

Tony Garnier's utopian Cité Industrielle, which he proposed in 1904, represented an attempt to reconcile industry and the modern city. In his idyllic retreat at the Villa Medici after winning the Grand Prix de Rome, Garnier dreamed of a world in which the architecture of mechanization would be perfectly integrated into the urban fabric. But Garnier's was a perverse innocence, for what his handsome color prints reveal is the dissolution of the city as a social site, to be replaced by a megastructure entirely geared to the requirements of production.

URBAN FACTORIES

The most spectacular industrial structures in France were built either within the context of urban programs related to the production of the new energy sources—gas, electricity, and compressed air—or because their location in the city called for a particular architectural treatment.

The production of gas for illumination had gotten a slow start in Paris in 1820, following various experiments in covered passages. In 1855, the half-dozen gas companies that had appeared between 1820 and 1830 merged, forming the Compagnie Parisienne d'Éclairage et de Chauffage par le Gaz. The generation of factories constructed during the Second Empire and in the following years all had gas tanks of fairly simple design, made up of cast-iron posts, sometimes doubled up, which were simply connected at the top by a polygonal framework, which might have circular openings, like the Vaugirard gas tank of 1868. By the 1880s, cast iron was no longer used, and the tanks became larger. In 1910, the tanks were as large as 240 feet in diameter and more than 160 feet high, as at the Landy factory in Saint-Denis. The recognizable structure of gas tanks, their rectangular-link lattices braced by Saint Andrew's crosses, their monumental scale, and their proximity to cities have made them a symbol of the urban industrial landscape.

Electric lighting made its first appearance in Paris in 1889 at the central market of Les Halles, where a part of the basement had been converted to accommodate the generators. After Paris was divided into distribution sectors in 1894, the architect Paul Friésé designed several factories that are remarkable metal structures. One of the most important, on the former Rue des Dames, exhibits on the gable end a large arch of solid sheet iron from which the floors are suspended, thereby creating an interior span of roughly seventy-five feet. As electric lighting evolved and the Métro appeared, many substations were built, a number of them by Paul Friésé.

Beginning in the 1890s, compressed air was distributed in Paris, through a network developed by the Compagnie Générale d'Air Comprimé, chiefly to power hydraulic elevators and the clocks at the main intersections. The great hall that Joseph Leclaire, an engineer, built on the Quai de la Gare in 1891 to house the compressed-air generators is a fine example of an urban industrial structure. The street facade has iron sections and stained-glass windows, while the side facades are braced with large Saint Andrew's crosses forming a lattice. Another interesting factory for the same company is at 132 Quai de Jemmapes, built by Friésé to house electric boilers and generators. The coal was delivered directly from barges along the quai, then conveyed to bins under the roof.

The former elevator factory designed by Pierre Chabat and built in 1887–89 at the corner of the Quai de la Rapée supplied the reservoir beneath the Place Saint-Pierre in Montmartre. The external iron sections were contrasted with an infill of brick and terra cotta, including striking ceramic motifs representing the arms of the city of Paris. Unfortunately, the building was recently dismantled.

LATER INDUSTRIAL BUILDINGS

The many industrial buildings constructed after 1880 present designs that are notable for the boldness of their architectural solutions. Constraints imposed by the urban context—regulations concerning common walls, facades, and decoration—contributed greatly to the success of these buildings. The extensive use of metal framing allowed unencumbered space at ground level and permitted natural light into the workrooms. Metal facades and internal supports translated into common exterior configurations and covered interior courtyards that resembled traditional architectural typologies, yet were singular in their expression.

One line of descent, through the workers' colonies and the phalansteries, inspired the Rue des Immeubles-Industriels of 1872–73, where the ground floor and the mezzanine are supported by a metal framework. The first iron-framed facade appeared in 1878 in an apartment house at 5 Rue de l'Aqueduc in Paris. This structure was applied after 1885 to commercial buildings, in particular, to textile warehouses, where a great deal of natural light was needed to judge colors accurately. Examples of these are 13 Rue d'Uzès in Paris, built in 1885–86 to designs by Gustave Raulin for a fabric shop, and 23 Rue du Mail, which was also built in 1885.

There are many other kinds of industrial structures in which iron and steel played a major part. The most typical of these are the anonymous head frames of the mines, raising their delicate black silhouettes against the flat landscape. Designed to support the guide pulleys for the elevators in the mine shafts, they incorporate into a common typology—a vertical structure with angled braces—a wide variety of detail. Examples survive near Anzin, Lens, and Montceau-les-Mines, but most of them are abandoned today, the last working coal mine in the northern region of France having closed in 1990. Some will be preserved as evidence of the miners' toil and as landmarks of the industry.

THE INDUSTRY OF FINANCE

The Industrial Revolution and the rise of capitalism were intimately associated. As wealth was increasingly produced and distributed, money entered into circulation as an instrument of development rather than something to be hoarded. The public's savings had to be tapped and put at the disposal of entrepreneurs. Two complementary institutions evolved in this sector: the bourses, or stock exchanges, and the banks. The Paris Bourse was built to designs by Théodore Brongniart in 1807–15. Constructed on a rectangular plan, it is surrounded by a portico of Corinthian columns that gives it a noble and imposing appearance, although this composition never took hold as a canonical model for bourses. Étienne Labarre covered the central court with a glass roof in 1823. Among the first of its kind, this glassed-in court, which effectively became the trading floor, was replicated everywhere in buildings dedicated to the exchange of money. The Bourse was expanded in 1903, with two symmetrical wings in the exact style of the original architecture.

The Marseilles Bourse, built from plans by Pascal Coste, is an important structure whose location on the Canebière, a stone's throw from the port, testifies to the major role that trade played in the economy of the city. The first stone was laid in 1852. The edifice derives its majesty from its composition, featuring an arcaded base above which Corinthian columns are crowned with an attic. The Lyons Bourse, built to plans by the architect Dardel in 1860, combines the styles of the Venetian Renaissance and the French eighteenth century. Another monumental structure, the Le Havre stock exchange, which no longer exists, had a prominent dome designed by Brunet-Debaines. Joseph Bouvard's Bourse du Travail of 1888–92 is

Opposite, top: The Sudac compressed-air factory in Paris is a particularly spectacular industrial building, thanks to the expressive metal structure that animates the facade.

Opposite, bottom: Designed by Paul Friésé, a specialist in industrial architecture, the Grands Moulins in Corbeil combines a vast complex of granaries and flour mills. The tower housing the elevator system rises above the complex like a belfry.

Right: Some commercial buildings at the end of the nineteenth century had facades composed almost entirely of glass, as at 13 Rue d'Uzès in Paris.

also worthy of mention. The facade is rather ordinary, but its glass-roofed court, supported by triangular beams, is particularly handsome.

Unlike stock exchanges, which were public buildings and fairly few in number, banks—both headquarters and branch offices—spread throughout France in the nineteenth century. Until 1850, the institutions were very personalized, and the bankers—Rothschilds, Mallets, Hottinguers, and others—conducted their business in private *hôtels particuliers.* The great credit institutions began during the Second Empire: Crédit Foncier in 1852, Crédit Industriel et Commercial in 1859, Crédit Lyonnais in 1863, and the Société Générale in 1864, to name only the principal banks. They grew rapidly, initiating branch systems between 1870 and 1880, while most also constructed headquarters in Paris on a large scale. The Crédit du Nord, founded in 1866, was one of many regional banks that also developed a network of local offices.

The banks' primary function was to accommodate clients and their transactions. This required tellers' windows in a hall that usually had a glass ceiling. The investment of loans, sales of securities, and payment of dividends also required lines of tellers' windows and many counters. The second function of banks was to safeguard valuables in rooms containing safety deposit boxes, which were sometimes distributed over several levels with metal floor gratings. All of these activities required scores of clerks, who had to be housed in large office spaces. Over the course of the century, these employees tended increasingly to be women.

The banks' prosperity depended upon the confidence that they instilled in their clients; thus, they willingly invested in decorum, in order to assert their wealth and project a sense of security. Even in the case of branches or smaller institutions, the banks' facades were always ostentatious to some degree. Arcades were a recurring element, signifying a public, mercantile space, and facades were often enlivened by columns, pilasters, caryatids, and pediments. Respectability and credibility were desirable virtues, ostensibly reflected in styles meant to recall the great banking centers, such as Renaissance Italy and Flanders. Inside, the halls served to lead clients to the services at various windows, but they also created monumental spaces that would reassure clients of the power of the institution that held their money. The halls were treated luxuriously, and the effects of the expensive materials, carpets, illumination, and stained glass conspired, as in the casinos of the era, to create an environment that made material wealth seem easily accessible. Not only the great Parisian exemplars, but many banks and savings banks adopted similar compositions.

The Paris headquarters of Crédit Lyonnais was built in 1875–78. William Bouwens van der Boijen constructed, on the Boulevard des Italiens, a building with a windowed courtyard and a double stairway beneath a skylight, inspired by the stairs at Chambord; the ornate facade is adorned by a central pavilion with columns, caryatids, and a sculpted pediment. The edifice extends into the block through the securities room, a great navelike hall built by Gustave Eiffel's company in 1881–82 to resemble a shopping arcade or a department store. The vast offices were entirely open: "Partitions serve only to allow the staff to read their newspapers," claimed Henri Germain, the founder of Crédit Lyonnais. The complex was completed on the side of Rue du 4-Septembre in 1908–13 by Victor Laloux and André Narjoux, who replaced the earlier dome with another, much larger one. Unfortunately, the great hall was recently divided into two floors.

With a similar monumental hall beneath a glass ceiling, the Comptoir d'escompte de Paris, today the headquarters of the Banque Nationale de Paris, was built on Rue Bergère in 1882–88 to designs by Édouard Corroyer. The floor is paved with translucent glass tiles, which allow the securities room on the floor below to be illuminated. The facade is distinguished by a monumental pavilion graced by three female figures—representing Industry and Commerce flanking Confidence—sculpted by Étienne Millet. The most spectacular glass dome, however, is still that of the Société Générale, at 29 Boulevard Haussmann, built in 1906–11 to plans by Jacques Hermant. The dome is supported by pendentives that are also of glass. The stained glass, the bronze metalwork, the marble tellers' windows, and the polychrome mosaics on the floor endow the space with a sumptuous quality. The Nancy branch of Crédit Lyonnais also has an extremely beautiful glass ceiling by the master glazier Jacques Gruber. The Société Générale branches in Bordeaux and Nancy exhibit similar features.

The branches of the great banks, though less monumental than the Paris headquarters, tend to reflect the architecture of the main offices and to display a degree of monumental opulence in their facades. This is the case, for example, with the Crédit Lyonnais branches in Dijon, Angoulême, and Caen. The savings banks also manifested a certain investment in their architecture, as evident in the banks in Tours, by Jean Jacquemin, of 1864; Dreux, by Vidière and Avard, of 1893; and Montargis, by Brochon, of 1904.

Opposite, top: A detail of the pediment of the Crédit Lyonnais headquarters in Paris, whose symbolic statuary conveys the sense of prosperity proper to a bank.

Opposite, bottom: The stained glass in the lobby of the Société Générale headquarters helps to create an opulent atmosphere infused with the mystique of money.

Steam and Speed: Train Stations

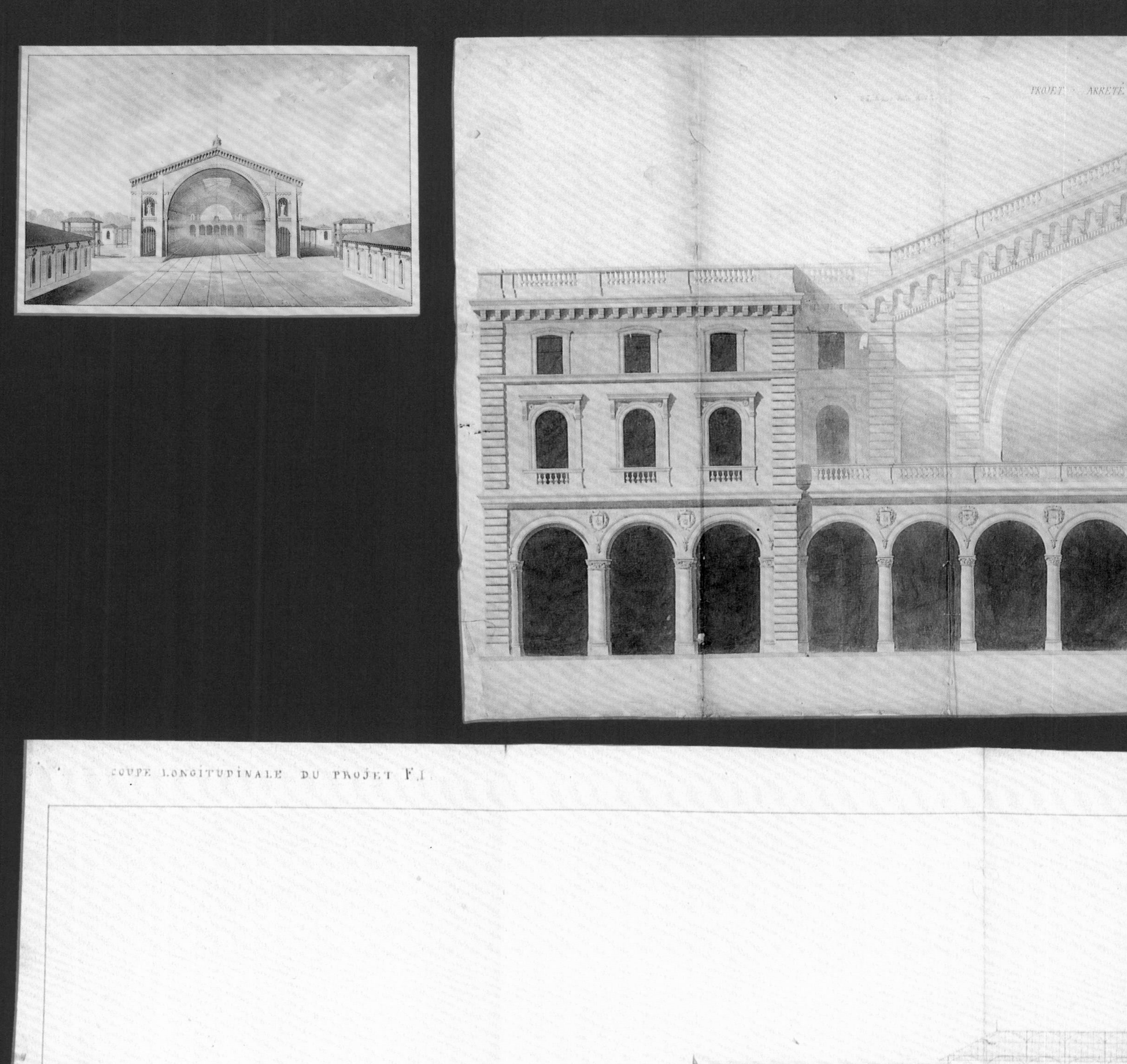
PROJET ARRÊTÉ
COUPE LONGITUDINALE DU PROJET F.I

LE 11 SEPTEMBRE 1847

The importance of rail transportation to the Industrial Revolution gave nineteenth-century train stations a special architectural status as the most visible and spectacular expression of the new technology of the time. Steam locomotives, with their plumes of smoke and potent metal bodies, were pure products of industry, images of the alliance between steel and coal. Théophile Gautier saw them as such, in 1868, when he wrote of a journey by train that he had taken some years earlier.

> *We were saying, in our traveling compartment, accompanied by administrators and engineers of the line, that the stations would soon become humanity's cathedrals, the place of attraction, the meeting point of nations, the center where everything would converge, the nucleus of gigantic stars whose iron rays would reach to the ends of the earth. We added that the train stations would give rise to the new architectural form that had been so vainly sought, because this building did not exist among the ancients and had to adapt to unknown needs. As the architecture of antiquity developed from its temples, that of the Middle Ages from its churches, so will ours arise from the station.*

The station's function was not only to distribute the flow of passengers and goods, it was also a symbol of travel, of the freedom to move, of the modern age.

THE SYSTEM OF STATIONS

In France the typology specific to train stations took a while to develop. The first "docks," a term borrowed from the world of navigation, were built in the then-current Neoclassical style, transposing the pediment and columns of the temple front to the station's facade. London's Euston Station, which was inaugurated in 1837, featured a monumental propylaeum in a solid Doric order. The basic typology of the nineteenth-century train station—a block housing the passengers' services and a covered concourse containing the platforms—was established with the construction of Liverpool's Crown Street Station in 1829–30, from plans by George Stephenson, one of the pioneers of the railway in England. The station comprised a small structure along the platforms and a wooden roof over the tracks. Thus, the station's functional program was articulated through two distinct elements: a traditional building housing the ticket windows, the waiting rooms, and the baggage areas; and a shed containing the concourse, as spacious as possible, so that the smoke emitted by the steam engines could be dispersed. The basic requirements of the program guided the technicians, architects, and engineers who collectively defined the railroad station as a building type.

The rapid and continuous increase in the number of rail lines and passengers meant that early stations were frequently rebuilt to accommodate the growth. Most of the earliest docks were rebuilt after about twenty years, and it was not unusual for a station to be rebuilt two or three times in the course of the nineteenth century. As the network of railways grew, the number of tracks and approaches to the stations multiplied. The sheds therefore expanded, and their roof spans—originally of wood, then of metal—became gigantic. The multiplication of the number of services provided to the passengers also required new structures, which were attached to the station itself. Three classes of waiting rooms, shipping offices, lobbies, shops, restaurants, and hotels all became part of the station complexes. In France, it was the practice to process the passengers and baggage before they entered the platform area. After checking their bags, passengers waited in an enclosed room that corresponded to the class of their ticket. The waiting rooms were off a vast lobby, while the platforms remained physically separate from the station block.

At the same time, the characteristic layouts of the buildings and platforms were being revised. Small and medium-size cities kept the traditional arrangement of the so-called transfer stations, the intermediate points between the larger hubs. The typical transfer station was built along the platforms, generally on one side only, and a roofed structure open at both ends spanned the width of the tracks. The stations lent themselves to a variety of architectural effects, but within a fairly limited stylistic range. A central block with a clock above it

Chapter opening spread: The main hall of the Gare d'Orsay in Paris, today a museum. This was the first station in France designed exclusively for electric-traction trains, although the enormous glass-roofed concourse follows the established model developed to accommodate steam locomotives, whose billows of smoke would be dispersed in the vast space.

Preceding pages: The first great train station in France—Paris's Gare de l'Est—shown in drawings by François Duquesney, 1850. The station was enlarged and its facade doubled with an identical design in 1933.

The large, semicircular window of the Gare de l'Est reveals on the facade the presence of the vast train shed, a compositional formula that would be repeated in many stations throughout France. In the foreground, allegorical statues represent the Seine and the Rhine rivers.

was usually flanked by two symmetrical wings, which often divided departure and arrival areas. Various kiosks—such as shelters on the platforms, toilets, and information desks—completed the main building, along with freight storerooms and water tanks for the locomotives. In the large hub cities, a station with a blind side was the rule, with departures and arrivals taking place on separate sides of the main building. But there were different plans, depending upon whether the buildings were located alongside the tracks, grouped at the railhead, or both.

Those building the stations thus faced several problems. The engineers were challenged to devise a system of roof framing that would both be economical and permit a very wide span. The stations' architectural identity lay in their great glass-covered concourses. Painters responded keenly to the particular quality of light that resulted from the high windows. Claude Monet, for example, made a number of paintings of the Gare Saint-Lazare. The station's urban placement, however, required that it be accorded the status of a public building, and that the contradiction between the platform area and the main building be resolved. At the heart of the discussion concerning the architecture of train stations was the question of how the glass shed would be expressed on the station's facade. And to this end, the stations of nineteenth-century France artfully combined skill and science, structural elements and decorative motifs.

THE EXAMPLE OF PARIS

The train stations of Paris, comparable to those of London in the same period, provided the architectural models for the rest of the country. The first generation of stations, built from 1837 to 1848, were designed within Neoclassical architectural strictures. An arcade at ground level opened into a lobby leading to the waiting rooms and the baggage check. The shed was not visible from the outside. The station's monumental expression derived from the application of classical orders: pilasters, pediments, and cornices. The roofs were generally of wood, but roofs combining wood and metal appeared as early as 1837. In 1837, the engineer Antoine-Rémy Polonceau perfected a very economical roof-frame system, which was applied for the first time on the Paris–Versailles Left Bank line and became immensely popular, especially in French stations. Polonceau's system was remarkably long-lived: it was used in the 1887 expansion of the Gare Saint-Lazare. The first station to have an all-metal roof frame was Euston Station in London, built in 1837.

In the early 1850s the second generation of stations appeared, exhibiting the features of the modern train station. Paris's Gare de l'Est of 1847–52 is particularly noteworthy in this respect. Architect François-Alexandre Duquesney designed a building in which the articulation of the platforms and services is clearly expressed by a large, semicircular window in the middle of the facade, above a portico in the Florentine style. A statue representing the city of Strasbourg, the end of the line, has pride of place at the peak of the gable. Inside, the eight tracks are roofed with curved Polonceau trusses nearly one hundred feet across, designed by Jacques Sermet, an engineer, and made by the ironworker Jacquemart. The platforms were shortened in 1900, then again in 1924–31, when the station was expanded. During the latter project, the architect Bernaut achieved a stunning duplication of the main building, replicating the earlier facade exactly, while treating the interior in an Art Deco style. The design of the Gare de l'Est, combining a ground-floor arcade with a frontal lunette, was widely employed in France thoughout the nineteenth century and established the Rationalist paradigm for train stations. One of the railway specialists of the time, Auguste Perdonnet, was implicitly referring to this solution when he cited "the architectonic decoration" of train stations.

> *The architecture of a monument must reveal its intended purpose. The train stations, especially the termini, also have their specific architecture. Besides the peristyle, what most often characterizes the principal facade is a monumental clock and, when the facade terminates the station, a great arch or immense gable that describes the shape of the roof over the passengers' concourse.*

In keeping with these recommendations, the Gare Montparnasse, built to plans by Victor Lenoir in

1848–52, displays on its facade a clock that divides the gables of the two roofs directly over the departure platforms and the arrival platforms—so directly that a locomotive whose brakes had failed came to a halt on the other side of the great window, providing the subject for a justly famous photograph.

As rolled iron came into general use in the 1860s and roof systems improved, roof trusses became significantly longer and the platform areas could take on the monumental proportions appropriate to the railway's importance. The Gare Saint-Lazare, rebuilt in 1852–54 by an architect, Alfred Armand, and an engineer, Auguste Flachat, had Polonceau trusses more than 130 feet across.

The Gare du Nord in Paris is notable for both its monumental facade and the elegance of its metal-and-glass shed. Jacques-Ignace Hittorff brought his knowledge of Greek architecture to the design of the facade, which displays statues representing the cities served by the Chemin de Fer du Nord, the northern railway. The roof of the main train shed, one of the largest in France, is supported by slender cast-iron columns.

As technical advances made it possible to increase the size of the glass-covered spaces, the main building, too, became more monumental. The Gare du Nord represents one of the most successful attempts to transcribe the space of the great hall into the design of the facade. The earlier station, built in a Neoclassical style in 1842–46 by the engineer Léonce Reynaud, had a double concourse covered by a wooden roof that was supported by a center row of cast-iron columns. The facade had been taken apart and reassembled in Lille. In its place, the architect Jacques-Ignace Hittorff, in 1861–65, constructed a huge station from plans drawn up by Léon Lejeune, the architect for the Chemins de Fer du Nord. The facade presents sequences of Ionic pilasters on either side of a central arch flanked by two smaller arcades. The careful attention given to the proportions and the details and the many statues placed along the roofline make this structure the epitome of the archaeologizing Neoclassicism so dear to Hittorff. The windowed arcades do not open directly into the concourse, designed by the engineer Couche. The shed is no less remarkable for the simplicity and breadth of its roof, which rests on four rows of imposing cast-iron columns; tie beams are completely absent, replaced

Above and left: The facade of the Tours train station, designed by Victor Laloux in 1899, reiterated—nearly a half-century later—the composition inaugurated in the Gare de l'Est. The clock provides a focal point, which is emphasized by robust masonry pillars.

Right: The Roubaix train station is representative of a group of handsome stations in a Rationalist mode built, in the north of France at the end of the century. The metal-and-glass gable is flanked by pavilions in the Louis XIII style.

SNCF GARE DE ROUBAIX

by supporting brackets that branch out at the top of the pillars. The total width of the covered space is nearly 230 feet, half of that covering the middle section. As was his custom, Hittorff chose a different color for each section of the roof frame.

Compared with the Gare du Nord, the Gare d'Austerlitz, rebuilt in 1865–69 to designs by Louis Renaud and the engineer Sévène, seems unresolved, with its two separate courts for departures and arrivals separated by an office building. The interior, however, contains a magnificent shed with a vault spanning 168 feet. The Polonceau-type trusses rest on delicately worked brackets. The glass screen that closes off the end of the platform is noteworthy. It appears that the concourse was inspired by the great hall of the Forges du Creusot, built by Schneider et Cie. Constructed in 1904, the metal catwalk that crosses the bay at the third-floor level was a spectacular addition to the departure hall.

The second reconstruction of the Gare Saint-Lazare, by Juste Lisch in 1885–89, gave it a new urban facade that entirely masked the glass-roofed concourses and would have suited a city hall or a museum just as well. The Hôtel Terminus occupies a separate building on Rue Saint-Lazare, but is connected to the main block by an attractive metal passage. The juxtaposition of stations and hotels, in fact, became increasingly common in the last years of the century, introducing a complete dissociation between the station facade, now treated like that of a residential block, and the shed, in which all the expression of the station's technical identity became concentrated.

A MONUMENT IN THE CITY

By around 1880 train stations in France were gaining in monumentality what they were losing in originality. The disappearance of any indication of the glass-roofed shed on the facade made possible an eclectic architecture that allowed for a great deal of decoration. This shift also confirmed the urban status of the station, which was raised to the rank of a major city monument, disconnected from its technical origins. The Metz train station, built to plans by J. Kröger in 1903–8, rather heavy-handedly asserted the new political status of the city, then under German domination. Its pink sandstone facing, its solid massing dominated by a belfry, its *Rundbogenstil* (round-arched style), and its symbolic decoration all combined to make the station a local symbol of Wilhelm II's expansionist policy after 1890. By contrast, a utilitarian Neoclassicism was especially popular in Prussia, in the great frontier-post train station (today out of service) in Nouvel-Avricourt, near Blamont.

Compared with this progressive monumentalization, the Rationalist approach initiated by Duquesney in the Gare de l'Est continued to work as an exemplary solution. The stations built by the Chemins de Fer du Nord between 1880 and 1900, many of which have unfortunately been destroyed, exhibited windowed gables flanked by side roofs. The stations of Amiens (1878), Arras (1898), and Calais are gone, but Roubaix's station, built in 1905, provides a very attractive example of this plan. The station in Le Havre, built to plans by Lisch in 1880, displayed a metal-and-glass gable that was embellished with brick and glazed terra cotta, recalling the best industrial architecture of the period.

The Tours station, built to designs by Victor Laloux in 1900, displays a fairly artful compromise. Two metal arches entirely filled with glass are supported by cylindrical masonry piers; the side buildings are barely visible. This station, recently painted blue, stands out as one of the century's most successful examples of railway architecture. Laloux reinterpreted this arrangement three years later in Paris's Gare d'Orsay, but adapted it to the narrower constraints of the site and the urban context, while responding fully to the replacement of steam locomotives by electric traction. This station, its all-metal skeleton built in record time, is flanked by passenger hotels built in stone. The main block of the station, which extends the length of the platform and contains the ticket windows and waiting rooms, is marked by so-called thermal windows—large arched openings derived from the model of ancient Roman baths—which both let light into the passengers' area and indicate the presence of the concourse. The decorative treatment of the great metal vaulted ceiling, almost entirely masked by staff coffers, reveals the architect's intention to

Opposite, top: The basic program for nineteenth-century train stations included a ticketing hall, baggage areas, waiting rooms, and, on the second floor, an apartment for the station master. This is a design of 1856 for a modest station on the Ardennes line.

Opposite, below: The length of a station's wings was related to its importance. As in this example in the Loire Valley, stations were originally located on the outskirts of the cities and towns they served.

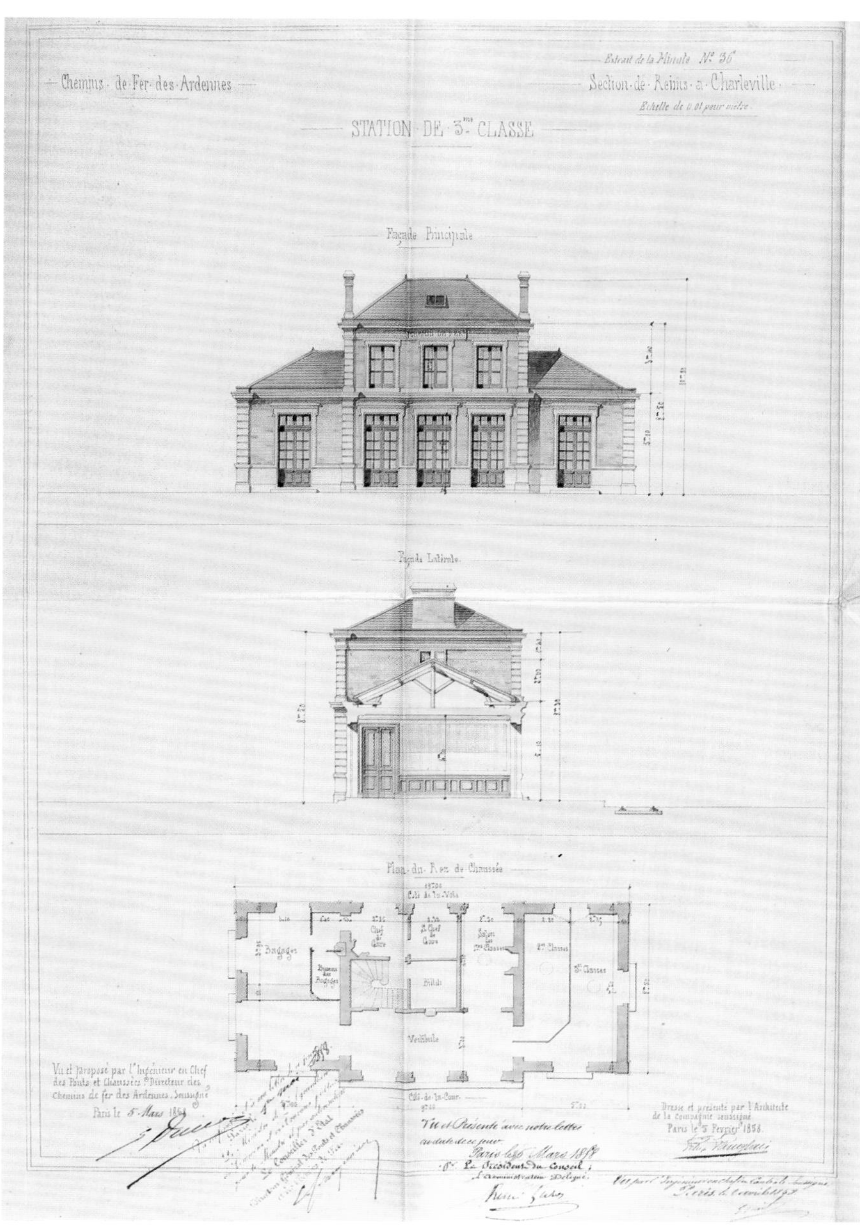

design a composition appropriate to the monumental environment of the station, bearing in mind that the vault's function, unlike in earlier stations, was no longer to disperse smoke. As the theoretician Julien Guadet wrote: "No more steam, no more smoke, and since then, the train station as such could be a hall, I might even say a drawing room."

Paris's Gare de Lyon, built in 1900 to plans by the engineer Denis and the architect Marius Toudoire, is less subtle in its design, but it introduced a new element into the vocabulary of the train station, one that would endorse the station's monumental status for more than half a century. The campanile, which serves only to support a monumental clock, recalled the belfry of the typical town square in the north and the campanile of the Italian *piazza,* and established the station as the new urban hub.

The more common principle of the transfer station, composed of a glassed concourse open at both ends, lent itself well to an architectural compromise between the monumental station and the Rationalist impulse to express the shed. One such station is the particularly monumental Bordeaux–Saint-Jean station of 1898.

This project, designed by S. Choron, chief engineer for the Compagnie du Midi, is composed of a main building that follows the axis of the platforms and is punctuated by pavilions. The central block houses the station restaurant and divides the departure and arrival sections. But the pièce de résistance is its great glass roof, more than 180 feet across, and covering an area of nearly 183,000 square feet. It was, in its day, one of the largest train sheds in the world. The firm of Daydé and Pillé won out against the best structural metalworkers of the time in an open competition for the contract. The glass roofs of the Dijon and des Brotteaux stations in Lyons were built to the same design.

The Compagnie du Midi also built many wide metal roofs for nonpassenger buildings and sometimes for less important stations. These roofs were usually between fifty and eighty feet across. Polonceau trusses were used in the stations of Morcenx (1863), Bayonne (1867), and Hendaye (1881). By the end of the century, arched trusses were the rule, as at Dax (1894), Nérac (1900),

The Valençay station was designed in a Renaissance Revival style, in keeping with the region's architectural context.

Mont-de-Marsan (1902), Langon (1903), and Biarritz-ville (1910).

Some of the same features used in the Gare d'Orsay appeared in the La Rochelle station, built to plans by Pierre Esquié in 1922. Great lunette windows articulate the highly structured facade, and a monumental campanile rises like a lighthouse in the middle of it. One of the last great monumental train stations in France, the Gare des Bénédictins in Limoges, built to designs by Roger Gonthier in 1925–29, expresses the space of its stilted central dome by means of a segmental arch on the facade. Though late, this station employed the typology of the late-nineteenth-century station, complete with its campanile, and kept to the characteristic decoration of stations of the period.

THE STANDARD STATION

The increasing monumentalization of train stations ought not to overshadow their standardization, which nevertheless allowed for virtually infinite variations. The Neo-Renaissance style became almost conventional in small-town and rural stations, allowing the railway architecture to be integrated into most contexts and still retain a specific identity. Thousands of stations throughout the country, large and small, display this typical disposition.

Every railway company, in fact, nearly every line, had its own style of station. Overall, there were four types of station, depending on the density of the expected passenger traffic. The first-class stations were only in the big cities and exhibited individualized designs. The elements of the program—lobbies, ticket windows, stationmaster's office, waiting rooms for each of the three classes, shipping offices, and, always, the stationmaster's apartment on the floor above—were the same across the different types, but given more or less importance. The passenger area comprised a central block flanked by wings of variable size. One or more bays could be added to the wings, as needed. The smaller stations had no wings at all, and all the services were concentrated in a single area, although the minimum requirements of waiting room, ticket window, and baggage check were always respected. The standard plans drawn up by the railway company engineers were usually adapted to local conditions, including the facade materials, which varied according to the expression considered desirable for the building.

Efforts to adapt regional styles to railway architecture were particularly justified in cities with characteristic architecture of their own. Thus, Vitré's station is Neo-Medieval, Valençay's is Neo-Renaissance, and Nancy's is Neoclassical. The stations built at spas and in resort towns evoked fanciful associations and were exempt from the generally accepted Rationalist code. Cauterets's wooden station, for example, reflects the rusticity of the surrounding landscape. This Picturesque and regionalist vein continued into the 1930s. Examples include the station of Senlis, of 1922, designed by G. Umbdenstock in a Neo-Medieval style; Hendaye's station in a Neo-Basque style; and Deauville's station of 1930, with its Norman roofs and half-timbering.

Naturally, the interior decoration of stations relates to travel. This type of iconographic program was characteristic of stations throughout France. Destinations were a common theme; for example, all along the departure concourse of Paris's Gare de Lyon is a fresco representing the panorama of the cities crossed by the Paris–Lyons–Marseilles line. A station is also a gateway to a city, and so must display what makes its city famous or otherwise special. And, finally, the station's importance as a focal point of the city is expressed by the opulent decoration of the restaurants and hotels that are part of it. Le Train Bleu, in the Lyons train station, is a restaurant that is justly famous for its interior. Thirty

The vast shed of the Bordeaux–Saint Jean train station, completed in 1898, is one of the largest in France.

painters from the regions served by the line collaborated on the decoration, which depicts Paris and southeast France amid a riot of gilt staff. The Tours and La Rochelle stations have mosaic panels representing places in their regions. As Louis Vilmorin rightly observed in 1957, "What is extraordinary is that these extravagant decorations contain, within their wild ostentation, a substantial truth that defies the delicacy of beauty and taste with a display of 'Republican opulence.'"

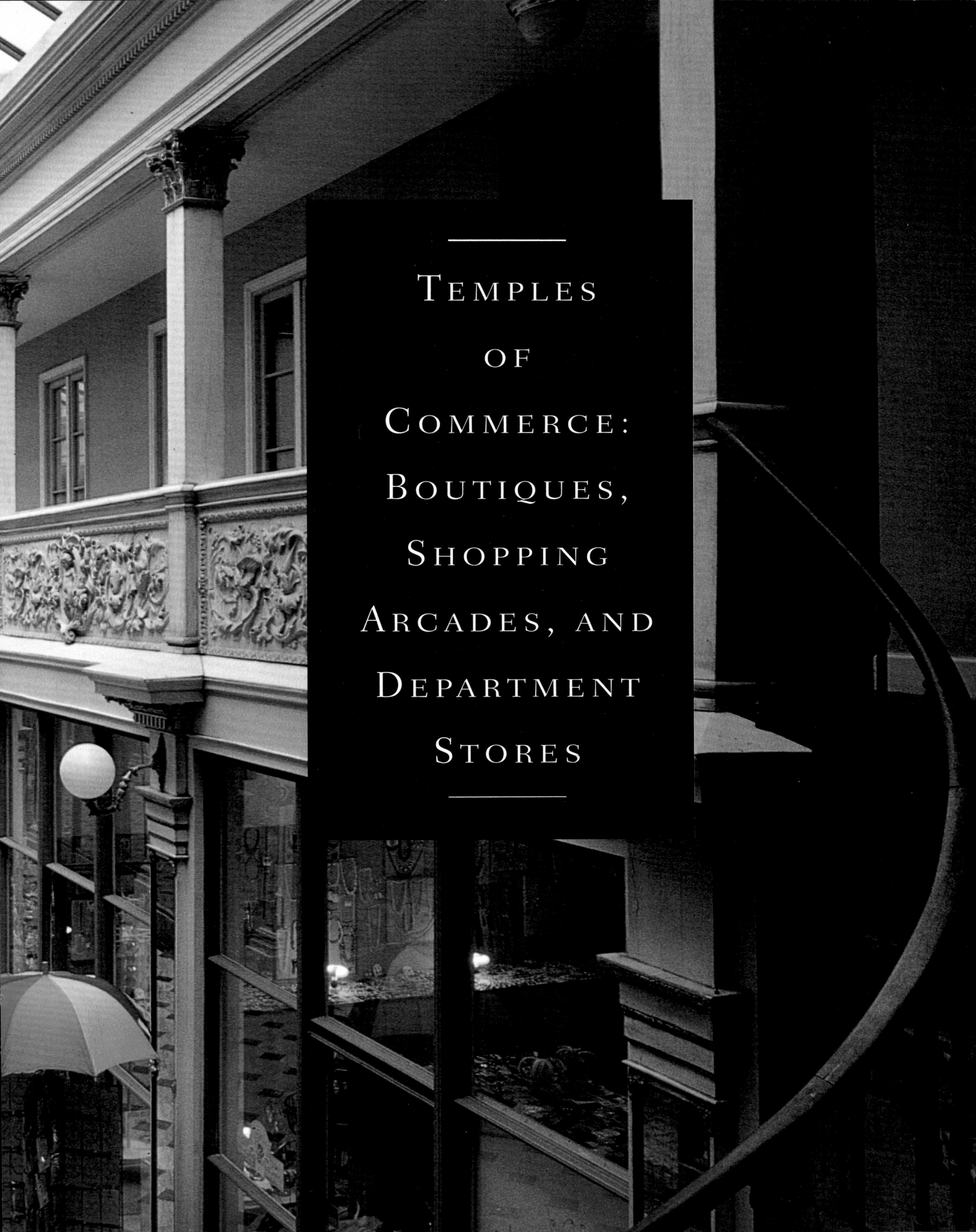

Temples of Commerce: Boutiques, Shopping Arcades, and Department Stores

MAISON DES MAGASINS REUNIS
MAISON DES MAGASINS REUNIS
MAISON DES MAGASINS REUNIS
MAISON DES MAGAS
CONFECTION
MENAGE
MODES
MAGASINS REUNIS

VIARD-GARDIN
MAISON DES MAGASINS REUNIS

The nineteenth century in France witnessed the triumph of a mercantile society. In the wake of the Industrial Revolution, trade and commerce intensified, bringing an unprecedented profusion of goods to the marketplace. The system of marketing to consumers became a sophisticated enterprise, requiring specialized building types and methods of display and defining a new relationship between the public and the ever-widening array of accessible merchandise. The intrinsic seductiveness of an object was enhanced by the allure of the place where it was offered for sale. As the activity of shopping became a popular diversion among the middle and upper classes, a variety of mercantile buildings developed to meet the demands of commerce.

BOUTIQUES

The luxury trade represented the vanguard in the new expression of commerce. In the eighteenth century, specialty shops sold goods made by famous manufacturers and skilled artisans. Luxury boutiques of the nineteenth century kept the traditional layout, in which a counter or tables extended around the room. Their interior decoration, however, became more lavish by the end of the century, with mirrors, wainscoting, and paneling that imitated those of drawing rooms and libraries. To attract customers, signage and storefront displays became more and more elaborate. The facade and the interior served to advertise the boutique's wares, to distinguish it from other establishments, and to create its image. Signage became an integral part of the architecture. Production and exchange were separated once and for all, with the commercial function taking over the space of the store. Artisans no longer worked under the customer's gaze, but rather in the back of the shop or in the mezzanine. Honoré de Balzac observed this change in *César Birotteau* of 1837:

> *I put my desk, the till, and a pretty cabinet in the mezzanine. I am turning the present back of the shop into the shop. . . . Our workers will be in the attic; passersby will no longer see the labels being glued on, flagons being unstopped, phials being corked. That's good enough for Rue Saint-Denis, but for Rue Saint-Honoré—it's out of the question! Bad form. Our shop must look like a drawing room.*

The most remarkable instance of the new type of shop that appeared in the early nineteenth century was the novelty store. The word *novelty* referred to fashionable items and accessories, as well as unusual and rare curios. Novelty resided in Paris: "Luxury goods that are not made in the capital are not well received in the provinces," wrote a contemporary. Luxury goods were also called "Paris goods." Novelty stores were an important stage in the shift from the specialty shop to the department store, prefiguring the latter in the variety of goods for sale and the method of merchandising, in which a variety of goods were openly displayed and all integrated into a single building. In 1825, a chronicler described the advent of the department store as follows:

> *The time is not long past when this kind of establishment began to attract the public's attention. It is less than twenty years ago. In the beginning there were few such, today they are beyond counting and every week new ones open. . . . The arrangement of the goods on display is done with taste, refinement, sensitivity, and skillful harmonizing of colors unmatched in any other country.*

In 1850, there were four hundred novelty stores in Paris.

Beginning at mid-century, commercial architecture exploited the advantage of iron construction, which allowed unencumbered floor areas, larger openings for doors and windows, and transparent glass roofs. Traditional shops were transformed, their interior spaces expanded, and their windows enlarged. Larger commercial floor areas could be accommodated in new structures, in which masonry walls, partitions, and pillars were replaced with cast-iron columns attached to iron beams. Although it is difficult to pinpoint the date of the first installation of an iron-framed commercial interior, it probably occurred in France in the late 1830s.

Chapter opening spread: This shopping arcade in Autun, built in 1848, is one of the most beautiful in France, and also one of the most original, with its gallery running the length of the second floor.

Preceding pages: Joseph Hornecker's Magasins-Réunis in Épinal was an early incarnation of the department store, which followed the arcade, or covered passage, as the modern building type of the retail trade.

In 1800 the Passage des Panoramas in Paris launched the fashion for shopping arcades, which were covered passages through city blocks. Nearly sixty such passages would be built in France. This early example had a simple roof with glass skylights.

There is at least one known example of a ground floor altered in this way, at 17 Rue de la Paix, in 1842. Likewise, the houses built on Rue Rambuteau had iron beams; this was ascertained when they were torn down some years ago.

The development of this arrangement, first on the mezzanine, then on the higher floors in the 1860s, was accompanied by a technical innovation in the load-bearing skeleton. The cast-iron post-and-lintel system became increasingly widespread, gradually becoming more explicitly expressed in the composition of the facade. In 1867, for example, a building by E. Noël at 9 Rue Beaurepaire, in Paris, employed a plate girder as a beam supporting an all-glass mezzanine. A great many stores used the system. The appearance of steel at the century's end allowed the spans between supports to become wider, almost eliminating columns and posts. For example, the 1903 Nouvelles Galeries in Le Mans, designed by Paul Auscher, had a trelliswork girder nearly one hundred feet across, which supported the entire facade.

SHOPPING ARCADES

In the early nineteenth century, industrialization not only revolutionized the mechanisms of distribution, but also introduced the concept of competition. The number of shops multiplied rapidly, and they tended to be grouped into various spatial configurations in order to attract customers. Arcaded streets that aligned shops along a sheltered walkway were an old tradition in some European countries, but they were never very widespread in France. In Paris, the Rue des Colonnes and the Rue de Rivoli, and, in the provinces, Chambéry's Rue de Boigne are rare examples of the revival of this time-honored arrangement.

The shopping arcade, or covered passage, of the nineteenth century was a novel architectural solution to the new demands of the marketplace. It emerged at a time when shops were achieving their commercial and architectural identities and the first large novelty stores were making their appearance. Integrating various types of luxury shops along a glass-roofed walkway, arcades produced a new form of commercial public space, the precursor to today's shopping mall. These covered shopping arcades were successful, first in Paris, then in many cities throughout France and Europe. In this formula the public space as such existed primarily as a site for the presentation and display of merchandise, but conversely, the shops and their frontages constructed the space and gave it public status. Thus, arcades were more than just covered commercial streets, they were complete, self-contained mercantile spaces, with stores, entertainment, cafés, restaurants, banks, and so on, where the nineteenth-century bourgeoisie could find within reach everything their hearts desired. Representing a new way of life, arcades corresponded to the rise of a capitalist, mercantile society. As one observer put it:

> *Ever since the arcades were established, a new kind of industry has arisen, its avowed aim being to satisfy certain sensual needs that seem to be more imperious and widespread than one would have believed among society's leisure class. In order to support establishments wherein is lavished the luxury of which I speak, and which is not the only one of this*

kind in Pairs, there must be a great consumption of the goods that are sold there.

The arcade functioned as a public drawing room, where people could display their riches, a place to see and be seen. It became a microcosm of the city itself. One author had a character observe in 1834:

Is an arcade not a summary of an entire city? The Eldorado of the indolent who spend all their time there, and could spend their lives there without having to put their noses outside the glass dome. Don't they find everything they require to satisfy every need of their animal, intellectual, even passionate natures?

The rise of shopping arcades in Paris happened over two fairly brief periods: first from 1823 to 1828, and then from 1839 to 1847. In the rest of France, they were built over a longer stretch of time, between 1825 and 1880. The earliest structure of this type was the "wooden gallery" of the Palais-Royal, built in 1786. This temporary construction that closed off the fourth side of the Palais-Royal gardens displayed spatial organization very similar to that of the future arcades, with facing rows of individual stores. There was no glass roof but rather a series of windows beneath the overhang of the roof. The first true shopping arcade came somewhat later: The Passage Feydeau was built in 1791 on land belonging to the convent of the Filles-Saint-Thomas. With windows set into the roof, rows of shops, and its function as passage through a constructed block, it had all the features of the future arcades, though the Passage du Caire of 1799 and the Passage des Panoramas of 1800 are more developed examples of the type. The Passage du Caire was built at the same time as the street of the same name—celebrating the very recent Egyptian campaign—on the site of the convent of the Filles-Dieu. The Passage des Panoramas was constructed through the gardens of the Hôtel de Montmorency to allow easier access to the rotunda that had just been built to house the first scenic panorama painted in France, a major attraction. The passage was later extended and side arcades added. Both of these passages are fairly modest efforts,

The Passage Choiseul, of 1826, is one of the longest in Paris. This theatrical loggia is located at one end of the arcade.

with little decoration. Instead of glass roofs, they had only skylights in wooden roofs. The first glass roof appeared in 1808 in the Passage Delorme, setting the standard.

The interior walls, parallel to the axis of the passage, were always treated as architecturally composed and decorated facades. The principal facades were defined by the repetition of identical storefronts. Lightweight materials, such as wood, plaster, and glass, were often used in the construction. The glass roof, virtually the defining feature of the arcade, enclosed the interior promenade, providing strollers with protection from the elements, while its transparency opened the space to the outdoors. The decoration displayed the Neoclassical vocabulary of the period, as well as a wide range of figural elements related to commerce. A statue of Mercury surveyed the scene from its pedestal in the middle of Paris's Galerie Vivienne, another looked down the Passage de L'Argue in Lyons, and his silhouette still hovers over the entrance to the Galeries Véro-Dodat in Paris.

The Galerie Véro-Dodat is a strikingly handsome example of a fashionable arcade from the Restoration period. The refined decor includes elegant brass storefronts and remounted paintings on the ceiling.

THE FASHION FOR ARCADES

Arcades were the rage during the Restoration period. In Paris, more than twenty of considerable size were built within the five years between 1823 and 1828. Among these, the Galerie Vivienne, of 1823, designed by François Delannoy, was distinguished by the complex sequence of its spaces and its elegant decor. Its neighbor and rival, the Galerie Colbert, was built three years later with even greater opulence by J. Billaud, though it was never as successful. In the same year, the Galerie Véro-Dodat, named for its promoters, stunned the public with the lavishness of its gilt bronzes, mirrors, and remounted canvases. Nirot's Passage du Commerce was one of the first to open outside of Paris.

In Lyons, in 1825, the Passage de L'Argue was built from V. Fargues's design on the site of an earlier alley. Well situated in the center of town, and with its ninety-six shops, theater, and rotunda, it bears comparison with the galleries of Paris, and was instantly a huge success. In 1856 it was cut in two by Rue du Président-Herriot (formerly Rue de l'Hôtel-de-Ville). Two other major arcades later opened in Lyons. The Passage de l'Hôtel-Dieu, designed by the architect Dubuisson de Christot, was built in 1840 on the site of a butcher's shop belonging to the hospital. This arcade, more than four hundred feet long, twenty-three feet wide, and nearly fifty feet high, was the largest in France. In 1960, it was replaced by a street. In 1857, in the center of Lyons, the Passage des Terreaux was built through a handsome building on the square of the same name to design by Jean-Étienne Giniez. Bordeaux followed the trend, though somewhat tardily, with three arcades, all on Rue Sainte-Catherine, the city's major commercial artery. The Galerie Bordelaise, built by Gabriel-Joseph Durand in 1831–34, has lost some of its original splendor, but it remains a beautiful example of Neoclassical architecture, its austerity set off by a fairly ornate decor in red, white, and gold. Situated diagonally through the block, the passage includes ground-floor arcades, a balcony along the second level, and a cornice crowning the upper floor.

The second generation of arcades in Paris was built between the late 1830s and 1848 off the grand boulevards or near the train stations. The Passage Jouffroy, which opened in 1845 at the same time as the Passage Verdeau, is noteworthy for the refined design of its facades and its glass roof in a herringbone pattern, as well as for its unusual layout, forced by the particular configuration of the lot. It is still today one of Paris's liveliest arcades. The same cannot be said of the Galerie de la Madeleine, which opened in 1845 on the square of the same name. However, its fine architecture by Théodore Charpentier is worth a visit, and the building on the square into which the passage opens is a classic example of 1840s architecture, with ornament sculpted by J. Klagmann.

The most beautiful French arcade of this period is without a doubt Nantes's Passage Pommeraye. A notary public named Pommeraye commissioned the spacious passage to connect the Grand Théâtre and Rue Crébillon—the center of the carriage trade in Nantes—to the lower part of town and the Bourse de Commerce. It was designed by Jean-Baptiste

Buron and Hippolyte Durand-Gasselin and inaugurated in 1843. But Pommeraye was ruined by the undertaking, and he died in 1850 following a tragic bankruptcy. The superb arcade remains, a monument to commerce and its pomp. The upper part of the arcade resembles Paris's Galerie Vivienne, but is more highly decorated. One enters through a portico into the vivid brightness of a three-story, glass-roofed atrium. The proportions of the volumes, the effects of light and shadow, the handsome railings of the balconies, the somewhat strange decoration—the space is populated with statues of adolescent girls and boys in languid, dreamy postures—everything comes together to make this a uniquely fascinating place.

The most notable arcades elsewhere in France are Auxerre's Passage Manifacier, of 1869, by G. Roux; the Passage de l'Industrie in Fontenay-le-Comte, of 1839–42, by Garnereau; and the Passage du Théâtre in Mulhouse, of 1867–68, by Senaire. Autun's Passage de la Halle, of 1848, presents an unusual layout, with second-floor galleries under the glass roof. A similar configuration occurs in Vichy's Passage Giboin of 1880. The Passage Boyer in Carpentras, built in 1846–48 by a goldsmith of that name, has the proportions of an actual street, with a glass roof over the fourth floor. The late addition of narrow sidewalks accentuates the effect.

Shopping arcades succeeded as commercial entities because of their inherent attractiveness and their adaptability to different urban conditions. The arcades of the first half of the nineteenth century emerged as private, speculative development sponsored by individuals or partnerships. Not only were the arcades easier to develop and control and more profitable than shopping streets, they allowed the most to be made of a piece of property by filling the interior courts of blocks with retail stores, which greatly enhanced the value of the venture. The ideal situation for an arcade joined its attraction for shoppers with the advantages of its function as a passage, or shortcut, for pedestrians.

Blending public space and commerce, shopping arcades excited great enthusiasm because they represented the new urban experience that took shape in the first half of the nineteenth century. The development of arcades coincided with the fashion of promenading that arose during the Romantic era, and that Balzac memorialized:

> *Oh! Wandering through Paris! What a charming and delightful existence! Strolling is a science, the gastronomy of the eye. To walk about is to vegetate, to stroll is to live. . . . To stroll is to enjoy, to collect impressions, to marvel at sublime tableaux of unhappiness, love, and joy, pleasing and grotesque portraits; it is to plunge one's gaze deep into a thousand existences: to be young is to desire everything, to possess everything; to be old is to live the life of the young, to wed their passions.*

Arcades were particularly suited to this activity because they provided beautiful stores and numer-

The Passage Pommeraye in Nantes, inaugurated in 1845, is remarkable for its vast, glass-ceilinged central space, which is occupied by a monumental staircase. As was typical of shopping arcades, the Neoclassical embellishments refer to commerce.

ous comforts for pedestrians, while attracting a diverse public that was perfect for people watching.

Their capacity to offer the quintessential experience of city life naturally brought the arcades to the attention of the great social reformers of the Romantic era. Although he was referring to the great galleries of the Louvre and Versailles, rather than to shopping arcades, Charles Fourier, the leading theorist of the utopian movement, discussed the structuring role that he hoped to see the "gallery-streets" play in his communal cities and phalansteries.

Structurally, the few bazaars—from the Persian word for "covered market"—built before 1850 very much resembled arcades. The bazaars were usually more spacious and more spatially complex, organized around a court or a large glass-roofed central hall that was surrounded on one or more floors by galleries supported by cast-iron columns. The galleries were reached by one or more monumental stairways. Bazaars displayed a diverse array of goods for sale, anticipating the assortment of merchandise that would later be found in the department stores. One chronicler went so far as to compare the bazaars to the exhibition salons of the period: "For the art lover, they are at all times practical branches of museums, and permanent exhibitions of all the products of the national industries." Today, most of these precursors of department stores are gone. The finest examples in Paris were the Bazar de l'Industrie Française, by Paul Lelong, which opened in 1829, and the Galeries du Commerce et de l'Industrie, by Jean-Louis Grisart and Joseph-Antoine Froelicher, inaugurated in 1838. Bordeaux's Bazar Bordelais, designed by Joseph-Adolphe Thiac and opened in 1835, was a commercial failure, despite its fine decoration and spacious salesrooms and performance spaces. It was replaced in 1893 by a department store, the Nouvelles Galeries, built to plans by Paul Auscher.

THE DEPARTMENT STORES

Following their stunning success in the first half of the nineteenth century, shopping arcades lost much of their popular appeal after the 1850s. By that time they seemed incompatible with the new approaches toward urban planning that were transforming the cities in France. The prospects undertaken in Paris under Haussmann's prefecture, beginning in 1853, and the same principles applied later in the provinces were based upon broad, straight boulevards made possible by the razing of built areas. Compared with these avenues, the more intimate arcades looked small, humble, and a little antiquated. Émile Zola's 1863 description of the Passage du Pont-Neuf is far from flattering:

> *This arcade is thirty paces long and two wide, at most: it is paved with yellowish, worn, loose tiles, which always exude an acrid dampness; the glass roof covering it, set at a right angle, is black with grime. . . . The Passage du Pont-Neuf is not a place to stroll. People take it to avoid the long way around, to save a few minutes. It is used by busy people whose only concern is to go quickly and straight ahead.*

The retail trade no longer had to exercise restraint in calling attention to itself. With the birth of the department store, goods were laid out directly for the inspection of would-be purchasers, in grand temples to consumption that presented themselves as urban monuments.

Beginning in the Second Empire, glass roofs appeared with more frequency over commercial spaces, following the examples of the arcades inaugurated half a century earlier. Metal structures began to appear in the large novelty stores, for example, in Au Colosse de Rhodes of 1856 and Au Colosse d'Hercule in 1861, with spectacular arched metal girders. Several of the department stores specializing in novelties and built in this period had large covered central atria surrounded by galleries. This was the case of Au Coin de la Rue, of 1864, so called because of its corner location at 8 Rue Montesquieu; La Belle Jardinière, of 1866–67, whose two glass roofs were supported by decorated girders; and À la Ville de Saint-Denis, of 1869, the first to offer its customers the use of an elevator.

The first department store with truly monumental architecture was the Maison des Magasins Réunis on the Place du Château-d'Eau (today the Place de la République), built to designs by Gabriel Davioud in 1865–67. With its large windows, massing, and prominent roofline, the overall effect recalled Lefuel's Louvre. Davioud was working within two constraints: the fact that the building would have to be convertible into apartments if the enterprise failed, and its location symmetrical with the Prince-Eugène barracks, a very austere structure. The commercial formula of the Magasins Réunis was still very similar to that of the arcades, in that it brought together in one place independent businesses that were situated around galleries that opened onto a central court. The large court, originally open to the sky, was treated as a garden. It was covered in 1875 for a temporary tenant, the Myers circus.

All the features of the modern department store were joined for the first time at Bon Marché. Founded in 1852 by Aristide Boucicaut and his wife, Marguerite, the store gradually took over most of the block bounded by Rue de Sèvres, Rue Velpeau, Rue de Babylone, and Rue du Bac. A new building, designed by Alexandre Laplanche, was erected on the corner of Rue de Sèvres and Rue Velpeau in 1869–72. Its monumental entrance was decorated with sculptures, and large windows filled the facade. The interior was organized around a series of glass-roofed courts, the largest of which contained a handsome two-flight spiral stairway, like that at Au Tapis Rouge, inaugurated two years earlier. The construction, however, was traditional, with the iron nowhere to be seen. The building was extended along Rue Velpeau in 1872–74, and this time the design was by Louis-Charles Boileau, the son of architect Louis-Auguste Boileau and an enthusiastic convert to metal architecture. He used Laplanche's basic elements, a double-helix stairway beneath a central glass roof, and a glass navelike space. However, the visible metal parts, in particular the small columns supporting the galleries and glass roofs, are frankly asserted and elegantly treated so as to maximize the effects of transparency and light. The glass roof is actually composed of two layers, which made it possible for the lower, visible layer to be made of decorative stained glass that masks the structure and creates a thermal buffer. The all-metal framework, made by Gustave Eiffel's company, posed a new architectural interpretation. Boileau justified his part:

> *Such a monument, which cannot seriously be compared with buildings of stone, must eschew any and all imitation of them and be considered from another point of view entirely. If I may be permitted an almost paradoxical exaggeration, the better to make my point, I would say that this point of view ought to consist of imagining not the solid parts of the building but the hollow part the building envelops, that is, rather than attempting to cause the light to play off plastic shapes, one must set the light against itself in the ambient air circulating through the structure, and, by means of its profusion or its economy, create flashes, glimmers, and glints that cause light to sparkle in space, just as one brings out the fire in the crystals of candelabra by cutting different prisms into them. In this concert of light, the solid architecture will be like the setting of a semiprecious stone: It must count just enough to cause to vibrate as intensely as possible the full interior light that, passing through the glass surfaces and surrounded by half-lit depths, become gayer, more sonorous, fuller, so to speak, than the pure and simple light outdoors.*

Boileau later built a second building in the same spirit, also in two sections, along the Rue du Bac, in 1879–87. It was "a compact building with five floors and two basement levels, as broadly lit as possible in all its areas and laid out in such a way that at least three of its floors, ground floor, first floor and second floor, given over to sales, make up just one hall, a single space that can be taken in, so to speak, with a single glance." Today, the store is more or less intact in its structure, but the essential original effect has been spoiled by the alteration of the decorative elements.

Most of the department stores built in the nineteenth century were inspired by the principles demonstrated at Bon Marché. They relied on a combination of the decorative qualities of metalwork and the effects of space and light made possi-

Opposite, top: The multicolored glass dome of the Grands Magasins du Printemps in Paris invites the customer into a dreamlike environment geared to the enhancement of the merchandise on display.

Opposite, bottom: Bon Marché was one of the first department stores to employ modern merchandizing methods. Its sales floors occupied an entire city block.

ble by glass roofs. The Grands Magasins du Louvre, built in 1876 into a section of the Grand Hôtel du Louvre, represented a somewhat special case, because the project included the conversion of an existing building. But the overall layout, with its glass-roofed courts, is not very different from that of a department store.

Paul Sédille's new Grands Magasins du Printemps was a turning point in department-store design. Jules Jaluzot's store had burned down on March 9, 1881; while sales continued in the surviving areas of the ground floor, the store was rebuilt in a few months, occupying the entire block between Rue du Havre, Rue de Provence, Rue Caumartin, and the Boulevard Haussmann. Sédille decorated the principal facade, on Rue du Havre, with arcades and statues portraying the four seasons; the entrances were marked by elegant corner rotundas with bulb-shaped cupolas, which in turn bore campaniles—a theme that quickly became standard in department-store design. This beautiful facade was diminished when four additional stories were built. The lateral facades have large vertical windows divided by masonry pilasters. The entire interior structure is made of iron, including the floors and the piers. The store is organized around a great glass-roofed hall, crisscrossed by walkways; the arched girders, resting on iron posts, appear to support a roof of multicolored stained glass. Whereas in the Bon Marché building the cast iron seems to melt into the stucco decoration, the use of metal in the Printemps hall was breathtakingly overt, in that it revealed every last rivet and angle iron. As a magazine of the time wrote:

> *In this spacious hall, decoration comes into its own. Space must be enlivened and warmed by color accents, with bronzes, gilt, and glazed terra cotta, which shine in here like precious stones beneath the shadow of the upper eave, adorned with painted strapwork. . . . Lining the balustrades of galleries and stairways, wood mixes with the iron of the construction and the oak of the furniture. Finally, the various marbles are framed in iron panels in the balustrades, and columns of rouge de Languedoc, with white marble bases and capitals on pedestals of polished Épaillon rock,*

support the transverse bridge-gallery and the landings of the great stairways at either end. With the great stained-glass ceiling, whose decorative colors soften the glaring vertical light, these are the elements of decoration and color of the Printemps's interior hall.

At night, this wonderland of color was lit by electricity. The glass-roofed hall has been divided into additional floors, but the pieces of stained glass have been reused in a beautiful glass dome.

In no building was the combination of interior iron framework and a monumental stone exterior as ostentatious as in the Grands Magasins Dufayel, built to plans by Gustave Rives in 1892. Behind a vast sculpted pediment at 26 Rue de Clignancourt rose a palatial lobby that was crowned with a majestic metal dome with stained-glass inserts and extended into a glass-roofed hall nearly two hundred feet long. As in the Printemps building, the metal skeleton was visible to the last rivet, and the hollow iron pillars contained the ducts, but here the decor was more emphatic, no doubt because it was designed for a more general clientele. The exterior facades still exist, but the interior was completely renovated after the store went out of business.

Bon Marché and Le Printemps served as models for a number of stores that opened in France beginning in the 1890s. The best known is probably the Nouvelles Galeries chain. At first just a bazaar, then a shopping center called Grands Bazars Réunis, the company grew, beginning in 1894 with the opening of the Nouvelles Galeries de Bordeaux on the site of the Bazar Bordelais, on Rue Sainte-Catherine. Other stores soon opened in other cities, in particular, Montpellier, Amiens, and Rouen in 1896, Le Mans in 1903, and Bourges in 1905; between 1902 and 1908, the architect Marcel Lamaizière built stores in Saint-Étienne, Grenoble, Belfort, Clermont-Ferrand, and Valence. All these stores exhibit the characteristic composition, with stone facades displaying pilasters that flank large windows, corner rotundas, and a great deal of decoration. The Le Mans store is an exception, because it took over existing buildings, while the store in Bourges stands out by virtue of the treatment of its corner rotunda, which contains an arched window as high as the rotunda itself. The Dames-de-France, a chain bought by Galeries Lafayette, are known throughout the south of France, with branches from Chambéry to Bayonne, as well as in Toulouse, where the 1904 store built to plans by Georges Debrie is noteworthy for its large glass doors and windows. The Magasins Réunis chain is also regional. Founded by Antoine Corbin of Nancy, it was established in Troyes in 1894 and in Paris in 1906. The Nancy branch, of 1907, was designed by Lucien Weissenburger and, though in the classical mold, was a model for the Art Nouveau artists of the School of Nancy, one of whose chief patrons was Eugène Corbin, Antoine's son. In fact, the museum of the School of Nancy was installed in Corbin's own home, and in 1934 he left his important collection to the city. Of the stores built in Lorraine, none of which still exists today, the one in Toul, by Weissenburger, had distinguished Art Nouveau facades that combined metal and brick.

The use of metal reached its climax with the 1903 reconstruction of the Samaritaine, the store on Rue du Pont-Neuf founded in 1869 by Ernest Cognacq and Louise Jay. The architect, Frantz Jourdain, who had designed the installations of the earlier stores, was an inveterate and fierce opponent of the classical academy. In his view, the new store provided an opportunity to elaborate an architectural manifesto that would be both Rationalist and in the Art Nouveau mode, as well as to create the ideal store that he had helped his friend Émile Zola to imagine when Zola was writing *Au bonheur des dames* in 1882. Like other department stores, however, this one had to be built economically, quickly, and spectacularly. The design called for a standard organization around a large covered court, more than 120 feet by 60 feet in area, crossed by walkways; there are five stories of galleries around the court, and the glass roof above the court is higher than the surrounding roof. The decoration drew on nature for its motifs. But Jourdain showed audacity in revealing the metal skeleton on the facade, as Victor Horta had just done on Innovation, a store in Brussels. The angular severity of the lintels and posts, similar to that of Chicago's Schlesinger and Meyer store (now Carson Pirie Scott store), which

The Galeries de Jaude in Clermont-Ferrand was modeled on the Parisian department store. Light entered through tall multi-pane windows, until electric lighting rendered them obsolete.

Louis Sullivan had just completed, and Jelmoli, a store of 1898 in Zurich, was softened by the exuberant cast-iron decoration, concentrated on the capitals of the piers and the superb awning over the entrance, and by the floral motifs on the spandrel panels, which alternate with the names of items for sale in the store, painted in gold letters. The store's name, Samaritaine, appeared in a mosaic by Eugène Grasset across the pediment above the main entrance on Rue de la Monnaie. As the critic Edmond Uhry remarked in 1907,

> *by using iron . . . he was able to reduce the number of support points to a minimum, allowing in an abundance of air and light. . . . His system is frankly stated in the facade with posts and crossbars; angle irons, embellished with iron and copper ornamentation, mitigate any rigidity arising from such a system of construction. The upper parts of the webs of the beams and posts are decorated with friezes and panels of glazed lava, which is impervious to bad weather, conceals the joints, and is not too easily reached by dust from the street and smoke from the neighboring houses. On the lower parts are panels of very hard wood from Vicado, sculpted by Janselme, which rest on bases of Bigot sandstone and frame copper plaques worked in repoussé and hammered by Schenck, and gold mosaics.*

On the Rue des Prêtres-Saint-Germain-l'Auxerrois, two corner turrets, as at Le Printemps, signaled the building's presence from afar. The treatment of the turrets' bulbs was unusual: The frames of the glass tiles were joined in a cluster that formed a small campanile with plantlike branches. The store, which occupied an entire city block, was built in several stages between 1905 and 1910, the last part, on Rue Baillet, presenting a simpler decorative treatment. The store acquired a building on Rue de Rivoli and then, in 1912, renovated the interior and reworked the facade to be in keeping with the facade on Rue de la Monnaie.

No sooner was it completed than Samaritaine, Paris's Art Nouveau masterpiece, was criticized, despite its great architectural qualities. Indeed, some found fault precisely with its over-the-top fantasy and exuberance. Art Nouveau was already going out of style. Jourdain defended himself by explaining that

> *a department store of our day must not be afraid to be "garish": On the contrary, it is right that it should attract the gaze and stimulate the customer's eyes. This explains the brilliance, the violence, if you will, of the decoration, which may be unusual, but is considered and carefully combined.*

The facade on the quai and the corner turrets were unfortunately torn down when the store was again extended in the direction of the quai, a project carried out by Jourdain and Henri Sauvage in 1926–28 in a geometric Art Deco style, after Jourdain's first design, with Art Nouveau overtones, was rejected.

In exactly the same spirit, the Grand Bazar on Rue de Rennes, part of the Magasins Réunis group and designed by Henri Guitton of Nancy, joins Rationalist construction in the spirit of the 1889 exposition with the decorative vocabulary introduced by Art Nouveau. The Grand Bazar's architectural qualities are evident less in its interior, treated with fairly conventional sobriety, than on its facade, which is enlivened by the combination of half-timbering and a curtain wall of elegant woodwork. The few solid areas were masked with "panels of black glass, etched with a sandblaster, the bottom filled in with gold; the ironwork is painted dark green, almost black, resulting in an effect that is both rich and sober, somewhat recalling Japanese lacquers," as reported in *L'Architecte* magazine. The facade was edged at the top with a crest, "with a very decorative silhouette that must attract the attention of passersby, executed in mass-produced U irons and T irons, in metallic ribbon, with copper decorations pierced and in repoussé, and accented in some areas with gold."

At the turn of the twentieth century, the typology of department stores was well established. Builders began to experiment with a new material, reinforced concrete, which was starting to compete in every area of construction. Metal was indispensable in commercial architecture, both because it allowed support points to be reduced to a minimum, and because it made possible the construction of the vast glass roofs that were necessary to illuminate the stores' interiors. In this period, however, cement was becoming a more economical alternative. It was easy to work with and permitted spacious open areas, when cement posts were combined with cement beams or floors. Around 1902, Paul Auscher built two stores for Félix Potin, in which he took advantage of the plasticity of cement. The Galeries Lafayette, founded a few years earlier, built a new store in 1910–12. The first section, of 1906–8, by Georges Chedanne, still used steel posts; the second, by Ferdinand Chanut, used only reinforced concrete. The middle section is occupied by a huge rotunda with a glass dome. Here, cement becomes as light as metal, and the stained-glass roof, which seems to burst naturally from the piers, is a wonder of its kind. A monumental flaring stairway, the equal of the Opéra's, once rose to the second floor, but was unfortunately dismantled in 1974.

The last department stores to exploit metal's plastic properties were the new Printemps and the Bazar de l'Hôtel de Ville. After designing a new

La Samaritaine was one of the last department stores built in Paris. The Rationalism of the facade, with its exposed riveted metal structure, is tempered by glazed panels with floral motifs.

stairway for Sédille's Printemps in 1905, René Binet built a second store along Boulevard Haussmann in 1907–10. The exterior was very similar to that of the store built twenty-five years previously, while the interior was organized around two large octagonal courts, each more than eighty feet across; the skeleton was made entirely of metal. The space beneath the glass roof rose to the seventh floor. The dome was decorated with stained glass in blue and green tones: "The effect is such that visitors instinctively raise their heads and stop, stunned by the play of the curving balconies, which achieve maximum richness with their miradors," wrote *L'Architecte* in 1911. Binet emphasized vertical circulation by accentuating the elevators and creating small balconies that were suspended around the periphery of the hall, "onto which the decorative effect extends, most of the shafts being treated uniformly, as a sowing of golden flowers climbing up vines." As in contemporary department stores, flowers provided the basic decorative motif, here executed by virtuoso ironworkers. Binet's Printemps was destroyed by fire in 1921.

Part of the Bazar de l'Hôtel de Ville was renovated in 1904–5, then in 1912 by Granon and Roger; its central court was quite modestly decorated, not unlike many stores built in that period in the provinces. According to one source, "to enable it to be built more quickly, the iron roof was designed to be completely independent of the masonry, like a giant box whose space will be filled at one's leisure. Thus, to the profound stupefaction of the curious who had been waiting about for some time, the roofers set their hands to the roof before the stone was put in place." Despite its large glass surfaces, the new facade remains effectively faithful to the original architecture, with its corner rotunda flanked by stone pilasters and its sculpted decoration.

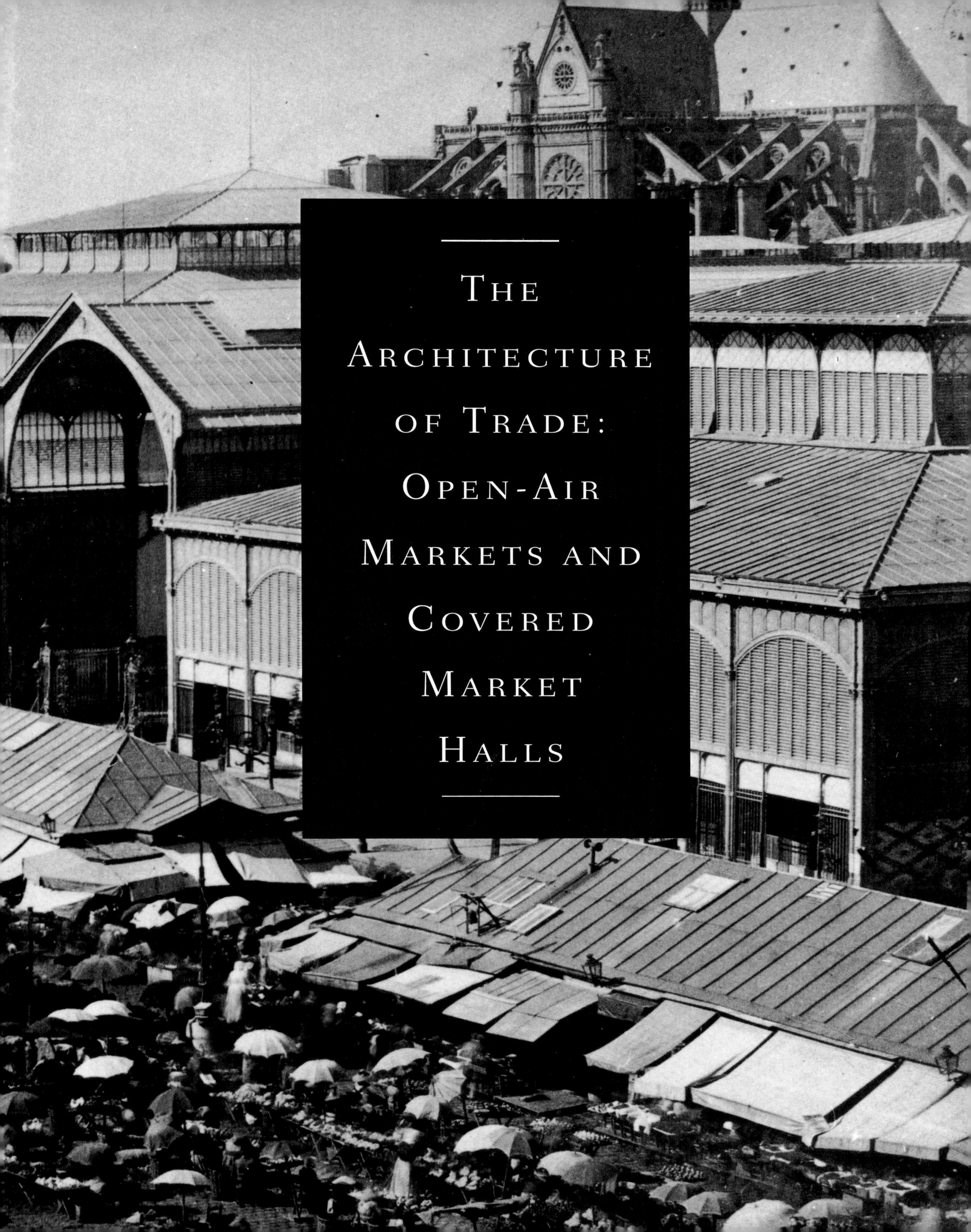
The Architecture of Trade: Open-Air Markets and Covered Market Halls

The massive development of metal *halles,* or covered market halls, beginning in the 1850s, accompanied the growth in trade in France and the redefinition of urban functions. The basic "umbrella" typology, which combined a metal skeleton that left the space unencumbered, a partial glass roof, and walls of iron framing glass and brick, took shape in 1853 with Victor Baltard and Félix Callet's Halles de Paris. This revolutionary prototype was followed throughout France, spawning a group of structures that are remarkably homogeneous. Its typology descended from two models. Traditionally, in France, markets were outdoor sites of exchange—squares and crossroads—before they were buildings. This arrangement emerged as a result of a mild climate and an active trade in agricultural and craft goods. As early as the Middle Ages, there were small *halles* displaying a typical form of architecture, usually composed of simple roofs, often with wonderful timberwork, that rested on wood or sometimes masonry posts. This elementary type was the model followed in Richelieu's new city of 1630. The *halle,* thus defined, of vernacular origin, is distinguished by its large roof and minimal walls. It was meant to be freely accessible and adaptable to many uses.

In contrast with this model, the Mediterranean market was traditionally a spacious square in the open air, surrounded by porticoes or arcades. The market activity was withdrawn from the bustle of traffic areas, concentrated instead in a central location. The two models were not mutually exclusive. Until the early nineteenth century, Les Halles in Paris was mostly contained in a small square under the open sky, but it also included a certain number of freestanding structures—usually for luxury goods, such as linen, leather, and meat—with porticoes. The term *market* most often described open-air places where perishable goods were sold, whereas *market hall* and *covered market* were used for covered or enclosed spaces.

A MODERN SOLUTION

At the end of the eighteenth century, the system of trade began to change in France. Whereas markets, inscribed in a given territory, had been intrinsically local, they became an integral part of a larger network for the distribution of goods associated with a major evolution in the number of exchanges. Because of their central role in providing goods to the public and in the mechanism of price formation, markets became critically important in the sphere of economics. The demands for profit, efficiency, and convenience gradually wove a web of customs, rules, and laws that would in turn influence the architecture of markets. This functional logic operated on three levels: the market stall, scrupulously demarcated by a modular outline that was the same for all; the space for circulation, which had to mesh efficiently with maximum profit; and the overall organization, informed by a desire to control the exchanges and to keep the whole enterprise separate from the street.

In this arrangement, however, two requirements conflicted: the need to enclose the markets, in order to contain them and to protect the interior from bad weather, and the desire to make them as open and accessible to customers as possible, to respect the traditional custom of selling in the open air, and to invite sufficient ventilation. Two architectural solutions developed around this contradiction. The first, the arcade, referred to Roman architecture. It expressed the ambiguity between open and closed and at the same time served to unify and connect the market and the urban context. The second solution was the monitor, or raised skylight, which had shuttered openings that controlled ventilation and light and which signaled from afar the presence of commercial activity. The image of the Roman basilica reappeared, complete with a dramatic roof and a vast interior space magnified by the height of columns rising straight up to just beneath the roof beams.

Whereas around 1780 it was still considered normal for a market hall to be a monumental work, intended to contribute to the embellishment of a city, this idea was weakening in the early nineteenth century. The architect Bruyère, director of works in Paris, wrote the following in 1810: "The architecture of the retail markets may be very simple, and yet imposing by virtue of its mass, its attractive organization, and the purity of its shapes. Such buildings ought always remain strangers to the luxury of onamentation." Thus, the monumental

Chapter opening spread: Émile Zola called Les Halles, Paris's famous marketplace, "the belly of Paris." In the foreground stands the Marché des Innocents. The dome of the wheat market, today the Bourse du Commerce, is visible in the background.

Page 168: An overview of Les Halles, as seen from the church of Saint-Eustache.

Page 169: A section drawing of a market pavilion designed in 1853 by Victor Baltard and Félix Callet, revealing the delicate tracery of the metal structure.

Opposite: The grain market in Blois, which has a Renaissance-inspired masonry facade that conceals a roof structure of iron and wood.

aspect of market architecture was contradicted by the prosaic character of trade.

Market halls constructed during the Empire were direct descendants of the models proposed by the winners of the achitecture prizes in the late eighteenth century and by Claude-Nicolas Ledoux, but without their tendency toward large-scale compositions. The *halles* had to be adapted to their particular sites, often by turning to local styles. In 1813, a good number of Paris's thirty-odd markets found themselves crowded into overlapping parcels of land. The ideal of the market isolated in its site was much easier to achieve in small towns and villages, where there was no lack of space, but for financial reasons the covered market was sometimes incorporated into the town hall, where it occupied the ground floor. These features are common to most of the covered markets built in the first half of the nineteenth century, including Victor Baltard's Halles Centrales, their culmination. The covered market in Blois, built by Jules de la Morandière in 1845, is one of the finest examples of the period's municipal architecture. It combines a handsomely wrought exterior of stone and brick and a mixed roof frame of iron and wood that is interesting as a transitional design between the two materials.

THE FIRST METAL MARKETS

As the architectural features of the covered market were becoming defined, the experimental use of metal for roof frames found fertile ground in this type of building. The first such application of metal was in the reconstruction of the roof frame of the Paris wheat market. This structure, notable both for its circular shape and for its location in the middle of a newly developed area, had been built in 1763–69 from plans by Nicolas Le Camus de Mézières, with an open central court more than 130 feet in diameter. In 1782–83, it received a remarkable wooden roof, designed by Jacques-Guillaume Legrand and Jacques Molinos. The roof was completely destroyed by fire in 1802. To prevent the recurrence of such a disaster, it was decided to rebuild the roof with metal, after various designs for masonry vaults and plaster-covered frames were reviewed. The architect François-Joseph Bélanger, who had already proposed a metal roof in 1783, following several trips to England, was able to persuade the municipal officials of the advantages of a dome of this type. The project received final approval in April 1808. The construction technique derived equally from those of masonry bridges and of the first large metal bridges. Curved cast-iron frames were bolted together so as to form fifty-two quarter-circle trusses, intersected by fifteen rings of the same type of frame. Thus, the vault displayed coffers of decreasing sizes, like the Pantheon in Rome. Light and ventilation were provided by a large glazed lantern, and the conditions of both were improved in 1838 with the addition of side windows. When the wheat market was converted to the Bourse du Commerce in 1888, part of the building was torn down, but the structure of Bélanger's roof was retained. Alençon's covered market, built in 1806–12 by an engineer named Barthélémy, who used the Paris wheat market as a model, also has a metal dome, which was added in 1865.

This excellent example, however, was rarely followed. The majority of market halls built in the first half of the nineteenth century had wooden roof frames. The first market with a metal roof frame was the Marché des Blancs-Marteaux in Paris, though the original roof frame of 1813–19 was of wood. Peyre and Dubut replaced the original frame in 1837–39 with a zinc-covered iron roof, another innovation at the time. By contrast, the Marché de la Madeleine, designed in 1824 by Marie-Gabriel Veugny and completed in 1838, was conceived with an internal structure made entirely of metal, having

two rows of cast-iron columns nearly forty feet apart. The central portion of the roof was raised to allow ventilation and light. The framework of special cast-iron members was visible only from inside, as the building presented a Neoclassical stone facade on the street.

LES HALLES

The construction of Les Halles in Paris initiated a long series of covered markets inspired by this model. After receiving the Prix de Rome in 1833, Victor Baltard, son of Pierre Baltard, the architect of the Lyons courthouse, was commissioned in 1843 to build the central market. The plan was to rebuild all of the existing structures that made up the market, and there was much discussion about whether it should be moved from its time-honored location. In 1845, Baltard visited England, Belgium, Holland, and Germany, noting in particular the English market halls, especially that of Hungerford, built in 1835. His first design, of 1845, was in a Neoclassical style, but the design he submitted three years later, in collaboration with Félix Callet, an official city architect, exhibited a magnificent metal roof structure inserted into a masonry building designed in the Rationalist manner. In its concept of a masonry exterior with a meticulously designed metal interior structure, the complex resembled Labrouste's Bibliothèque Sainte-Geneviève, then nearly completed. In the case of the market hall, the use of metal addressed the concern for sanitary conditions, the need for unencumbered interior space, and the desire to reduce the risk of fire. Upon final approval of the design in

The markets of Les Halles in Paris were made up of independent pavilions separated by covered streets, forming a city within the city.

1851, Baltard, leaving nothing to chance, consulted the engineer Joly, who had built the Gare de l'Est and the Gare de l'Ouest (Montparnasse).

Among the competing designs submitted during this period, Hector Horeau's were also distinguished by their use of metal roof structures. The use of metal became a key issue, however, when the first completed building of Les Halles was brutally criticized. Instead of a lightweight metal roof alighting on four corner buildings of stone, what the Parisians saw was a massive, enclosed structure. The roof frame, an iron structure with decorative motifs bolted on, was not visible from the exterior. Nicknamed "the Market Fort," the building aroused such hostility that work was halted on June 3, 1853.

In the wake of this controversy, some forty architects and engineers presented alternative designs. The aim was to find an architectural solution characterized by lightness and transparency, like London's Crystal Palace, built for the Great Exhibition of 1851, or the recently inaugurated train stations. As Baltard wrote: "A deep infatuation with metal construction, of which train stations were interesting specimens, dominated the public's taste and caused them to turn away from buildings of stone." Napoleon III himself wanted an architecture inspired by that of the stations, if Haussmann is to be believed:

> *The Emperor, delighted with the Gare de l'Est, . . . imagined the central markets built like the kind of covered concourse that shelters the trains' departures and arrivals. 'I need huge umbrellas, nothing more!' he said to me one day, as he instructed me to receive and sort for his consideration the preliminary plans that he had invited, and sketched for me, with a few pencil strokes, the silhouette he had in mind.*

His testimony is supported by newspaper reports of the day. For example, the *Moniteur universel* wrote, on December 17, 1853:

> *What chiefly struck the Emperor, when, a few months ago, he visited a work site to which he attaches a great deal of importance, was the possibility of applying to the construction of Les Halles a system like that followed for our most important train stations. Indeed, this method of construction, based upon the use of cast iron and iron, is as well suited to the former as to the latter, since it offers the advantage of leaving the space completely open to air, light, and circulation, which is as desirable in the covered markets as in the train stations. In addition, it is much less costly.*

Alfred Armand and the engineer Eugène Flachat had just completed a large, much-admired concourse for the Gare Saint-Lazare. They were asked to "prepare a design for the central markets that applies the same principles, but adapting them to this new purpose." Unable to agree, Armand and Flachat presented two different proposals. Armand's included two variations on a spacious roof supported by cast-iron columns, the facade composed of simple metal arcaded armatures. Flachat's design was bolder. It, too, included a large roof, but this one rested on three-strut Polonceau trusses nearly 270 feet across, longer than anything achieved at the time. Despite its industrial appearance, the design created quite a stir of approval, and some believed that Baltard used it as a model for his own final design. One of these was Viollet-le-Duc, who wrote, a few years later: "The city of Paris could congratulate itself for commissioning one of its most renowned architects to adopt, for the construction of the central markets, the overall ideas and designs of an engineer." Among the designs presented by other architects and engineers—all of which employed metal roof frames—Hector Horeau's, which reproposed a design previously published in 1850, was notable for the span of its cast-iron trusses more than 280 feet across. That solution, too, was plausible, and very daring, since Horeau was more of an enthusiast of metal architecture than an actual technician.

Baltard and Callet did not remain idle: In twelve days, they prepared three new designs, all of them proposing metal structures. In his *Mémoires,* Haussmann claimed to have guided the architects' hands, by having done "a sketch absolutely identical to the imperial sketch of the elevation of these groups of buildings, or rather of these spacious 'umbrellas' separated by streets . . . and also covered by raised roofs with large gables," and by having required Baltard to use "iron, iron, nothing but iron!" Haussmann may or may not have played a part in the final design, but his political support was certainly a determining factor in Baltard and Callet's success. The new project was definitively approved in April 1854, following the presentation of a scale model. It included ten buildings with all-metal structures, including the structures of the cellars. In each building, cast-iron columns nearly twenty feet apart and more than thirty-two feet high supported a roof with a glazed monitor. The spandrels sported cast-iron rosettes or punched-iron garlands that contrasted with the simplicity of the trellis-work girders of the roof frame. Light and ventilation were provided by vertical windows fitted with slats of frosted glass or louvers. The buildings were enclosed with panels of brick laid in decorative patterns, alternating with metal columns. This appears to be one of the first important examples of the combination of the two materials.

The first block of six buildings was inaugurated in 1858, with construction of the next four staggered until 1874. The simplicity and the elegant design of the structure, not to mention its scrupulous execution by Joly's firm, immediately excited the admiration of contemporary observers, and gave a strong impetus to the use of metal in architectural practice. Émile Zola made Les Halles the center of his novel *Le Ventre de Paris,* written in 1872, describing the market sometimes as a living being—"a great central organ beating furiously, spurting the blood of life into every vein"—sometimes as "a modern machine, outsized, . . . intended to digest a people, a gigantic metal belly, . . . with the elegance and power of a machine"—at still other times as a forest:

> *The shadow, dozing in the hollows of the roof, multiplied the forest of pillars, expanded to infinity the delicate ribs, the prominent balconies, the transparent louvers . . . there was . . . a whole blossoming, a monstrous flourishing of metal, whose stems rising in flares, and branches twisting and knotting covered a world with the leaflike lightness of a century-old forest.*

Zola ended by echoing Victor Hugo:

> *It is an odd thing to come upon, this bit of church framed in this advance of iron; the latter will kill the former, iron will kill stone, and the times are near. Look, it is an entire manifesto; it is modern art grown up, face to face with ancient art. Les Halles are an outstanding work, and yet only a timid revelation of the twentieth century.*

THE DIFFUSION OF THE MODEL

The result of this success was the proliferation throughout the country of copies of Les Halles. The duplication was rapid. Some eight hundred covered markets are estimated to have been built in France and its colonies, not counting the *halles* exported to countries in South America and those borrowed from the French model, like Barcelona's. In Paris alone, thirty-two metal market halls were built within thirty years, sixteen of them inaugurated in the last five years of the Second Empire. Of the thirteen that survive, four are intact, and nine have been converted to other uses. The *halles* that still exist are those of Saint-Quentin (1866) and Secrétan (Baltard, 1868), the flower market (1874), and the marché de la Chapelle (Auguste Magne, 1885). The livestock market of La Villette, built in 1864–68, stands out because of its purpose and its colossal size. The writer Joris-Karl Huysmans rightly saw this building as one of the most important architectural expressions of its time, along with Les Halles, the Bibliothèque Nationale, the train stations, and the buildings for the universal expositions.

> *Here, metal attains proportions of grandeur. Enormous courses fly, broken by svelte columns that surge from the ground, supporting weightless platforms flooded with light and air. It is an enormous courtyard, into whose flanks thousands of animals disappear, the vast plain whose covered sky hovers above a feverish commercial activity, incessant comings and goings of livestock and men; it is a series of immense buildings whose dark colors*

The market hall of Lusignan, of 1846, was a few years earlier than Baltard's design for Les Halles. Baltard borrowed from it the traditional typology of piers supporting a roof structure with a raised monitor, but used wood and iron in place of stone.

and rakish yet tough appearance suit the tireless and bloody industries practiced there.

The original three blocks were recently reduced to two, when the site was converted into an exposition center and public park.

The capital's prestige certainly played an important part in spreading the model of Les Halles. Every small market town wanted its own *halle.* The half-century during which these metal-covered markets were built was marked by an active policy of municipal construction. The design of Les Halles lent itself wonderfully to adaptation, which was facilitated by the detailed plans that Baltard published in 1863 in his *Monographie des Halles centrales,* and by the publication of numerous markets in the specialized press. For instance, the market in Lusignan in the department of Vienne, built in 1856 by L'Héritier et Rose fils, provides a handsome example of a traditional covered market in stone and wood. It is exactly contemporary with Baltard's *halles* and very similar to them in its general design, with its roof topped by a monitor for ventilation. Instead of cast-iron posts and an iron roof frame, however, masonry piers support a wooden roof frame. Beginning in the early 1860s, the metal market halls began to appear, becoming more popular than the stone markets. The market of 1861 on Rue Buisson in Lyons and that in Nancy of 1862 are among the first of this kind.

The diffusion of the Halles model was also facilitated by the fact that it could easily be designed by local architects or engineers, who could interpret the basic plan as needed or desired. The firms specializing in metal construction also contributed greatly to the proliferation of market halls, experienced as they now were after numerous projects. For example, Joly's construction firm, which built Les Halles in Paris, also built, between 1854 and 1878, the livestock market of La Villette, the Saint-Honoré market hall, and fifteen other neighborhood *halles* in Paris, as well as the covered markets of Montpellier; Lille; Rouen; Constantine, Algeria; and Pointe-à-Pitre, Guadeloupe. The firm founded by Armand Moisant was responsible for the markets in Rennes (1871), Troyes (1872), Parthenay (1878), and Sens. Although the type established at Les Halles in Paris was faithfully repeated, the covered markets also display a wide variety of shapes and materials. A simple, compact version is most often found in small towns. There is a fine one in Melle, built in 1900 to plans by P. Mongeaud, who in 1896–1902 also built a market in Coulonges-sur-l'Autize, which deserves mention for the refined treatment of its entrances. In the more important cities, the *halles* usually follow the basilican plan, with strongly accentuated gables and side aisles. This design appears in the covered markets of Arcachon, Aubervilliers, Belfort (1906), Fontainebleau, Libourne, Lisieux, Niort, and in the Marché Victor-Hugo in Toulouse (built in 1890–91 to designs by Joseph Galinier; now demolished). When the site allowed, the market was sometimes extended into two or more buildings joined by covered streets identical to those of Les Halles in Paris. The cross street appeared in the market halls of Bayonne, Bordeaux, Bourges (1886), Cognac, Dijon, La Roche-sur-Yon (destroyed), Troyes (1872), and Vichy (demolished in 1930). There were through streets in Avignon, Lille, Meaux, Moulins (demolished in 1984), and Orléans (1882, demolished). In the more densely built urban areas, the market was often built up against a common wall, as in Tonnerre. The floor plans can be complex: hexagonal, as at Sens, or octagonal, as at Amiens, Auxerre (1901), Millau, Perpignan, and the Marché des Carmes in Toulouse (built to designs by Charles Cavé in 1891–93; demolished in 1965). And finally, a shelter reduced to a roof supported by columns was commonly found in villages and towns. Variations on these themes allowed the *halles* to be tailored to the different situations presented by their contexts. It is equally remarkable, however, that the variety of shapes all fit within a narrowly defined architectural rubric that brings into play a limited number of elements. The success of the formula of Les Halles no doubt resided in the flexibility that allowed it to be copied, yet altered and adapted to local needs, with subtle but countless stylistic variations.

Nevertheless, one can distinguish two generations of metal market halls. The first and most widespread followed the Parisian model very closely, in both overall morphology and in details like the arcaded armature of the facade and the roof frame with tie beams. The second generation began in the 1890s with the introduction of steel and the development of roofing systems that were triangular and free of tie beams, leading to new approaches in the technical design of the covered markets, even though the overall organization remained the same. Decoration became more elaborate as well. Although iron and cast iron remained the basic materials, glazed lava, tile, brick, terra cotta, and masonry allowed for ornamentation and polychromy that would become increasingly refined into the early twentieth century.

One of hundreds of examples, the market in Marans, in Charente-Maritime, built in 1881 to plans by a Reims firm, Reinneville et Triaud, is typical of the architectural quality that these market halls can display, even in small towns. Above a decorated brick base, reinforced with stone piers, the glass infill is enhanced by cast-iron moldings. The very simple capitals are crowned with cast-iron lions' heads. Light marquees with the city's coat of arms shelter the entrances. Inside, a central monitor rises from a fine roof frame of punched iron.

The Decline of the Covered Market

Despite their many advantages, covered markets did not always answer their users' needs and desires. Quite often, the tradition of the open-air market proved to be so deeply rooted in custom as to cast some discredit on sheltered markets. It was also the case that by the end of the century people began to weary of their sameness. Around 1900, the architectural theorist Julien Guadet wrote: "Alas, if you have seen one, you have seen them all! And it is no small disappointment to the traveler, when he visits one of our cities in the Midi, for example, to find there the inevitable copy of Les Halles in Paris. As if a market could be identical at the latitudes of Lille and Marseilles." This phenomenon accompanied a slow but consistent decline in the use of covered markets after 1876, to the point that a certain number of leases signed with private promoters were broken. The result was that fewer markets were built around the turn of the century, but with a greater wealth of details, and colored materials, including stained glass, were introduced. Of the second generation of *halles,* the Belfort market, built by the architect Doré in 1906, displays exceptionally elaborate gables, an attempt to assert a monumental status. One particularly noteworthy example is Lyons's enormous livestock market, built to designs by Tony Garnier in 1907–14 on the model of the Galerie des Machines at the Exposition Universelle of 1889. Its span of nearly four hundred feet entirely without intermediate supports makes this covered market a technological marvel without equal in France. It was recently converted to a center for expositions and events.

Most of the covered markets have survived the twentieth century, but there have been significant casualties, such as Vichy's, which was torn down in 1930. The increased real-estate pressure in the urban centers and the awareness on the part of municipalities of the value of good locations, occupied by what appeared to be no more than common sheds, led to what was practically an epidemic of demolition between 1970 and 1977, and which continues to some degree today. The most striking case is that of Les Halles, which were torn down in

Hundreds of covered markets were built in France in the wake of the Les Halles model.

Opposite, top left: The market hall in Coulonges-sur-l'Autize.

Opposite, top right: The Sainte-Claire market in Grenoble.

Opposite, bottom: The market hall in Sens, with its uncommon hexagonal plan.

1971–73, but one could cite many other markets that were lost in this same period, such as those in Toulouse (the Marché Victor-Hugo and Marché des Carmes), Bordeaux (the Marché Saint-Jean), Auxerre, Nevers, Angers, La Roche-sur-Yon, Poitiers, Bressuire, and Paris (the Marché des Batignolles, Marché Nicolle, Marché de l'Europe, Marché des Ternes, and others). The demolitions continue; witness the Langres market, torn down in 1989. Approximately three to four hundred market halls still exist in France today, some of them converted to other uses. In 1976, one of the buildings of Les Halles was dismantled without great technical difficulty and installed in Nogent, where it is now a center for concerts and cultural events, proof that this kind of building can easily be adapted to other purposes.

Left: The market hall in the tiny town of Marans, near La Rochelle, is unusual because of the delicate treatment of its ironwork.

Opposite: The market of Belfort was one of the last metal-framed market halls to be built in France. The zinc ornamentation that highlights the gable gives the hall a monumentality that was rare in this type of building.

ARCHITECTURE
AS
ENGINEERING:
BRIDGES,
AQUEDUCTS,
AND
VIADUCTS

VIADUC DE GARABIT
LIGNE DE MARVEJOLS A NEUSSARGUES
Mr Bauby
Mr Boyer
Mr G. Eiffel
N°1
N°2
N°3

The nineteenth century was a very prolific period for civil engineering because of the extraordinary development of systems of transportation. In less than a century, roads, canals, and railroad lines wove a dense network across France. Two factors combined to favor the tremendous growth in the number of bridges in France and the enormous progress made in their construction. The completion of the national system of roads in the first half of the century provided the initial impetus for bridges and viaducts. The laying of a railroad system beginning in the 1840s required even more and larger bridges than those in the road system, and these bridges demanded gentler grades and had less flexibility in adapting to the terrain. Thousands of structures were engineered in order to allow the railroad system to expand. The emergence of metal as a construction material—cast iron until the 1850s, then rolled iron, and finally steel beginning in the 1880s—made it possible to meet this ever-increasing demand both technically and economically, for economy was a key incentive to invention in bridge building.

Wood was by far the least expensive construction material, but wooden bridges were fragile and not very sturdy; they could bear only limited weight and all too often were unable to withstand rising waters, unless they had masonry piers. Timberwork bridge frames had fallen into disuse in the 1850s, except in Switzerland and the United States, which was abundantly provided with forests. Nevertheless, for reasons of economy, timberwork was fairly common in France in the first half of the nineteenth century, in particular for construction associated with the railroad lines. The first railroad bridges over the Seine were made of wood, with arches nearly one hundred feet across, and wood was still employed in the Pont de Grenelle in 1847.

STONE BRIDGES

Bridges had long been built of stone, and important progress in the design of masonry bridges had been made in the late eighteenth century, largely thanks to Jean-Rodolphe Perronet, founder of the École des Ponts et Chaussées in 1747. Perronet had achieved depressed arches with very wide spans.

Chapter opening spread: The Tanus viaduct over the Viaur River was the largest metal bridge built in France.

Preceding spread: Top: The railroad bridge in Bordeaux was one of the first great railroad bridges with a trussed structure, inaugurated in 1860. Bottom: The Garabit viaduct, completed in 1884 to designs by Gustave Eiffel, is a testament to the progress made in a quarter century in the technology of spanning deep valleys. Its arch is as high as Notre-Dame de Paris and the Colonne Vendôme combined.

Opposite: The viaduct of Fontpédrouse, built in 1908, was one of the last major masonry bridges built in France. The engineer, Paul Séjourné, drew inspiration from the Gothic builders to make the arches as lightweight as possible.

The arches of the Pont de Neuilly, of 1772, for example, were 128 feet across. Masonry bridges were considered reliable, resistant, and long-lasting, but they were difficult and expensive to build. They continued to be built throughout the nineteenth century—until the 1940s, in fact—especially in cities, for which they were considered particularly apt. The greatest stone bridge of the early nineteenth century is still the Pont d'Iéna in Paris, built by Lamandé in 1807–13. The location of the bridge, at the foot of the hill of Chaillot, where Napoleon's palace was to be built, required a work in ashlar, with depressed arches. It was initially only about forty feet across, but was widened for the Exposition Internationale of 1937 by the addition of side arches of reinforced concrete that respected the original stonework. The Bordeaux bridge, another work commissioned by Napoleon, was not completed until 1822. More than sixteen hundred feet long, it was for some time the city's only road bridge and an essential link on the route to Spain. The engineer Deschamps resolved the great difficulty of sinking the piers into the Garonne River. He lightened the load by creating longitudinal galleries within the arches and using light bricks of alluvial clay. In the first half of the nineteenth century, many bridges were built over the Garonne River and its tributaries: in Libourne, over the Dordogne; in Moissac, over the Tarn; in Agen, over the Garonne; and in Aiguillon, over the Lot, to name a few.

Perronet's approach was employed by the engineers Croizette-Desnoyers and Morandière in Paris for a number of road bridges, including the Pont de l'Alma in 1856, the Pont de Bercy in 1863, and the Auteuil viaduct in 1866, whose elliptical arches reiterated those of the Pont de Bercy. The Pont de Bercy was widened in 1904 to make room for the elevated Métro.

The first railroad bridges were modest spans of around fifty feet, but before long the great viaducts appeared, such as that of Chaumont, built in 1856; set into a magnificent landscape, it was more than two-fifths of a mile across and nearly 175 feet high, and consisted of three tiers of arches. The Morlaix viaduct runs directly through the city, which it overlooks from a height of 164 feet; its rough granite rustication is still impressive. The Cize-Bolozon viaduct, of 1875, in the department of Ain, strongly resembles that of Morlaix, but rises in a wilder landscape. In 1855, the first 50-meter (164 feet) span was achieved, in the Nogent viaduct over the Seine River; it was rebuilt using reinforced concrete following World War II, in a design quite close to the original. As for the arches, nineteenth-century builders used systems very similar to Perronet's. The piers, however—the most fragile element of the work—were significantly improved. Vicat's 1820 discovery of hydraulic cement, that is, a cement that sets under water, made it much easier to build the foundations of bridges. Compressed air was used to lower metal tubes, then actual caissons, below the water level to solid ground. This solved the problem of sinking the foundations of the piers in a river.

Bridges designed for the passage of canals are an architectural curiosity. Like railroads, canals must be built as nearly as possible on the horizontal. When they cross rivers and streams, they require canal bridges, or aqueducts. Until 1890, the handful of aqueducts built in France were of masonry. The first appears to have been the Fresquel aqueduct, near Carcassonne, for the canal du Midi, completed in 1810. Other works that deserve mention are the Digoin aqueduct over the Loire River and that of Guétin over the Allier River, both built by the engineer Jullien before 1837. In the south of France, the aqueduct at Agen over the Garonne River dates to 1840, and that at Bézier over the Orb River, not far from the famous stepped locks at Fonserannes, to 1857. Because metal was more watertight and could span a wider waterway, it began to replace stone for aqueducts at the end of the nineteenth century. The largest metal aqueduct is still that of Briare, over the Loire River, built in 1890–96 by the firm of Daydé et Pillé. Its entire length, of about 2,067 feet, is very elaborately decorated with period lamps and the coats of arms of the cities through which the canal passes. The Roquefavour aqueduct, near Aix-en-Provence, built in 1842–47 by the engineer Mayor de Montricher to bring water to Marseilles, is worthy of the Pont du Gard, whose system of tiered arches it borrowed, along with its vigorous stonework. The aqueduct is much longer than the bridge and, at about

272 feet high, quite a bit higher. It is still one of the nineteenth century's most famous viaducts, comparable to the great railroad bridges. Among the finest aqueducts are those that deliver water to Paris from the diverted waters of the Loing, Dhuis, Vanne, and other rivers. The Vanne aqueduct, built between 1867 and 1875, exhibits particularly interesting concrete arches that cross the shallow valleys of the Essonne River.

At the end of the century, the engineer Paul Séjourné raised the technique of masonry bridges to a new level that has remained virtually unsurpassed. Following an exhaustive analysis of the large masonry bridges, Séjourné was largely responsible for establishing the model for these structures, which comprise arched spans widened with small arches. The function of the carrier arch is clearly dissociated from that of the small piers that support the road platform. The Pont Antoinette—named for his wife—built in 1883 over the Agoût River, near Lavaur, is a perfect example of the quality and technical success of his work. With the arch of the Pont Adolphe in Luxembourg, built in 1899–1903, Séjourné achieved a span of 278 feet, a record he broke five years later with the Plauen bridge in Saxony. The previous record, a span of 238 feet, had been held for five hundred years by the bridge at Trezzo over the Adda River, built in 1377. Another important bridge, the Pont des Amidonniers in Toulouse, had arches that, as in Luxembourg, were doubled lengthwise. The Fontpédrouse viaduct, built in 1908 in the Pyrénées-Orientales, is equally stunning, with its Gothic references and imposing size.

These large spans, however, were unusual. A masonry bridge more than about 130 feet in length generally required several arches and as many piers and foundations, which were often tricky to build. Furthermore, the templates necessary for the arches added to the construction costs. Séjourné's doubling of the arches in the Pont Adolphe allowed the same template to be used twice. The loads were lightened when piers were set on the carrier arch to support the road with small arches, effectively reducing the weight and therefore the cost of the masonry.

An Attractive Alternative: Suspension Bridges

At the turn of the nineteenth century, it appeared that a particularly low-cost alternative to the masonry bridge had been found in the application of the principle of the suspension bridge. Such bridges are considerably lighter than those of stone, and the use of wrought-iron cables and chains made very long spans possible. Some fifty suspension bridges were built in the United States between 1796 and 1808. In Europe, Thomas Telford had initiated significant improvements with his magnificent bridge over the Menai Strait, built in 1818–20. Its double road, supported by four rows of double chains, soared across 579 feet in a single thrust.

The first suspension bridges in France were built simultaneously by Joseph Navier, an engineer of the Ponts et Chaussées, and by Séguin Frères, industrialists from the Annonay region. Jules Séguin, aided by his four brothers, Marc, Camille, Paul, and Charles, headed a firm that was at the forefront of technical progress. In 1826, they built the railroad line from Saint-Étienne to Lyons, the first in France to incorporate railroad tunnels, and in 1827 Marc and Camille devised the celebrated multiple fire-tube boiler with which the first French locomotives would be equipped. After two trips to England, in 1821 and 1823, Navier published *Rapport et Mémoire sur les ponts suspendus.* In it, he defined the basic features of suspension bridges, detailed each part, specified the most practical methods of calculation, and recalled experiments on the strength and resistance of various materials. That same year, taking up the idea of the American suspension bridge as illustrated in several publications, the Séguin firm, with Marc in the lead, built a test bridge nearly sixty feet long and twenty inches wide, near the family's factory. Four cables, each one made up of eight strands of wire, held up the platform. This modest construction allowed the brothers to test the fabrication of the cables, measure the resistance of the materials, and try out the system's sturdiness. The next year, on property they owned in Saint-Vallier, they built a second bridge using the same principles, this time with a span of about one hundred feet, which allowed them to test

From 1825 to 1850, suspension bridges like this one, over the Rhône River in Tournon, offered an attractive alternative for crossing large spans. Promoters of the system, the Séguin brothers built almost two hundred suspension bridges in France, including this example. Here, the support for the suspension cables takes the form of a classical triumphal arch.

certain systems, such as the part played by the wood parapet in keeping the road rigid. This experiment turned out to be the prototype for the first large suspension bridge built in France, at Tournon, over the Rhône River. Urged by the engineer Plagniol, the Séguins were granted a concession to build the vehicular bridge, but at their own financial risk. The structure, composed of two bays roughly 250 feet long and nearly fourteen feet wide, was inaugurated on August 25, 1825. It was torn down about 1965, but a second bridge in Tournon, built in 1849 by the Séguin firm, still exists.

As for Navier, he had observed that suspension bridges allowed great spans to be crossed inexpensively, and without such distances presenting obstacles. On the contrary, according to him: "The difficulty of these structures lessens with the greater width of the arches, and success is all the more assured the greater the endeavor and the more daring it appears. . . . One could easily build an arch 500 meters [approximately 1,640 feet] across with supports 30 meters [approximately ninety-nine feet] high." Suspension bridges also offered significant economic advantages. Only slightly more costly than arched bridges of wood, they required neither templates nor scaffolding; furthermore, they were easily repaired.

In order to complete his demonstration, Navier applied his principles to a project for a Paris bridge that would be suspended from wrought-iron chains and cross the Seine River in front of Les Invalides. Its span of more than five hundred feet was similar to that of the bridge over the Menai Strait, and would have been attractive, with its Egyptian-style piers roughly fifty feet high. The work began in 1824, but two years later, as the road was being assembled, a water main broke, a section of the foundation was flooded, and work had to be halted. At the same time, the city council realized that the suspension piers would spoil the view of Les Invalides, and the project was canceled.

Navier's setback operated to the advantage of the Séguin firm. They had elected a more pragmatic path and a slightly different construction principle, employing wire suspension cables, rather than chains, from their earliest experiments.

The success of the bridge at Tournon marked the beginning of the golden age of the suspension bridge. The public authorities encouraged these structures, seeing in them a way to "stimulate projects that could provide employment to workers," while replacing the ferries that were still common in small towns with toll bridges, the concessions for which were granted to private firms. The number of suspension bridges in France can be estimated at more than four hundred in 1886, the year in which the state bought back all the concessions that were still in effect. Many of these bridges had been built by the Séguin firm, which was responsible for 186 bridges throughout Europe. The spans of these bridges are between 263 feet and 656 feet, with the median being around 361 feet.

The most important bridges built in France were those of Beaucaire, built by the Séguins in 1829, and of Cubzac, over the Dordogne River, built in 1839, by Émile Martin; both bridges had several bays. The longest spans were obtained at the bridges of La Roche-Bernard, built by Leblanc in 1835–39 (650 feet); Saint-Christophe over the Scorff River, built by Leclerc and Noyon in 1847 (602 feet); and La Caille, which still exists today, on the road between Annecy and Geneva, built in 1839 by Belin (599 feet). Few suspension bridges in operation today remain in their original condition. Many in the Rhône Valley, such as the bridges of Donzères and Givors, still have wooden road coverings.

Generally, the suspension piers are of masonry. Builders freely indulged their architectural fancies in the design of the piers, with a certain predilection for the form of the Neoclassical triumphal arch, which lent itself well to the placement of suspension chains and symbolically expressed the crossing of rivers. The Pont de Seyssel over the Rhône River, for example, is supported by a central arch that also marks the border between two departments of the country. When the piers were not joined at the top, the column motif was naturally selected, preferably in an austere, "masculine" style, such as Tuscan, Doric, or Egyptian. The surviving piers of the bridge in Remoulins, along with the bridge's small toll booths, display an attractive Neo-Grec style. Neo-Gothic elements, like pointed arches, or Neo-Romanesque features are rarer. The bridge of La Caille offers a striking example of the translation of medieval architecture to bridge design, with suspension piers in the shape of crenellated towers.

With no particular consideration of style, several engineers attempted to replace masonry with iron in the suspension piers. The most remarkable instance of this transition is Émile Martin's 1839 bridge at Cubzac over the Dordogne River, which is supported by great conical pylons made of cast-iron frames. The pylons, high enough to accommodate the sailboats running up to Libourne, were reused in 1886 when the bridge was changed from a suspension system to one of girders. The principle of so-called rocker bars was devised out of a concern for economy. The cables were supported by a simple cast-iron rocker bar, articulated at the base. First used by the Séguin firm in 1832 for the bridge at Bry-sur-Marne, and thereafter widely employed, such as in the Saint-Georges footbridge in Lyons, rocker bars were soon proscribed for bridges with more than one bay.

The fashion for suspension bridges ended abruptly in the early 1850s. Several accidents had already cast doubts on their sturdiness, and the catastophe at the bridge at Angers in 1850 marked the beginning of the end. On April 16 of that year, a battalion of the eleventh light infantry regiment marched across the bridge. The rhythm of their march vibrated with such a frequency that it caused the bridge to collapse. Two hundred twenty-three men died. The fact-finding committee attributed the accident to three causes: the force of the

No longer in use, this transporter bridge over the Charente River is the last survivor of its type. These great turn-of-the-century works of civil engineering were erected at the entrances to ports. Passengers and vehicles were carried in cabins suspended by cables to the platform.

wind, the passing of the troops, and the extensive corrosion of the mooring cables. Twenty days later, the bridge of La Roche-Bernard over the Vilaine River was blown away in a storm. It was, at the time, the largest bridge in France.

"A useful and remarkable invention nearly ceased to exist," observed Brissaud, who sought technical solutions to save suspension bridges, in 1865. The suspension bridge was given a second chance in America, where the early introduction of steel into the manufacture of cables and the use of much heavier and more rigid roadways led to the modern suspension bridge, such as New York's Brooklyn Bridge.

Stimulated by the extension of local road systems, in particular in the south of France, the construction of suspension bridges started up once more in the 1890s, with improved cables. The first bridge to be so renovated was over the Allier River, at Saint-Ilpize, in 1879, by the Arnodin firm. The same firm also constructed several spectacular transporter bridges that allowed estuaries and ports to be crossed without the waterways themselves being encumbered. Following the construction of two bridges—in Bilbao, Spain, in 1893 and in Bizerte, Tunisia, in 1898—five were built in France: in Rouen in 1897, Rochefort in 1899, Nantes in 1902, Marseilles in 1908, and Bordeaux in 1913 (never completed). The Bizerte bridge was reassembled in Brest in 1908. The bridge at Le Martrou, near Rochefort, is the only one still standing; it was closed in 1967, but it is designated as a historical monument.

Other interesting works by Arnodin include cable-braced bridges designed by the colonel of the army engineers, Gisclard; some of these, like the bridge at La Cassagne, in the Pyrénées-Orientales, of 1908–9, are among the only suspension bridges in France used by the railroad. As in the transporter bridges, the suspension pylons are of metal, and the braces partly replace the suspension cables, according to a formula much used today.

THE RISE OF METAL BRIDGES

Metal bridges gained extraordinary popularity in the nineteenth century. In 1779, cast iron was used experimentally in the Severn River Bridge in Coalbrookdale, England, afterward spreading rapidly throughout Great Britain, where iron was produced inexpensively. By 1830, some thirty cast-iron projects had been built in England, while France lagged behind.

The Pont des Arts in Paris, of 1802, was the first bridge in which metal was employed, even though similar designs had been formulated in the eighteenth century. In 1801, commissions for three new bridges over the Seine River had been granted to a private firm, with the work to be carried out under the direction of the engineers of the Ponts et Chaussées. The firm that had been retained built the first bridge of timber and the next two of metal. The Pont des Arts, so named because of its location between the Louvre and the Collège des Quatre-Nations, was designed by Louis-Alexandre de Cessart, then senior inspector general for the Ponts et Chaussées, assisted by his student Jacques Dillon. Their first design, presented in April of 1801, had eleven iron arches resting upon a row of timber pilings. Each bay was composed of iron curved into arcs; pivot pins articulated at the midpoints of the arcs acted as braces, and a series of intermediate arches connected them. The concept was simple and economical, similar to the technique used for roof frames, and appropriate for a light walkway with a straight wooden roadway. Following comments from the board of the Ponts et Chaussées, who desired a "more homogeneous" design, Cessart and Dillon replaced the timber pilings with cast-iron columns. In the end, the piers were made of stone, to better withstand the ice carried by the Seine in winter; this quadrupled the cost originally estimated. The Pont des Arts was instantly successful: sixty-four thousand people crossed it on the day it opened. The architectural choices and the use of iron, however, were criticized, in particular by Percier and Fontaine, Napoleon's trusted architects, so much so that the emperor apparently declared in 1810, concerning the bridge: "I can imagine that in England, where there is little stone, they might use iron for large bridges . . . but in France, where there is so much of everything!" Demolished in 1980 and rebuilt in steel, the new Pont des Arts is almost identical to the original, but with one arch less.

The second metal bridge made by this firm was the Pont d'Austerlitz in Paris, inaugurated in 1806. Designed by the engineers Becquey-Beaupré and Lamandé, it had five contiguous arches, each one 105 feet across, supported by stone piers. As with the Pont des Arts, cast iron had been chosen over stone for financial reasons, but the piers remained of stone. Each arch was composed of large cast-iron voussoirs that extended to the straight roadway. Improperly repaired and fatigued by intense use, it was demolished and rebuilt in stone in 1854. Contemporaries praised "the beauty of its proportions, the noble simplicity of its architecture, and the magnificence of its location."

Until the mid-1840s, relatively few iron bridges were constructed in France. The largest, the Pont des Saints-Pères, was in Paris, across from the Louvre. In 1829, Antoine-Rémy Polonceau had conceived a highly original design consisting of arches made of curved planks, inserted into elliptical cast-iron tubes. The roadway was supported by circles of decreasing diameter. Completed in 1834, the bridge brilliantly illustrated the structural possibilities that metal offered, and it remained in service until 1935, when it was replaced by a concrete structure. Yet, its construction principles were subsequently only sporadically applied, for example, in Lyons's Pont de La Mulatière of 1843, which no longer exists; a bridge in Seville, Spain; and a small bridge, recently restored, over the Lanterne River in Conflans-les-Bourguignons, in the Haute-Saône department. As Polonceau himself remarked in 1839: "When one considers the advantages that cast-iron bridges present, one is led to wonder that so few have been built in France, or even in England, where they are so accustomed to working with cast iron and where it is so inexpensive." He attributed this to the excessive cost of cast iron, "and the difficulty and unreliability encountered in our foundries of applications of this kind." The cost of the only two cast-iron bridges then existing in France was close to that of stone bridges. The lack

In 1802 the Passerelle des Arts in Paris inaugurated a long tradition of metal engineering works. The method of assembly of its cast-iron arches was derived from carpentry techniques. The original was demolished in 1980 and replaced with a nearly identical copy.

of confidence in cast-iron bridges was induced by cracks and other problems that had arisen in the existing examples.

The rapid development of the French iron industry in the 1840s encouraged the construction of a number of cast-iron bridges, which continued to be built into the 1870s, most often as road bridges in cities. Some examples of these are the Pont Saint-Louis and Pont de Solférino of 1858 in Paris; the bridge in Argenteuil; the bridge over the Rhône in Tarascon, of 1852; bridges in Avignon and Nevers; and the Pont de Sully in Paris, of 1874–76, one of the few to survive. These bridges usually exhibited either molded panels or arched armatures supporting the roadway. The spans tended to be about two hundred feet long.

The capacity to produce rolled iron in industrial quantities, beginning in the 1840s, spurred builders to design bridges of sheet iron rather than cast iron. The Conway Bridge, in Wales, built in 1848, displayed a new solution for railroad bridges. It comprised double girders made of riveted sheets, between which the trains passed. In France, Eugène Flachat used this technique widely, for the bridges of Clichy and Asnières—the latter is famous as the subject of several of Monet's paintings—both built in 1852, and for the bridges he built for the Compagnie des Chemins de Fer du Midi, in Langon, over the Garonne River, in 1855; in Moissac, over the Tarn River, in 1857; and in Aiguillon, over the Lot River. The spans of these bridges, which were inspired by George Stephenson's Britannia Bridge, were about 230 feet long.

TRUSSES AND TRUSSED ARCHES

In the mid-1850s it became apparent that the use of the truss, a structured form composed of a series of contiguous triangles, provided ample resistance with less weight and less wind resistance than the simple iron girder or voussoired cast-iron arch. An almost limitless variety of truss formulas were developed in the nineteenth century to meet the demand for increasingly long and high bridges. The first large bridge of this kind was that in Kehl, over the Rhine River, completed in 1859, followed by a bridge of 1856–60 in Bordeaux. The foundations for both structures were set upon compressed-air metal tubes, a first in France for a technique that was to be so important in the future. The Bordeaux bridge, with a total length of 1,640 feet, was begun by the firm of Nepveu, then completed by that of Pauwels, to plans by Stanislas de Laroche-Tolay and Regnault. Gustave Eiffel was the foreman—his first entrepreneurial responsibility. Lattice bridges of this type, which were simple to calculate and to build, their uprights alternating with large Saint Andrew's crosses, became widespread in France, as did multiple trusses, especially in medium-size works built for the railroads. Several large viaducts also displayed these principles: for example, two bridges in Cubzac, the railroad bridge of 1886 and the road bridge of 1879–84; the viaduct of Évaux over the Tardes River, inaugurated in 1885; and the viaduct of Les Fades of 1901–9. The latter is noteworthy for its masonry piers more than three hundred feet high. The construction as a whole would seem disproportionately large, were it not set amid the wild grandeur of the Sioule Valley.

Beginning in the mid-1850s, it became increasingly common to use very high metal piers—less expensive than masonry piers—to span deep valleys. In 1858–62, with the Saarne viaduct in Fribourg, Wilhelm Nordling introduced the use of piers made of cast-iron tubes overlapped and wind-braced by iron bars. The viaducts of Le Busseau d'Ahun and Cère, both built in 1864 by the engineer Moreau and the firm of Cail, applied the same principle. Cast-iron piers were employed especially felicitously in a series of four viaducts on the Commentry–Gannat railroad line in 1867–70. All four were designed by Thirion and Nordling; the two larger were built by the firms of Cail and Fives-Lille, the other two by the young Eiffel company. For greater stability, the piers flare out into arcs of circles. The combined effect of suppleness and strength is remarkable.

Adapting the classic arch shape to metal construction opened new possibilities for spanning deep valleys. Rolled iron began to replace cast iron in the mid-1850s, in bridges with fixed-end arches. The Pont d'Arcole in Paris, built by Alphonse Oudry in 1854–55 with a span of 263 feet, was the first large bridge to be so constructed. By the end of the century, steel was replacing iron, allowing

The need to span deep valleys with railroad bridges suggested the use of tall metal piers for the great viaducts. Those of the 1867 Rouzat viaduct over the Sioule River are made of iron tubes that flare at the base to increase their stability.

wider spans. Generally speaking, and this remained true into the 1920s, arched road bridges in cities were decorated with end arches, which were different from the main arches, whose only function was to support the sidewalk, and which were decorated appropriately to the type of bridge and its site. On the other hand, the high cost of the pier foundations made it desirable to reduce their number; this was possible if the arches' spans were longer, especially when there was a specific natural obstacle to be cleared. This gave rise to the trussed arches, whose Rational yet elegant forms produced some of the most spectacular works of the nineteenth century. The advent of this type of bridge was signaled by the Maria Pia viaduct over the Douro River in Porto, Portugal, built in 1875–77 by Théophile Seyrig and Eiffel's firm, winners of an international competition. A crescent-shaped trussed arch 525 feet long crosses the river in a single arc, bearing a straight truss on metal piers. Its power and lightness were unprecedented. Eiffel repeated his success in 1880–84 with the Garabit viaduct, a private contract following the success of the Douro project, which was built in conjunction with a small local railroad line between Neussargues and Marvejols in the Massif Central. For financial reasons, and to avoid a detour of about seven and one-half miles, Eiffel fashioned a vast arch 541 feet wide to cross the valley at a height of 394 feet. Garabit is without question the most famous engineering feat in France. Its almost magical absence of mass, its delicacy and balance, and its spare elegance make it a masterpiece of metal architecture.

High arches with wide spans were inappropriate for urban sites, however, and this led to an interesting variation, introduced at the end of the century: the suspension of the road from the arch. This arrangement, which was very popular in Germany, was employed in France for many bridges, including the beautiful bridges built by the firm of Daydé et Pillé, such as those at the Gare d'Austerlitz in Paris, of 1903–7, and at La Roche-Bernard, of 1910. The latter did not survive World War II.

Another variation of the truss is the cantilever, which consists of a beam projecting from a supporting tower with a counterbalancing beam behind it, joining up with a similar cantilevered unit projecting from the opposite side. The most impressive bridge with this type of structure is the Forth bridge in Scotland, built in 1882–89 with a fantas-

Left: Eiffel's Garabit viaduct is one of the finest examples of civil engineering in France. In a single span, its trussed arch of 520 feet soars across the Truyère, today an artificial lake.

Opposite, top: The viaduct over the Viaur River, in the Aveyron department, displays an unparalleled power.

Opposite, bottom: Paris's Austerlitz viaduct is composed of a broad arch from which the platform for the Metro tracks is suspended. The structure was endowed with handsome ornamentation.

tic span of 1,079 feet. The Tanus viaduct of 1897–1902 over the Viaur River, near Albi, was modeled after it. Initially conceived in 1876 as a straight-girder bridge, then as an arched bridge like the Garabit viaduct, the Viaur viaduct was finally made the subject of a design competition. The solution proposed by the Société des Batignolles and its head of design, Pierre Bodin, was a single span about 722 feet across. Less well known than the Garabit viaduct, this great three-hinged steel bridge is nevertheless one of the most stunning in France. Its very simple lines and widely spaced triangulation make it difficult to comprehend its scale, but the contrast between it and its natural surroundings is worthy of Garabit. Also deserving of mention is a project for a bridge over the English Channel that was presented in 1889 by the firms of Schneider and Hersent, in consultation with the engineers of the bridge over the Forth. It would have entailed large spans of 1,640 feet joined together.

The principle of the cantilever was also employed for more ordinary bridges, whose arched shapes were equally elegant. Paris's Bir-Hakeim viaduct of 1903–5 is made up of two hinged right angles that rest on abutment piers. What makes this bridge unusual is its upper level supported by slender steel columns, whose Art Nouveau design has unfortunately been altered. The decoration by Formigé, the architect of Paris's elevated Métro, is wonderful. The Pont Mirabeau, designed by the engineer Resat in 1893–96, is another fine example of the type. The side brackets were deliberately overloaded with brick arches to balance the weight of the main brackets, which are articulated at the crown. The result is a flattened overall line that works well within an urban setting. The decoration is also notable, with gilded bronze statues. The Pont Alexandre III, built in 1898–1900 by Resat for the Exposition Universelle of 1900, also presents an almost horizontal road, which allows the view between the riverbanks to be seen. The construction technique harks back to that of the earliest cast-iron bridges. The arch is made up of fifteen trusses comprising voussoirs of molded steel bolted together. The decoration is also exceptional, relating to the location of the bridge and to the part it was to play in the exposition. The pure line of the arch, which is articulated at the springers, is emphasized by a frieze, while that of the road is marked by a series of garlands and masks that echo the rhythm of the connecting stanchions. The entrances to the bridge are punctuated by four ornate masonry pylons.

CONCRETE

In the early twentieth century, steel seemed to be the ideal material for works of civil engineering, small and large alike. Indeed, over the first half of the century, new uses were continually found for steel, though without substantive innovations in form or technique. Calculations were increasingly refined, due to the increasing improvement in the quality of steel, and there was progress in construction processes.

But if metal was the material of choice for bridges throughout the first half of the twentieth century, reinforced concrete gradually came into common use for small and medium spans. Several structural engineers in France developed reinforced concrete simultaneously in the late nineteenth century, but François Hennebique was the first to use it for a major project, at Châtellerault, in 1898–1900. In the following years, Hennebique built several similar works—notably over the Rhône River at Pyrimont—before taking on the Ponte Risorgimento in Rome, in 1908–11. The Roman bridge had a span of 328 feet, a record for this type of construction. Some works of the first decade of the century combined reinforced concrete and masonry. The Pont des Catalans in Toulouse, built by Séjourné in 1904–10, for example, has stone arches supporting a road of reinforced concrete. Although they emerged during the nineteenth century's ferment of invention, concrete bridges belong to the history of the twentieth century.

The Châtellerault bridge was, in 1900, one of the first large reinforced-concrete bridges built in France. François Hennebique's firm designed the bridge as a manifesto for the qualities of the new material, which was the firm's specialty, although its basic form was similar to that of earlier metal structures.

INDEX

Page numbers in *italics* indicate captions.

BIBLIOGRAPHY

Association française pour l'histoire de la justice. *La Justice en ses temples, regards sur l'architecture judiciaire en France.* Paris, 1992.

Bowie, Karen. *Les Grandes Gares parisiennes du XIXe siècle.* Paris, 1989.

Dallemagne, François. *Les Casernes françaises.* Paris, 1990.

Deswarte, Sylvie, and Bertrand Lemoine. *L'Architecture et les Ingénieurs, deux siècles de construction.* Paris, 1980.

Drexler, Arthur, ed. *The Architecture of the École des Beaux-Arts.* New York: Thames and Hudson, 1978.

Foucart, Bruno, ed. *Viollet-le-Duc.* Paris: R.M.N., 1977.

Grenier, Lise, ed. *Villes d'eaux en France.* Paris, 1985.

Hautecoeur, Louis. *Histoire de l'architecture classique en France.* Vols. 3–4. Paris, 1955–57.

Hitchcock, Henry-Russell. *Architecture: Nineteenth and Twentieth Centuries.* Rev. Ed. Baltimore: Penguin, 1977.

Kohlmaier, Georg. *Das Glashaus: ein Bautyp des 19.Jahrhundert.* Munich, 1981.

Latour, Geneviève, and Florence Claval. *Les Théâtres de Paris.* Paris, 1991.

Lemoine, Bertrand. *L'Architecture du fer, France XIXe siècle.* Seyssel, 1986.

_____. *Les Halles de Paris.* Paris, 1978.

_____. *Les Passages couverts en France.* Paris, 1989.

Loyer, François. *Architecture in the Industrial Age.* New York: Rizzoli, 1983.

_____. *Paris, la rue.* Paris, 1987.

Marrey, Bernard. *Les Grands Magasins.* Paris, 1979.

Middleton, Robin, ed. *The Beaux-Arts and Nineteenth Century Architecture.* Cambridge, Mass.: MIT Press, 1982.

Middleton, Robin, and David Watkin. *Neo-Classical and 19th Century Architecture.* New York: Abrams, 1980.

Mignot, Claude. *Architecture of the Nineteenth Century in Europe.* New York: Rizzoli, 1984.

O'Brien, Patricia. *Correction ou Châtiment: histoire des prisons en France au XIXe siècle.* Paris, 1988.

Pevsner, Nikolaus. *A History of Building Types.* London, 1976.

Pinchon, Jean-François, ed. *Les Temples de l'argent.* Paris, 1992.

Prade, Marcel. *Ponts et Viaducs au XIXe siècle.* Poitiers, 1990.

Trachtenberg, Marvin, and Isabelle Hyman. *Architecture from Prehistory to Post-Modernism.* New York: Abrams, 1986.

PHOTOGRAPH CREDITS

©R.M.N.: C. Jean, 108 (bottom); Musée d'Orsay, 8, 9, 29, 50–51, 61, 68–69, 84–85, 86, 87, 90, 92, 152–153, 182–183; Musée du Louvre, 106–107

Marco Polo. F. Bouillot: 11, 12, 16 (left), 20, 21, 22–23, 26–27, 30, 32, 39 (right), 46, 47, 48–49, 58, 66–67, 71, 72 (bottom), 72–73, 78, 80–81, 90 (bottom), 93 (top and bottom), 94 (top and bottom), 95, 96 (right), 98 (bottom), 104–105, 108 (top), 111, 116 (bottom), 119, 126 (bottom), 135 (top), 136–137, 141, 142, 143 (top), 157, 161 (top and bottom), 164 (top and bottom), 177 (top), 180–181, 184, 191, 194, 195 (top and bottom); Ph. Hallé: 13, 14–15, 16 (right), 17, 19 (top), 24, 33, 42, 43, 44–45, 53, 56, 72 (top), 88, 96 (left), 100, 101, 102 (top and bottom), 112–113, 116 (top), 117 (top and bottom), 124, 127, 128, 129, 130, 132 (bottom), 144–145, 149, 150–151, 158, 171, 177 (bottom), 178, 187 (top and bottom), 189, 196–197

B. Lemoine: 6–7, 25, 28 (ENSBA), 34, 36, 37, 38, 39 (left), 41, 75, 82–83, 98 (top), 120–121, 122 (bottom), 126 (top), 132 (top), 133, 135 (bottom), 138–139 (archives SNCF, top and left private collection), 143 (bottom), 155, 156, 163, 166–167 (document BHVP), 168, 175, 179, 193

Other sources: cliché archives de Paris, 169; © Giraudon, 59; Photo Pierre Pinon/IFA, 65; © photothèque des musées de la ville de Paris, Musée Carnavalet, 115, 122, 123; © E. Revault/Archives photographiques/CNMHS, Paris 54, 55, 62, 74; © Roger-Viollet, 77, 172